travel with children

cathy lanigan

foreword by maureen wheeler

lonely planet publications melbourne oakland london paris

Travel with Children
4th edition – February 2002
First published – May 1985

Published by
Lonely Planet Publications Pty Ltd ABN 36 005 607 983
90 Maribyrnong St, Footscray, Victoria 3011, Australia

Lonely Planet Offices
Australia Locked Bag 1, Footscray, Victoria 3011
USA 150 Linden Street, Oakland, CA 94607
UK 10a Spring Place, London NW5 3BH
France 1 rue du Dahomey, 75011, Paris

Printed by SNP SPrint (M) Sdn Bhd
Printed in Malaysia

Photographs
Cover images: penguin family (David Tipling) and street signs (John Borthwick) courtesy of LPI. Giraffe courtesy of DGUSA. Child in dunes courtesy of Maree Conroy.
Many of the images in this guide are available for licensing from Lonely Planet Images.
Web site: www.lonelyplanetimages.com

ISBN 0 86442 729 8

Editor: George Dunford
Designer: Karen Nettelfield
Senior Editor: Martine Lleonart
Publishing Manager: Martin Heng

Thanks to: Bridget Blair, Jane Hart, Jenny Jones, Isabelle Young, Jane Pennells, David Kemp, Mark Germanchis and Maureen Wheeler

authors

AUTHORS

cathy lanigan

After many family car trips checking out the Australian outback and beaches, Cathy took off overseas and between jobs as a journalist travelled to Europe, Asia and bits of the Middle East and Africa. After stints as a student, politician and festival organiser, Cathy settled down to a career at Lonely Planet. In recent times, Cathy and her partner John have travelled in Europe with their 13-year-old foster child, Ali, and half-way around Australia with their baby, Zoe. When not travelling, they hang out in Gippsland, Australia. Cathy co-ordinated this book and wrote the introductory chapters and Australasia destination profiles.

michael s clark

Michael and his wife Janet took their first trip with daughter Melina when she was just five months old. The three, Melina riding in dad's backpack, crossed fields of lava rock on a moonless midnight to witness lava rivers flowing into the sea on the coast of Hawaii's Big Island. Since then, the family has grown by one with son Alexander adding to the chaos and joy of family travel. Many trips later, baby backpack and stroller have been replaced by travel games, kids' journals and new passports.

When not on the road, Michael teaches English to international students in San Francisco and Berkeley, California. He has written for the *San Francisco Examiner* and is co-author of Lonely Planet's *New York, New Jersey, & Pennsylvania* and *Myanmar (Burma)* guidebooks. Michael wrote the destination profiles for the Asia and North America chapters of this book.

siona jenkins

Siona Jenkins arrived in Cairo for six months of Arabic language study in 1989 and is still based there. She is now a freelance journalist, writing for the *Irish Times*, when not compiling guidebooks or helping to produce documentary films. She is also the mother of eight-year-old Leo, who has already clocked up several thousand air-miles in his short life. Leo had to shoulder such onerous tasks as walking in the Sinai mountains and camping in the dunes of Egypt's Western Desert in the name of his mother's travel writing. The Africa and Middle East destination profiles in this book were written by Siona.

robyn jones & leonardo pinheiro

Robyn – a farm girl from rural Victoria, Australia – spent a year as an exchange student in the Brazilian megalopolis of São Paulo. After training in Agricultural Science, Leonardo left his hometown of Rio de Janeiro, Brazil, to do post-grad studies in Sydney and check out the Australian surf. They met in Melbourne, where they now live with their two boys Alex and Nicholas. Robyn and Leonardo worked in the Amazon region for Lonely Planet's *Brazil* and *South America*, and wrote *Fiji*. Alex helped them research a new edition of *Fiji* and the Fiji and Tuvalu chapters of *South Pacific*. Then Nicholas joined in on the fun to research a new edition of *Brazil*. In between travels Robyn works as an architect and Leonardo studies for his PhD in biochemistry. The kids play wherever they are. Robyn and Leonardo wrote the South & Central America and the Caribbean destination profiles for this book.

rosie whitehouse

Rosie was born in Liverpool but grew up in London. Every summer her parents bundled her and her two sisters in the back of the car and drove them across Europe. It put her sisters off travel for life, but not Rosie! She studied International History at the LSE and after that she worked as a reporter and editor at the BBC. In 1990 Rosie decided to witness history first hand. She and her baby son left for post-revolutionary Romania where they lived in a Bucharest tower block. In 1991, now with two children, she set up home in Belgrade, then in the grip of wartime nationalist fervour. When pushing the kids in their stroller around Sarajevo, they heard the first shots of the Bosnian war. By the end of the war Rosie had three children, who summered in Dubrovnik and other holiday destinations deserted by regular tourists. Now she lives in London with five kids, all of whom regularly accompany their mother on writing trips across Europe. Rosie wrote the Europe destination profiles for this book.

THANKS

cathy lanigan thanks Rebecca Magalhaes of the La Leche League International for gathering breastfeeding information from around the globe. Also much appreciation to the crew in the LP office – Martine Lleonart, Martin Heng, Pete Cruttenden and George Dunford – for their trust and support. And a special thanks to Zoe for putting up with her mum being glued to the computer way too often, and to my partner John for entertaining her while I was.

michael s clark thanks his friends, parents and kids who offered their experience, and secret spots to consider. Special nods to Peter, Shannon & Nick Van Dyke, Marcia Condon, Like Lokon, Nadire Ozavar, Bill & Min Preston – and of course to his loving family – Janet, Melina & Alex. Also Tammy Fortin in the Oakland office for cheerful last-minute assistance.

siona jenkins thanks Leo for putting up with his mother's boring tendency to sit at her computer instead of playing Game Boy.

Thanks to everyone who wrote in with useful tips, advice and stories: Louise Anderson, Liz Allen, Sandra Bardwell, Jeff Barrons, Jane Bennett, Tracy Berno, Bridget Blair, Vivien Bortot, Mary Burns, Ericka Chemko, Damien Coghlan, Maree Conroy, Christine Curran, Carolyn & Ben Findlay, Carol De Giorgio, George Dunford, Jo Gregory, Sue Jacques, Kirsty Johnson, Kevin Jordan, Ben Judah, Claudia Koch-McQuillan, Tania Kutny, Debra Leung, Stephanie Levin-Gervasi, Jacqui Higgins, Charlotte Hindle, Adele Levinge, Mark Lightbody, Fiona Lovegrove, James Lyon, Kylie McBride, Sharon McRae, Rebecca Magalhaes, Annie & Stéphane Marais, Sarah Mathews, Ringo Mollinger & Meik Touw, Deidree Noss, Morna O'Neill, Lyndall Parris (lmparris@bigpond.com), Steve & Kathy Peterson, Angela Price, David Quinn, Tim Rock, Sue Roedl, Cathy Sather, Bernadette Saulenier, Nancy Savage, Tanya Seaward, Edward Seco, Phillipa Schultz, Megha Singh, Dore Stockhausen, AA Tan-Keultjes, Staffan Thorell, Trisha Thornquist, Rosie Waitt, Crispin Walker, Elizabeth Wear, Mark Wilgar, Walter Will, Jane Wood and Rodica Woodbury.

part 1 ...BEFORE YOU GO

part 2 ...WHERE TO GO

When I first wrote *Travel with Children* my daughter Tashi was three years old and her brother Kieran was 12 months. Tashi was already a veteran traveller and Kieran was learning fast that 'home' was several places. Many people I met on the road or even at home were amazed that I would take my tiny children to Asia, Africa or South America, however I have always found these regions to be welcoming and accepting of children. Restaurants and hotels would bend over backwards to make the children feel at home. We met many local people who would relate to us immediately as children and family are so central to society in these regions. There is, of course, a natural concern about staying healthy in countries where clean water is not available and food may be an issue. We were always extremely careful about personal hygiene and food so both children suffered nothing more than the usual minor travel problems on our trips.

foreword

Lonely Planet co-founder Maureen Wheeler penned the original *Travel with Children* in response to requests from parents who wanted to keep travelling.

Outback trips have always been a real favourite with us. Although they are basically road trips, and children and long car rides don't always go together, the nights spent around a campfire, looking for shooting stars and comets, or just marvelling at the number and intensity of the stars, more than made up for the difficult days. The sense of space and distance in Outback Australia is an experience in itself, it is possible to feel really free in a landscape without boundaries or other people.

Having children is an adventure, watching them grow and growing with them is a journey. I showed them the world, but they also showed me things I would have missed or have become oblivious to. I remember the first time we took Tashi to Kathmandu, she was amazed at seeing cows in the streets and laughed when the cow lay down in the road and stopped all the traffic. I had become so used to seeing cows wandering around the streets in Hindu countries that I only realised how surreal it was then.

Kieran has learned to bargain in markets all over the world, culminating in a desperate pitch for a Masai shield in a bus station in Kenya. The African woman was so tickled by Kieran's spiel that they struck a deal – his children's books and little plastic cars in return for one very beautiful shield.

Tashi and Kieran are grown up now. They are both great travellers and Tashi has made several trips on her own or with friends. Kieran and I went trekking in Mustang last year and had a wonderful time. It is too early yet to say what effects all that travelling has had on shaping them, but I know that I learnt a lot and I am very pleased that we have shared so many adventures as a family.

The book has also grown up and after four editions it is the result of many families' adventures. While the idea of going to a resort with a swimming pool, full service and children's club is very appealing (a real holiday!), for those of you who yearn to explore the world becoming parents doesn't have to spell the end of your travel dreams. The anecdotes and information in this book will hopefully inspire you to embark on your own family adventures. For everyone who ever wondered if there was travel after children this book is for you – and your children.

Maureen Wheeler

about lonely planet

The story begins with a classic travel adventure: Tony and Maureen Wheeler's 1972 journey across Europe and Asia to Australia. Useful information about the overland trail did not exist at that time, so Tony and Maureen published the first Lonely Planet guidebook to meet a growing need.

From a kitchen table, then from a tiny office in Melbourne (Australia), Lonely Planet has become the largest independent travel publisher in the world, an international company with offices in Melbourne, Oakland (USA), London (UK) and Paris (France).

At Lonely Planet we believe travellers can make a positive contribution to the countries they visit – if they respect their host communities and spend their money wisely. Since 1986 a percentage of the income from each book has been donated to aid projects and human rights campaigns.

KEY to ICONS

The icons used in this book are designed to indicate information relevant to various age groups. Individual development varies greatly from child to child, so the ages given below are to be used as a guide only.

Babies: 0–18 months, still able to be carried or fits into a stroller or backpack. May still be breastfed and require pre-teething food.

Toddlers: 18 months–3 years, walking and talking, but not perfectly, so issues of both balance and communication will arise.

Older children: 4–12 years, can socialise and interact with other children, but may still require a watchful eye in some situations.

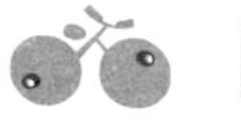

Teenagers: 13–18 years, 'too cool for school', keen to be independent and apparently bored by everything on offer.

WARNING

Although we give treatment guidelines for illnesses and first aid situations in this book, these are not intended as a substitute for medical advice. You are encouraged to seek medical advice wherever possible. Self-treatment should only be considered if you are in a remote area far from medical help. While the authors and publisher have made every effort to ensure accuracy, they cannot accept responsibility for any loss, injury or illness resulting from advice or information given in this guide.

INTRODUCTION

Travelling doesn't have to stop because you have children. Sure, with kids your pace of travel will probably be slower and you'll have to compromise to meet their needs but you'll also get an enormous amount of joy from taking children with you.

As a travelling family you get to spend time together and enjoy each other's company. You can make decisions with older kids, have lots of time to talk and share experiences together. And until they hit the teenage years, and sometimes even then, most kids thrive on having their parents around to do fun things with. If you want to spend quality time with your child, help them learn, grow and gain a better understanding of the world and humanity, then travelling is a great way to do it. There are so many fantastic things kids learn from travel – it can teach flexibility, appreciation of cultural diversity and that the world is bigger than your home town or city.

Travel with children provides insights into local cultures that you often just don't get travelling childless. In most cultures children are welcomed, if not revered, and will attract attention to themselves, and by default, you. And although your lives may be very different, you have parenting as a common bond with people all over the world.

That's not to say it's easy travelling with a child. It helps if you plan and take the right bits and pieces with you, including the right mental attitude. Like travelling with most people, you don't always get to do what you would like to all the time, in fact once you've got a child who's hit 'toddlerdom' you'll spend a lot of time compromising.

Health issues are often a major concern for parents taking their kids to developing world countries. Obviously you need to take precautions and do your homework before you go, but it doesn't have to stop you. The health chapter in this book – written by a doctor, with the bonus of tips from an experienced naturopath – provides a good starting point.

There are a few encouraging messages which keep coming through the stories in this book – the great rewards of travel for yourself and your children and the attitude that you just have to get out there and do it. You could spend a lot of time waiting until your child is the 'right' age to travel.

One of the nice things about this book is that it's not just one person telling you about travel with children – it's a whole community of people who have been travelling with their kids sharing their stories, offering their best tips and passing on practical information. This book has grown over 17 years and enshrines the knowledge Lonely Planet co-founder Maureen Wheeler gained travelling with her children in their first 15 years, as well as the experiences of Lonely Planet authors, staff and readers.

From bike riding with a toddler and a baby through China and Pakistan to camping rough around Australia with three small children, to breaking new ground hiking with a teenager in the US, the stories in this edition of *Travel with Children* are nothing short of inspiring.

There are stories from people who break all the stereotypes as well – travelling with a special needs child, as a single parent and selling all your possessions to travel around the world by campervan for a few years.

With a positive attitude and a bit of forethought there's no reason why you can't travel happily with kids. Things won't always go as planned of course, but then they never do with travel or with kids.

part

...BEFORE YOU GO

- planning
- getting there
- on the road
- health
- pregnant travel

PLANNING

The fun of travelling with kids can start at the planning stage. Planning doesn't mean having to map out your entire route and book every hotel but with kids in tow you do need to think ahead. If you've got the right equipment, have prepared your children as much as possible and done your homework about your destination then you're well on your way to making your trip work.

children's ages

Travelling with children of any age can have its own rewards and pitfalls. There is no right age to start travelling with children, your trip can be just as enjoyable with a newborn as it can with a teenager. However there are different issues to take into account depending on their age.

babies

Babies are portable and easy to entertain – a day in a museum is a possibility with a baby in a backpack or stroller. This is probably the only stage of a child's life you get to dictate where you go and what you do so make the most of it! Babies are usually of interest wherever you go and provide a great opportunity to interact with local people.

The downside of travelling with babies is that they require a lot of equipment – nappies, changes of clothes, carrying devices – and they like some kind of routine for naps, feeding and changing. They may also get you up at night which may cause you (or your neighbours) anxiety if you're staying in a hotel. There is also more anxiety with babies on the move – they can't tell you if they are too hot, too cold or get a stomach ache. However if you travel with the right equipment, tune in and respond to your baby's tired, hungry, bored signals, and take a good medical kit, you should circumvent most problems.

toddlers

Toddlers can be challenging to travel with; all that energy, trying to do everything and all the frustration of not always being allowed to. You need to be extremely watchful as they are inclined to pick up unsavoury objects, cuddle the fleabag cat or wander off when their eye is caught by something intriguing. They're also often fussy eaters and obstinate in their likes and dislikes. On the plus side toddlers bring a fresh interest to everything and give you the chance to see the world from a different perspective. Your choice of destination is more important with toddlers – it helps to choose destinations where they can run around freely for some of the day without getting into danger. It's also good to stay in places where you can feel free to childproof the room.

older children

From about the age of four, travel with children becomes a real pleasure. It can still be hard work and children of this age can get bored easily, but it's also very rewarding as your children now form their own impressions and relationships, and can tell you what they are experiencing. They will tell you what they enjoy, and planning trips can be more of a group effort with their likes and dislikes being taken into account, within reason.

teenagers

Teenagers are much more able to entertain themselves than younger children. They may enjoy some of the same things that you do and they'll also remember most of what they experience and get great educational value from it. Your evenings will also be less restricted as they are often able to stay up as late (or later!) than you do.

They're also at an age where you can really involve them in the planning of the trip and what you do from day to day. They will probably be very clear about where they do and do not want to go, and how many 'temple' days and 'ruins' days are a reasonable exchange for beach days or shopping days! Accommodation choices may be an issue as teenagers want more privacy and may not appreciate a family room. Taking one of their friends along, if that's a possibility, can make everyone's trip more enjoyable. See the friend section later in this chapter.

preparing to travel

There are loads of ways you can help prepare your kids for the trip before you leave. Giving them some information that helps establish some familiarity with your destination can go a long way towards coping when they get there and it might also get them excited about the prospect in advance. Encourage your children to be involved in planning the trip and where you'll be going as often as possible.

books

A month or so before you depart get as much literature as you can on the area you will be visiting. Get tourist brochures, guidebooks, books from the library – anything with pictures. Try to find books of legends or children's stories from the region. For a young child, even a travel brochure can be made into a story by explaining the pictures. You may be surprised at how much sticks. See the country profiles later in this book for kid-friendly suggestions.

film & television

There's nothing like a good movie to get kids excited about a place and give them a visual image of what it will be like, so hire some videos or DVDs before you go (see the suggestions in the country profiles later in this book). You can also watch television travel shows and other TV specials about places you'll visit, or get one of the videos of the Lonely Planet TV series (there are more than 40 destinations).

restaurants & outings

Take your kids out to eat in restaurants, go for weekend trips, take them for walks – in short prepare them for travelling. You can introduce a few different foods or flavours into your cooking and visit restaurants that offer cuisine that they will be exposed to while travelling. Although most young children will recoil on principle when anything new is offered, they will sometimes try new food in a new country when it is served up in a restaurant.

map

Pin up a map of the region you are travelling to and get older children to mark where they'd like to go. As you plan out your travels you can mark your route on it.

travel stories

Invite friends around to share their travel stories of destinations. You might have to choose people carefully so you get stories that will capture the children's imagination rather than bore them to tears.

travel tips

Try to get a picture dictionary in the language of your destination.

A reader, UK

learning the language

Learning some of the local language can be useful as well as enjoyable. Make it a fun and relevant activity like trying to talk in the language at the dinner table or use foreign words when you're driving in the car. It will help your children's confidence if they can converse with a few words, even if it's just hello, goodbye, please and thank you. Children usually pick up languages well, particularly young children. Whatever efforts they make will be appreciated by local people.

internet

Check out Lonely Planet's Web site www.lonelyplanet.com for loads of information about where you're travelling, as well as a chance to ask other travellers for tips and advice. Destination profiles give a very digestible overview of a country, the Kids to Go page of the Thorn Tree is the spot to ask questions about travelling with kids, and there are excellent links to loads of other sites. Tourist office Web sites are also a good starting point for information about the country you're visiting.

See the Web Site Appendix for more useful addresses.

documents

passports & visas

Many countries (such as Australia, UK and USA) require children to have their own passport, sometimes available at a reduced rate. There is the option for Dutch, German, and Canadian children to be added to their parent's passport until they are 16 (saving on passport costs), or they can have their own passport. Children of Dutch, German and Canadian parents but born elsewhere also have this option, but in addition require a passport from the country they are residents of if they need to gain re-entry there. Children with their own passports require visas just like adults and there are usually no reduced rates. However, if the children are included on the parent's passport, a visa is often only required for the parent, and in some places this can result in a considerable saving.

other documents

Check with your travel agent or the appropriate embassy whether any special documents are required for your destination. In Mexico, for example, authorities may require a notarised letter of consent signed by both parents permitting a minor (a person under 18 years old) to enter the country if travelling alone or with one parent. This rule is a direct result of the number of North American parents who run away to Mexico with their children in order to escape custody battles, however it applies to travellers of all nationalities.

costs

Travelling with children doesn't have to be prohibitively expensive though you will probably end up spending more money per person on places to stay, food and transport if you were used to travelling cheaply before you had children. Cleanliness somehow becomes more important with children, but you don't necessarily have to spend a lot more to find comfortable and clean options. In general, children up to the age of two can travel and receive admission for free or very little, and children between the ages of two and 12 receive discounts for most things. Once they're 12 travel with children will generally cost the same as another adult. See the country profiles later in this book for country-specific information.

what to bring

The first rule of thumb is to take as little as possible. Keep paring it down until you think it isn't nearly enough – it almost always is. Remember, in general babies' needs are pretty simple and wherever you go people have babies, so you can usually improvise. Detailed below are the pros and cons of some of the equipment you might want to consider taking.

From when they are toddlers it's possible for children to carry their own daypacks to take on the plane with them. It helps them feel involved and also

travel tips

Always remember to pack wet wipes for dirty hands, ice cream mouths, pen marks and seat cleaners at toilet time.

Louise Anderson, Australia

gets them to take responsibility for some of their own possessions. In a daypack they can carry their books and a few toys. You have to make it clear that it is their daypack and they carry it (when possible), so keep it light.

Babies require a fair amount of equipment though you can minimise it. Nappies, clothes, feeding equipment, a child safety seat if you plan to hire a car (though you may be able to hire a seat as well), a baby-carrier backpack or stroller and favourite toys are essentials. You may also want to consider a port-a-cot, portable highchair and bedding.

For toddlers you'll need a stroller (or backpack), child safety seat if you plan to hire a car and favourite toys and books. You might also want to consider a potty if they've just been toilet trained, a plastic bed sheet and their own feeding equipment.

The range of equipment requirements starts to reduce as children get older. Favourite toys and books including things like a Walkman (and plenty of spare batteries) with music or story tapes and computer games – can help with entertainment.

clothes

In most cases you can get by with two sets of the children's day clothes – ie, shorts, long pants, T-shirts, long-sleeved tops, jumpers – so that one can be worn while the other is being washed. Also take a jacket, extra socks and underwear, bathing suit, hat, pyjamas and perhaps a dress for girls. Make sure the clothes mix and match, don't show the dirt and that your children like wearing them. You'll need more clothes if you don't want to wash regularly but if you want to travel light these basics will be enough. Babies are more likely to make a mess of their clothes and will probably require three or four sets of their day clothes.

travel tips

The hot travel tip for older children is to bring a Game Boy – it doesn't improve their cultural experience but it keeps them happy for a few hours.

James Lyon, Australia

nappies (diapers)

If you're travelling in a warm climate there'll be times when babies can run around without nappies on, but for the majority of the time you'll need either cloth or disposable nappies. See the country profiles later in this book for information on nappy availability at your destination.

cloth Cloth nappies are easy to pack, reusable, relatively inexpensive and environmentally friendly. They can also double as bibs and towels. If you use cloth you'll need to carry a minimum of a dozen nappies. You may want to take a collapsible camping bucket for soaking and a bottle of tea-tree oil makes a good portable sterilising solution. Woollen or cotton nappy pants are best to minimise nappy rash if you're going to be in a warm climate.

disposable Disposable nappies are convenient but they're bulky and can be very expensive. Take a large bag full of disposable nappies from home and as they are used up, the bag can be used to carry purchases. Disposable nappies are light so they don't really affect your luggage allowance. Be sure to carry a roll of masking tape for when the tabs fail! Be aware that disposable nappies have a long-term environmental impact because they don't break down easily and contribute to the landfill problem – an issue of concern worldwide.

port-a-cots

You can take your own port-a-cot which airlines will carry free but with so much extra luggage already you may prefer to simply cope as you go along. In many countries you can buy one there or get something made if you're going to be staying around long enough or find that life without a cot is impossible.

> **travel tips**
>
> **On a recent trip we found the port-a-cot useful. It served as a safe, clean and familiar enclosure for our crawling baby – especially where the hotel rooms weren't clean.**
>
> Robyn Jones & Leonardo Pinheiro, Australia

bedding

For babies you might want to take two cotton sheets, one warm blanket, a mosquito net (in the tropics) and possibly a lambskin or something similar. Of course you don't need to provide all your own bedding wherever you go, but lambskins are a very good idea as even if the baby sweats a lot they never feel really damp. They are always soft and cuddly, and keep a child warm when they are cold and cool when they are hot. You can use lambskins under the sheet as well as on top of it. They are washable but you need a full, hot day to dry them.

For small babies cotton sleeping bags (the type that goes on like a nightgown over the head and arms, but fastens down the middle and are sewn along the bottom like a bag) are cooler than sleep suits, but protect the child from draughts and mosquitoes. Only a soft, light cotton material is necessary. A woollen sleeping bag is a good idea if you plan to go to cooler climates with a baby.

Waterproof sheeting is a very good idea for all small children. Even reliably toilet-trained little ones can have an occasional accident when they're very tired or in strange surroundings. The rubber backed type of cot sheet aren't as hot and sticky as having straight plastic under the sheet. The only problem is remembering to take it with you if you're moving around – it's worth having a check list of important things and ticking the list off before you close your bags.

> **travel tips**
>
> **Pack your young child's pillowcase to use in unfamiliar hotel rooms. It makes the bed seem more familiar and takes up much less space than a teddy bear.**
>
> Carol De Giorgio, Singapore

strollers & backpacks

A folding, reclining stroller can be a lifesaver. Obviously, a stroller is no good at all if you plan to go trekking on mountain paths, isolated tracks or beaches. It is strictly useful for day-to-day excursions to restaurants, shops, hotels and around towns, providing the footpaths are even. All-terrain, three-wheeler strollers will get you to more places but even they have their limitations. A stroller can be great in restaurants where the child can be strapped in an upright position to eat without having to keep them on your knee. It's also possible to sleep in it so you don't always have to rush back to your room for naps.

Backpacks are good for children who can sit up by themselves. You have two hands free and kids usually love them. The drawbacks are that they're not as comfortable for sleeping in and not all of them sit up by themselves to be used as a chair/restrainer in a restaurant.

For babies not yet sitting up there's the option of front pouches or slings (you can use a sarong, shawl or buy one custom-made). Babies love being carried in front and will often be lulled to sleep by your heart beat and movement.

There is a combined backpack/stroller on the market that may make life easier. It folds down into a backpack with retractable wheels and, with a bit of fiddling, springs into action as a stroller. They're available in Europe and in specialist camping shops in many other places.

feeding equipment

For babies bring bottles, teaspoon or baby spoon, plastic dish (wash in boiling water frequently), strainer (a tea strainer will do and is useful for straining fresh juice) and/or a food mulching device. Also bring several towelling bibs or a couple of soft plastic ones.

For toddlers, bring a cup with a spout, teaspoon (handy when you are only given a large spoon and fork in a restaurant), plastic bowl (for when you put together a meal yourself or give them a share of yours). Older children don't require any special equipment.

travel tips

Buy a small travel kettle to boil water to make up feeds. If you need to boil the water for ten minutes to purify it, invest in a small camping stove.

Rosie Whitehouse, UK

Despite the availability of highchairs in many restaurants there are many times when they are not available but you would love to have one. For children who can sit up unassisted, there are fold-up chairs that suspend from the table. The chairs have nylon or plastic seats and are light and reasonably portable. The problem with these is that they can only be used on certain types of table and then only if it's strong enough. See the country profiles later in this book for country-specific information on availability of highchairs and other feeding equipment at your destination.

favourite toys & books

These are really important to take but like everything else don't overdo it. You can buy things along the way. Choose toys that don't have small pieces that will inevitably drop on the floor of the plane/car/bus. An activity book and pencils; a Walkman with tapes of nursery rhymes, stories or music depending on the age of the child; a couple of favourite toys and books; as well as a new toy and book for the journey can all be useful. A lot of older children will be content for hours with a hand-held computer game. If you're travelling in countries where it's difficult to get English-language children's books, think about swapping with other travellers or getting someone to send you new ones if you're on a long trip. Make sure the books you take are ones they'll be happy re-reading!

friend

It raises a whole set of other issues but it can be worth considering taking along your teenager's friend on the trip. When they're at the age where everything is boring, it can make it all worthwhile if they've got a friend to talk to and explore with. Of course, then there's issues such as taking responsibility for someone else's child, the impact another child has on family dynamics and how other children who haven't bought along a friend react, but it's something to consider.

what to do about school

If you're travelling for an extended period of time with school-aged children there are a range of different options for schooling. You can organise with their school to get work in advance and take it with you; the children could attend a local or international school if you are staying in one place for a while; or they could attend cyberschool if you have an Internet connection or can access Internet cafes.

Check out dir.yahoo.com/education/k_12/alternative/home_schooling/ which has good links to lots of online and home schooling sites. As well as via the Internet, home schooling could be done via a correspondence course or you could develop your own curriculum. With a correspondence course you'll receive all the materials you need and the work will be graded. Developing your own curriculum means you can make it more relevant to your trip and adapt it to your child's needs and skills. It does mean more work for you – planning, teaching and keeping records. Really though, your trip will be an education in itself and there are plenty of opportunities for children to practise their reading, writing, maths, history and geography skills. See the Web Site Appendix for more ideas on home schooling.

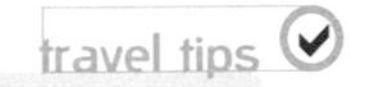

We're taking our son on a three-year, round-the-world trip. We're arranging a link-up with his high school via computer (laptop).

Edward Seco, Lonely Planet Web page

people

The people will be the most important memories your children take home and you will be surprised at how many they remember. In many countries tourism is definitely a two-way process and often you are the centre of attention.

attention

Travelling with children opens up a whole new world and it's quite likely your children will regularly be the centre of attention in another culture. They're likely to be talked to by adoring adults, given sweets and generally admired. You're likely to receive lots of praise and maybe some advice. In some cultures it's common for children to be passed around or to get admiring pinches on the cheek. Some children will love the attention, others won't. If your child has difficulty coping with the tactile affection, you can protect them from it as much as possible. Let your children set their own limits and support them. To keep them away from unwanted physical contact, they can always ride on your shoulders.

local children

One of the nicest aspects of travelling with young children is that, no matter where you are or what language is spoken, your children will make friends and communicate beautifully with the local children.

As they get older, children tend to need to have a common language before they can really play together for any length of time. Even a few words can go a long way. If you find yourself staying at a hotel where there are children of a similar age, your children will usually be so delighted to have other children to play and communicate with that you may not see them from one meal to the next.

> **travel tips**
>
> **If you should ever need help, go to someone who also has children. Children and people's adoration for them is truly a universal language.**
>
> Ericka Chemko, Canada

Despite the communication difficulties children do notice and study each other's behaviour. It is interesting to discover what your children are noticing and what they think of it. The beach is a good place to observe cultural differences and also one of the few places where your children can engage in noisy, boisterous games with the local children without relying on spoken communication.

One thing to be aware of on the beach is that although they may splash around happily in the shallows, some children are not taught to swim. Even if your children are good swimmers who don't need close supervision, keep an eye on the children they are playing with in case they are led out of their depth and experience difficulties.

culture

You may find that your normally outgoing, assertive two-year-old becomes very dependent and clingy when you first start travelling. This is normal. When everything familiar has disappeared they will hang on to what remains. Don't try to make them 'snap out of it', make friends with strangers or get them to stay with the lovely woman who runs your hotel and is longing for the chance to look after them. It will only make matters worse. Try to be extra comforting, take them with you wherever you go, tell them where you are going and what you hope to see there. Let them know that everything is perfectly normal and fine, and just give them a bit of extra coddling to reassure them. Generally it doesn't take too long for children to regain their sense of security.

If you are also feeling disoriented and a bit uncertain of what you are doing, especially if it is your first trip beyond a familiar environment, you may feel a little insecure yourself. Try not to let your children sense this. Stay close to your accommodation, make short walking trips in 'your neighbourhood', eat at your accommodation if you feel more comfortable there and only set off on excursions when you feel ready.

As a parent you are, of course, expected to know everything – you are the source of all wisdom and strength. No matter how vulnerable you are feeling, now is not the time to disillusion your children. Be decisive, even if you are not sure what it is you are deciding. If you need to find out something, ask questions of anyone you meet who is likely to have the information you require. Other travellers are good sources of information about places to eat, ways of getting to places, where to change money, etc, and they are usually happy to pass on what they have learned.

At some stage your children, depending on their age, may become upset by the poverty and suffering they see in some countries. Trying to avoid it, pretending it isn't there, or it isn't so bad, or suggesting that somehow these people are different and don't feel things the same way, are all doing your children a disservice and denying them the opportunity to use their travelling experience to its fullest extent. Of course, that doesn't mean that you should launch into a full political and ideological dissertation; it is generally enough to answer only those questions the children will ask, namely 'Why?'

Try to teach your children respect for the people they meet. The best way is by example – be aware of how you speak about the people you meet and how you talk to them. Apart from insisting that the standards you normally set are maintained, you must try not to give way to expressions of disdain when you are talking about the local people. This is something we like to think we don't do, but how often does some local frustration cause you to lose your temper or talk about 'these people' in less than affectionate tones? Remember that your children use you as their role model and will rely on you even more now that their world is totally different and their usual guidelines are gone.

The fact that 'grown-up' people don't understand English may cause your children some hilarity; they may feel superior when someone uses the wrong word or talks 'like babies'. It's a good opportunity to introduce your kids to the language of the country by teaching them a few basic words. You can make them aware of their relative position by asking them how much of the local language they can speak. See the country profiles later in this book for country-specific cultural issues.

GETTING THERE

getting there

air

Flights are never likely to be boring again once you start flying with children, in fact you'll probably be savouring the quiet moments. It can be hard work flying with kids, particularly young ones, but some good preparation can help make it manageable.

With small babies, the motion of the plane will often soothe them to sleep. Once they're over six months and more mobile, flying becomes more difficult simply because you have to work so hard to keep them happy – nursing them, playing with them, singing to them. With babies, whatever their age, you've got challenges like changing nappies in the cramped toilets and eating your meal with a baby on your knee. However even older babies will usually sleep for a good part of a long flight. If you've got the right equipment and entertainment to hand, and ask for help when you need it – you'll get a long way.

Toddlers can be hard going as travel companions; a long flight can be pure torture for an 18-month to three-year-old, not to mention their parents. Herculean efforts are required to amuse and distract them, and books, toys and snacks can only go so far. Hopefully they'll have a long sleep! Don't expect too much from your toddler. Remind yourself that the flight will eventually end and try not to be stressed by any negative reactions from other passengers. You'll probably never see them again! See the Travel Games Appendix for ideas on keeping the young ones amused on long haul flights.

travel tips

Even long flights are a short-term endurance test. If you retain your sanity, sense of humour and patience by the end of the trip there will be a real sense of achievement.

Jo Gregory, Australia

After three or four years old it does get easier. The children can amuse themselves with drawing and simple games. They can play with a few well-chosen toys, listening to the children's channel and even the movie will occupy them for a little while. They can feed themselves from their tray and the novelty of being offered drinks will usually keep them in good humour. It is also easier to persuade them to lie down and have a sleep.

Teenagers are much more self-sufficient and can usually be kept amused with in-flight entertainment and their own selection of books and music. Like adults they'll get bored as well but can cope with it much better.

fares & baggage allowance

Children under two years old pay 10% of the full adult fare on international flights, provided they are accompanied by a fare-paying adult. Only one 10% fare is allowed per adult, any other under-twos have to pay the children's fare. Children on 10% fares do not get a seat (they're expected to sit on your lap if necessary) or any baggage allowance. Nor do they get a meal, as you're supposed to bring food for them or let them pick off your tray.

Children's fares in relation to adult's fares vary to some extent. In general children are classified as being from two to 12 years of age for international flights, and three to 12 years of age for domestic flights. Children usually pay 50% of the scheduled adult fare or 67% to 75% of discount fares, which account for a high proportion of fares these days. The age of the child at the time of departure is the determining factor; so if your child passes the critical age while you're away that's no problem. Once your child has turned 12 all the discounts end; they're full fare from then on.

Necessary items for the baby during the flight can be brought on as cabin luggage. 'Necessary items' can be loosely interpreted, although it generally means food, nappies and clothes. Most (but not all) airlines will allow a stroller to be carried onto the plane. And it's very rare that there isn't a spare meal or two left over at meal times.

Although you cannot – officially at least – bring a baby's carrycot on board, the airlines will usually carry it free. They ask that it be collapsible if possible, but as long as it doesn't exceed 76cm by 40cm by 30cm that's OK. They don't specify what carrycots can weigh but as long as it's not over about 10kg you should have no problems.

Children over two get the full baggage allowance and if you're travelling somewhere tropical, where your clothes and baggage requirements are lightweight, you may find yourself with lots of spare baggage allowance which can be useful for bringing purchases home.

service

Airlines and airports offer quite a range of services and are usually very sympathetic to travelling parents', and their children's, needs. Some airlines really are better than others at catering for children; some give the distinct impression that the flight attendants' training is more inclined towards pouring the wine properly rather than coping with toddlers.

At the end of the day no amount of cheerful, competent, well-thought-out service can match lots of empty seats around you. The least crowded flights are often the best ones as far as flying with children is concerned. With a couple of seats to stretch over small children can sleep just as comfortably as they do at home. A good flight route can make a real difference as well; children dislike being woken up in the middle of the night in order to stand around some god-forsaken airport terminal even more than adults do.

Arrive at the airport early and try to be among the first to check in. This is important if you are going to have any choice at all in the seat allocation, although airlines often will try to give families more choice than other passengers.

If you require a bassinet you need to reserve this when you book your ticket (see sleeping for more information). If you require snacks rather than full meals for your child or yourself, book these with the airline at least 48 hours in advance. You can also order baby food, or bring it yourself and they will heat it up (see food & drink below for more information).

travel tips

To help expend energy in transit, we always carried two fly swats and some balloons that became balls once in the terminal. Instant tennis!

Adele Levinge, Australia

airports

Most airports have a parents' room where you can change and feed your baby; some are excellent, others are inconvenient and dismal. There has been a swing towards making these facilities available to parents rather than just mothers, so these days fathers too can change and tend to their babies. Some airports have family areas or play areas, ask in advance or at an information booth when you get there.

equipment for the flight

There is a fine balance between bringing everything your child might need and what you really do need. Below are some suggestions for things that are useful.

babies

- a rug or lambskin to sleep on
- nappies and nappy cleaning equipment
- plastic bags for dirty nappies, clothes, wipes, etc
- waterproof change mat
- food and drink
- at least one change of clothing and several bibs
- a few toys

Airlines carry disposable nappies but it is best to consider those an emergency supply only. Usually the crew will take away used disposable nappies but they must be in a plastic bag to meet health regulations.

Although there is usually a toilet in each section with a foldaway change table it can be difficult to hold down a wriggling child on a flat, hard surface in a cramped aeroplane toilet and change a nappy at the same time. It can be easier to lay the change mat on your seat and change the baby, unless it is really too disgusting and likely to make you very unpopular with other passengers.

For children over six months, toys that they can fiddle with seem to keep them occupied for a little while. Don't bring too many toys either – a handful of tried and true favourites is all that is necessary.

toddlers

- rug or lambskin to sleep on
- nappies or extra pairs of underwear
- wipes for nappies and cleaning up
- drinks and snacks
- a few toys and books

For those out of nappies take at least a couple of pairs of pants; accidents happen even to 'trained' children when they are excited, or worse, have to wait in line too long for a toilet.

Toys and books are great (see the Planning chapter for ideas) but bear in mind the limitations. Coloured pencils and notepads to draw on are useful though the cabin crew usually hand out games, books, pencils, etc, when your children board the plane.

Most children have a toy that must travel with them – a teddy, a doll, or some such friend. To avoid having to carry this; the baby and the bags, tie elastic around its neck, so that there is a loop. This loop goes around your child's wrist. It means that even if you have to carry teddy, the elastic loop can go around your wrist or over the stroller handle, and still leave your hands free. This tactic prevents the nightmarish possibility that you may inadvertently leave it behind somewhere.

Let flight attendants know what you need – they are generally happy to provide anything to make life easier for you, but simply don't know what. Visit the cockpit with slightly older children!

Claudia Koch-McQuillan, Australia

Other methods for coping with small children at airports include attaching a small but loud whistle to your child's jacket. If they get lost or even momentarily separated from you, they can give a good piercing blast. It gives them a sense of security, although you will probably have to dissuade them from using it at inappropriate moments and hope they remember to use it at the appropriate one! See the Travel Games Appendix in this book for game ideas on planes.

older children & teenagers

- books
- toys
- Walkman

As children get older the problems of entertaining them dwindle, but make sure they have adequate supplies of new or favourite books, toys and games. A Walkman with story and music tapes usually keeps them happy for a good part of the flight.

preparation for the flight

It is a good idea to plan for a calm, relaxed day for the 24 hours before your flight. Eat small, bland meals (nothing too taxing for the digestive system), go to bed early and try to stop children from becoming too excited. Get to the airport in time to organise everything calmly. Walk around and look at the shops and planes; talk quietly about going on the plane and what it will be like. Try to keep everything as relaxed as possible.

what to wear on the flight

Comfort is the main consideration in deciding what to wear. Regardless of where you're going or the expected weather, cover all possibilities in case of an unexpected stopover. A layer system of clothing works well.

If you want the children to look relatively clean and tidy when you arrive, carry their good clothes separately, but don't put them on too soon – when you are taxiing to the terminal is time enough, as children can often foil their parents' best-laid plans.

Parents need to be comfortable too and if you are travelling with small children remember that it's possible to get spectacularly dirty by the time you arrive. Sticky fingers, spilt food, regurgitated sweets, all have fewer places to go in a confined space and you may find yourself the main recipient.

seating

Where you sit can be quite important. Parents with small children are generally placed in the first row of seats facing the bulkhead. This has the advantage of more leg room so your child can play, and you may be seated with other sympathetic parents. The disadvantages are that generally the bulkhead seat row has fixed armrests which the tables fold down into. This means that even if you are lucky enough to score a vacant seat beside you, your child can't lie flat because the armrest won't budge. Even if there is a vacant seat, without an armrest that lifts you can't spread your child across their seat and your knee.

The other disadvantage is that if the plane doesn't have movie screens with each seat, then when the movie is on you are right beneath it. If you stand up, which you seem to have to do a lot with children, you are in everyone's way. It is also less easy to turn your light on for all those emergencies for which you need illumination, as this affects the picture for everyone behind. Finally, any other parents with babies will be right there next to you. If your children don't usually cry, sitting beside children who do cry might just set them off!

travel tips

The best time to scout for empty seats on an aircraft is just after the doors close prior to take-off. Quickly claim this prize by throwing self, child and possessions in general vicinity.

Jo Gregory, Australia

If it is to be a long flight you could ask for seats in the middle section with the theory that there are more seats in that section than between the aisle and the window. In the middle section you have more chance of being able to stretch out if there are vacant seats. You can also ask if it's possible to keep a vacant seat next to you for as long as possible. The cabin crew are generally very helpful and understanding with trying to find you extra seats if at all possible. Also if you and your family have three seats in a row of four and an individual stranger sits down in the remaining seat, one look at your contingent is usually enough to send them looking for alternative seating, so you .may still wind up with an extra seat. If you have two adults and two or more children you can always go on a scouting trip through the plane. You may find that by splitting up you can get very comfortably organised for sleeping.

comfort

Planes are very dry, which can make everyone feel uncomfortable. Take a spray-nozzled container filled with water to spray on children's faces; it feels nice and fresh and the children usually think it is a lot of fun. If you follow it with a moisturising cream, it does take the tight, dry feeling away. A chapstick is also useful for dry lips. Toothbrushes and toothpaste are good for when you want to freshen up.

If you find the dry air causes sore noses or sinus discomfort, try putting a scarf or handkerchief around a child's face, like a bandit. Something made of light material, lightly placed across their noses may cause some localised humidity and ease the discomfort.

sleeping

All airlines carry bassinets on long-distance flights, but they are only useful for very young babies. The bassinet either clips onto the bulkhead (the front wall of the cabin) or hangs above your head on certain designated seats in the window aisle. Their dimensions are between 58cm and 70cm long and about 30cm wide, and about 20cm deep. Bassinets are usually for babies up to 10kg. If you require a bassinet you must reserve it when you book your ticket. Many airlines offer safety belts for infants under two that are put around the child and attached to your seat belt. They're a good idea if your baby or child is sleeping on your lap, as well as for take off and landing.

Young children can sleep on a special lambskin or rug and older children will generally settle down and sleep when they are ready. The flight attendant will bring blankets and pillows to make them comfortable. Make sure they have a seatbelt around them so you don't have to wake them up if there's turbulence.

Take a sheet or cheesecloth to darken the bassinet, which is inevitably under the video screen. Take some Blu Tac to fasten the sheet to the wall – a bit like a tent.

Claudia Koch-McQuillan, Australia

food & drink

If your baby takes a bottle, then bring the bottle and most of their food. Although airlines will provide baby food upon request, it is best to be self-sufficient; if there are more babies than expected on the flight it can be quickly depleted. Also you may be delayed somewhere unexpectedly and your supplies may have to go further than planned, so take what you calculate you need and perhaps a bit more. For quick, easy feeding on planes and in airports, bring jars of baby food rather than cans. Try to bring enough clean bottles to last the journey. Although the water is generally purified, it is best to be on the safe side.

You may not always be able to get food and drink when you need it. If the children are ready for dinner about the time you'll be in the departure lounge then bring along some sandwiches, fruit or yogurt and have a picnic dinner or buy them a meal at the airport. Similarly, it's worth keeping snacks in your bag for when your children are hungry between meals and the cabin crew are busy.

Most airlines will supply a snack or children's meal, check when you book your ticket. Juice and soft drinks are freely available, but if you prefer not to give your children juice with sugar or preservatives you will have to bring your own. If two adults are travelling with a baby ask the cabin crew to delay one of your meals, so one of you can hold the baby while the other eats.

Everyone gets dehydrated on planes, so nursing mothers have to be especially careful to increase their fluid intake (not alcohol or caffeine though). Use the water fountains frequently, request glasses of mineral water or bring your own bottle and get it refilled.

One very important item for toddlers is a trainer cup (one with a spout) and it can be useful to pack two, just in case one gets lost along the way. If you just make a blanket rule that while on the plane all drinks must be drunk from the spout cup, your trip will be much drier. If you decide to bring snacks remember they will be spending quite a while in your bag; anything with a tendency to mush, crumble or become soggy is not a good idea.

time zones

Time changes can really disorient children. They will usually be tired anyway from the plane trip and their body clock alarm will be going off at odd times. They can become worn out and miserable (when they are not bouncing around in the early hours of the morning making you feel worn out and miserable). Although you may feel like just falling into bed when you reach your destination, if it is mid-morning on your new time you should try to keep going for the rest of the day. Relax and wind down, but try to make your bed time an appropriate one. The more quickly you can get on to the new time, the faster you will adjust. This doesn't mean that you have to keep your children awake come what may. They will probably nap anyway, but try to keep the going-to-bed rituals (bath, pyjamas, stories, etc) until the time when they will actually be going to bed.

If you arrive when it is early morning on the new time then aim to have the children sleep before or around midday for an hour or two, then wake them up and keep them awake until a reasonable bed time. They will then hopefully sleep through the night and be on their way to adapting to the time change within a few days.

Older children and teenagers who have travelled before are at least aware of what is happening. Although it is still hard to keep them awake when they really want to sleep, they are more likely to cooperate and they can lie down, reading or listening to a tape.

health issues

For information on motion sickness and ear pain during take off and landing see the Health chapter.

bus & train

Bus and train journeys can be a good way to get around with young babies and older children and teenagers. But making long trips by bus or train can be difficult with children when they've passed the tiny-baby stage and not yet arrived at the able-to-amuse-themselves stage. Children who are crawling or toddling usually hate having to sit still in cramped buses or trains without much room for movement. Buses sometimes lurch along in such a way that you really have to hang on to your children.

If you do have to make a long trip, and there is no way you can break it up into smaller sections, all you can do is treat it like a plane trip. Make sure you have all you need readily available – drinks, snacks, books, whatever you think will work.

Buses are often the most crowded and uncomfortable form of transport. You may have to hold your children for the entire journey. So if they are older than two, even if they would travel for free, it's probably worthwhile to pay for extra seats rather than economising by keeping them on your knee. Take all the food and drink you could possibly need. If you are travelling overnight make sure you take a blanket or warm clothes.

For comfort, where there is a choice of bus or train, trains are probably a better bet. If the trip is a really long one, an overnight sleeper, if available, is always the best way to do it. Children usually love sleeping on trains.

After a long trip, try to make sure that the next few days are spent somewhere nice and relaxing. Choose a comfortable place to stay where the children can run around and enjoy themselves. Unpack the bags, frequent the same restaurants, give the children and yourself as much time as you can manage to totally get the trip out of your system. While it may seem that the children have forgotten all about the trip an hour after getting off the bus, the next time you reach the bus station you may find them yelling that they don't want to go. Never plan too many long journeys. Where they are unavoidable, space them as much as possible.

Older children will, of course, be bored on long bus trips, but they will usually manage better for longer. Local people may talk to them, you can play all the usual travel games (see the Travel Games Appendix for ideas) and chat about what you are seeing to pass time. Have a treat for each hour after a certain period, even if it is only sweets or fruit, and take advantage of any stops. Always remember to make your children visit the toilet at every opportunity although kids are kids anywhere in the world and bus drivers always know what it means when you come striding up the aisle, child in hand.

car

Renting a car or taking your own can make life much easier for the travelling family. You can travel when you want and for as long as you want (or as long as the back seat passengers can cope with), you can stop for the toilet as required

 travel tips

If you've got young girls, a potty in the car boot can be very useful. It saves hanging on while searching for a toilet.

Mim Holland, Australia

and have breaks along the way at playgrounds and parks. If you hire a car check when you book that it has safety belts in the back and if you are not able to hire a child safety seat for babies and young children (or they're prohibitively expensive) then take your own. See the country profiles later in this book for country-specific information about child safety seats. See also the accommodation section of the On the Road chapter for information about travelling around by campervan or recreational vehicle.

drive time

How long you travel for depends on the age of your children. It can be easy to travel for hours with babies and young children if you leave when they're almost due for a sleep during the day or drive at night when they're sleeping; though the latter option can make for tired parents. With older children you can either pace yourself and not travel more than two to four hours a day or do a long stint of six to eight hours and then stop a few days when you get to your destination. You could also start very early in the morning, let the kids fall back to sleep in the car and drive for a few hours until breakfast time to give you a good start for the day. This is particularly useful if you're driving out of cities to avoid the morning peak hour traffic.

With older children and teenagers plan the driving with them. Before you set out for the next day get them to decide with you what time you should leave, how far you want to get and by looking at maps or guidebooks, where you should stop. Make sure you plan some time for physically strenuous activity in breaks during the trip, you might have to initiate it to make sure they run off steam. Lots of readers have suggested taking a soccer ball or Frisbee to throw around during stops. And even though being cramped in a car with kids saying 'How much further?' may drive you nuts at times, try to maintain a positive attitude and think of the drive as a part of the adventure, not a means to an end. Driving can be a great time to talk with your teenager, particularly for long stretches of driving when any other members of the family are asleep.

car entertainment

Travelling by car usually means you've got a bit more space for luggage. Make sure you're prepared for the journey with drinks, food, toys, Walkmans etc, without going overboard. Drinks and snacks make a welcome break from back seat monotony and a few well-chosen toys will keep boredom at bay for a while. Make sure you don't take toys with lots of little pieces that have to be picked up from the floor of the car all the time. It's useful for kids to each have a tray table so they can play games or draw on an even surface.

If you're doing a long trip, it's worth buying Walkmans to keep kids entertained. You could get some children's talking book tapes or if your children are older, you could get ones to play on the car cassette player that you might all enjoy listening to. Funny tapes can lighten up the journey. You could also take it in turns to pick the music on the car's tape deck, so everyone's not sitting there with headphones on for the whole trip listening to their own music. If you can't cope with the music, revert to the headphones. Make sure you take lots of extra batteries. Alternatively for entertainment you could be the talking book yourself – learn a long story or even tell a story about your childhood and then when you've got the kids really enthralled let on that it's you.

Rattles and musical toys are good for babies; and things with moving parts will amuse toddlers; for older children plastic figures can provide hours of entertainment; and for teenagers cards and travel games are useful. It can be a good idea to make a pocket that can hang over the front seats for toys to go into or have them pack everything into their own day pack. To relieve the tediousness of car travel, change seats every now and then; kids usually love it when an adult sits in the back with them, or, if they're old enough, they get to sit in the front. See the Travel Games Appendix in this book for loads of great car game ideas.

travel tips

A big, magnetic drawing board gives kids something to do that can have loads of drawings on it and isn't messy. It can also double as a table.

Staffan Thorell, Sweden

bicycle

In many countries bikes are readily available in touristed areas and are a good, fun way to get around. Most kids will love cycling and can handle reasonable length rides if you let them set the pace, take breaks and keep it fun. Bicycle touring is also possible with kids and they may even surprise you with their stamina. If you're contemplating bike touring make sure you do plenty of practice runs and day trips before you leave home to introduce your child to cycling so you know what they're capable of and can check your set-up. Lonely Planet publishes detailed cycling guides for a number of countries for those contemplating a reasonable amount of cycling.

equipment

Children can travel by bicycle from the time they can support their head and a helmet – usually at around eight months. There are some small, lightweight, cute helmets around, such as the L'il Bell Shell. To carry littlies means attaching a child seat or trailer. Child seats are more common for everyday riding and have advantages of being cheaper, easier to move as a unit with your bike, and allow you to touch and talk to your child while moving. Usually over longer distances disadvantages become more obvious, including exposure to weather, the tendency of a sleeping child to loll and less luggage space at the rear. The best makes – such as the Rhode Gear Limo – have features such as extra moulding to protect in case of a fall, have footrests and restraints, recline for sleep, and fit very securely and conveniently onto a bike rack.

With a capacity of up to 50kg (versus around 18kg for a child seat), trailers can accommodate two bigger children and luggage. They give better, though not always total, protection from sun and rain and let children sleep comfortably. Look for a trailer that is lightweight, foldable, conspicuous (brightly coloured, with a flag) and that handles well. It's also handy to be able to swap the trailer between bikes so adults can alternate towing and riding beside the trailer. Child trailers tend to be preferred for serious touring, but may be illegal in some places, so you should check with local traffic authorities before setting out. Trailers or seats are treated as additional luggage items when flying.

Be sure that the bike you attach a child seat or trailer to is sturdy and low-geared, to withstand – and help you withstand – the extra weight and stresses.

From the age of about four, children can move on to a 'trailer-bike' (effectively a child's bike without a front wheel which hitches to an adult's bike) or to a tandem (initially on the 'stoker', as the back seat is called, with 'kiddy cranks') – this lets them assist with pedalling. The tandem can be a long-term solution, keeping you and your child together while still allowing you to compensate if the child tires.

Be careful of children rushing into touring on a solo bike before they can sustain the effort and concentration required. Once they are ready and keen to ride solo, at about age 10 to 12, they will need a good quality touring bike, properly fitted (A$300, US$200, UK£130 up).

touring

Bike touring with children requires a new attitude as well as new equipment. Be sensitive to their needs – especially when they're too young to communicate them fully. In a seat or trailer, they're not expending energy and need to be dressed accordingly. Take care to keep them dry, at the right temperature and protected from the sun. For children who are cycling, it's best to go with the layered clothes so that they can be peeled off as you go.

Keep their energy and interest up. Make sure your kids have a water bottle each and that you take plenty of high energy snacks to sustain them particularly if you're cycling in an area without a lot of shops. Most kids will be happy riding for a reasonable time but when their enthusiasm is flagging try singing songs, telling stories, making games out of reaching certain points etc. (see the Travel Games Appendix for more ideas). When you stop, a child travelling in a seat or trailer will be ready for action, so always reserve some energy for parenting. This means regular stops at playgrounds and toilets.

Children need to be taken into account in deciding each day's route – traffic and distances need to be moderate, and facilities and points of interest adequate. Pick a route that follows designated bike paths or back roads without a lot of traffic. Make sure your children are aware of road safety rules and are wearing helmets. Given the extra weight of children and their daily needs, you may find it easier to leave behind the camping gear and opt for indoor accommodation or day trips from a base or series of bases. The very fit and adventurous may not need to compromise to ride with children, but those who do will still find it worthwhile.

See the Asia chapter for Dave Quinn's story about cycling the Karakoram Highway from China to Pakistan with his family.

walking & trekking

Walking can be an enjoyable way to get around for children – they can run, explore new things and be outdoors all day. It's important to make the experience as much fun as possible so they don't end up bored – talk to them about what you're seeing along the way, play make-believe games to make the walk even more of an adventure, sing songs, tell stories, look for animal tracks, take time out for photos or check out the Travel Games Appendix in this book for more ideas.

Children always enjoy it more when there are other kids their own age around, so it may be a good idea to try to organise a walk with other families. Combine a walking holiday with a few days by the sea – plotting the more strenuous activity first! Think seriously about hiring a car if you haven't brought your own so that you're not reliant upon infrequent or nonexistent rural bus services. Children can be slow to adapt to changes of diet, temperature and altitude, so before undertaking a route of several days it might be wise to first establish a base camp and do a number of day or half-day walks to break them – and yourself – in. See the Health chapter for more information on altitude sickness.

travel tips

Start by carrying younger kids on your back and they'll grow up loving it. Make sure you're fit yourself so you don't get tireder than the kids!

Sandra Bardwell, UK

what to wear

Dress your children in brightly coloured clothes so they are always easy to spot, and pin a whistle to their jacket, so they can signal you if necessary. Make sure your children know what to do if they get lost – sit in one spot, stay warm and blow their whistle, or whatever other instructions you give them. Use the layering system of clothes so it's easy to add or take clothes off. Make sure you protect yourselves against the elements and carry lots of high energy snacks and drinks with you.

In cooler weather blanket sleepers can make good walking clothes for small children. Add a hood, mittens and a sleeveless jacket, and kids are cosy from head to foot, and comfortable. If you are planning a cold-weather trek make sure children's shoes fit over the plastic 'feet' in the blanket sleeper. Many experienced walkers recommend tennis shoes or slip-on rubber boots with felt inner soles. Always have enough warm clothes with you, even if you don't think you might need them.

equipment

You will also need to carry additional equipment if you are walking with a baby – nappies, extra changes of clothes, baby food, feeding equipment and possibly bottles. Nappies are a tricky issue but if you use disposables it's best to carry them out with you and dispose of them safely. Burying them on the trail doesn't solve the problem as animals may dig them up. Cloth nappies pack quite well but if you're on a long walk you'll need to wash them for which you'll need a wash basin – you could use a collapsible camping bucket or pack other things into a plastic basin and take that with you; avoid dumping the soapy water where it might pollute a water source. If your baby is formula-fed you could fill bottles with boiling water each day at camp and add the formula when ready. Bring along pre-sterilised bottles or just cleaning and boiling the bottles will suffice.

when you're walking

Most children like to carry their own packs. These don't have to be expensive, but do have to be light and easy to carry. Children from three years of age can carry their own but there will certainly be some passing it on to the accompanying adults at times. Check that there are no uncomfortable lumps, let them carry their own snacks and drinks, a flashlight and one or two favourite toys. Make sure you have plenty of food and drink – they'll need more than they normally do during the day.

From about the age of eight they can carry their own pack for an overnight walk. Those a little older might like to have a book in it for moments at rest stops when grown-ups get boring. See the North America chapter for Mark Lightbody's story about walking with teenagers or the Asia chapter for Megha Singh's tale of trekking in Nepal with her family.

There's a simple rule of thumb for calculating what kids can carry on a walk: most can comfortably walk their age and carry half of it. In other words, a 12-year-old should be able to walk about 12km per day in moderate terrain, carrying a pack that weighs 6kg.

It's best to start off early in the day when children's energy levels are higher but still be prepared to carry young children for part of the trip as they tend to tire easily. Obviously for babies and toddlers a backpack or similar carrier will be essential, while older but still portable littlies can ride comfortably on their parent's shoulders or back. However, this soon becomes uncomfortable for you, and on rocky, steep or uneven surfaces it can become unsafe.

Don't try to cover as much ground as you would without children. This sounds obvious, but it's sometimes overlooked. Lots of rest stops are necessary, and bear in mind, too, that during the rest stops you will probably have to keep working – entertaining, feeding, washing, and trying to get the children to actually stop and rest for a while. Always carry an extra set of clothes in an easily accessible spot – children will always be able to find the one puddle of water or mud hole for miles around.

If you're walking to heights over 2000m you need to be aware of the potential problems of altitude and that very young children don't acclimatise to high altitudes as easily as adults. See the Health chapter for further information.

ON THE ROAD

on the road

making it work

Travelling with children should be mostly fun, but it doesn't happen automatically. Some forethought and a few strategies can make a big difference to the enjoyment level of the trip.

what to see

Museums, ruins and historic buildings can be fascinating and most things you want to do will have some appeal for children, though not in quite the same way. Statues are interesting anywhere and make great climbing frames, but be aware of cultural sensitivities – for example, you should *never* let your children climb on Buddha statues. Even temples and buildings can be made to seem interesting if you have a little bit of knowledge about them, which means that you have to be prepared. You don't have to know everything – dates and architectural styles are not what children are interested in – but the stories and legends associated with historical buildings, monuments and statues will appeal to them. See the country profiles later in this book for ideas on kid-friendly sites.

> travel tips
>
> **Churches, cathedrals and temples are definitely 'doing' places. If the kids can light a candle, drop in money or light incense this makes for a special and fun visit.**
>
> Liz Allen, Australia

Pick and choose the things you want to see. Children will quickly become immune to castles, Roman ruins etc, so take them to a selection of sights you don't want to miss. Guided tours are probably best avoided with younger children. Instead, go at your own pace, explain things along the way and let them follow their own interests. Teenagers may be happier to explore places themselves and meet you at a designated spot outside.

involving your children

Keep any younger children informed of your plans. Tell them where you are going, what you want to see, how you will get there, how long it will take – all the details. With older children and teenagers you can involve them a lot more; they can help plan where you will go and what you'll do. Let children have some local money and encourage them to make transactions (with your help if they need it). Kids are often amazingly adept at working out how much their money is worth in a number of currencies and it's great for their maths skills. If you've missed a train and you have to make alternative plans, discuss what's happening with the children so they're not just picking up that something's wrong but aren't sure what it is.

taking turns

With very young children you may enjoy a gallery visit more if you go solo, so if there are two adults you can split up. One can stay with the children and one can visit the museum, and the next day vice-versa. Some travelling parents take it in turns to have one day to themselves each week.

Once your children are a bit older you can take turns at each doing an activity. You choose to visit a museum in the morning, but in the afternoon they get to choose what they want to do, whether it is playing in their room, present shopping for friends, going to a playground or swimming pool, or doing some sightseeing. If you have a full day on a bus or in the car, make the next day a rest day, when you all relax and the children get to choose the activities.

You can extend this further and adopt a system where each family member has a turn at being the leader for the day, deciding what you'll do that day, where you'll eat and what you'll see. It spreads the responsibility, helps build a child's confidence and makes them feel like it's their trip as well. And you may end up doing some things that you wouldn't have done otherwise! If they have no idea of what there is to do in a place you'll need to give them some options, older children can get ideas from guidebooks and tourist brochures.

tiredness

Young children get very tired and – like everyone else – cope badly with life when they are in need of rest. Avoiding overtiring is easier said than done, but try to structure your day around your kids' needs. Think about what you want to do and then how best to do it. If it is a long bus trip to your destination, the morning may be the best time to go, when the children are fresh and cheerful, and the ride back may be a good time for them to have a sleep.

Don't fill your days with things to do; children need some unstructured playtime each day. Take a couple of hours each day to stay at your accommodation and let them fill in time as they please – whether it is playing with toys, drawing, reading, being read to or whatever.

space to play

Where possible, choose places to stay with your children in mind. Any kind of garden, verandah or safe space is worth having. A swimming pool is top of the desirable facilities – children can usually spend hours jumping in and splashing around and if they've had a hot sticky morning of sightseeing it can seem like heaven. A hotel room is not a very stimulating environment, but being able to sit on a verandah and watch people going about their business, or run around a small patch of garden chasing a butterfly, may make enough difference to avoid kids feeling trapped and frustrated. If you've got teenagers let them go out by themselves to a local restaurant; organise to have separate rooms in your hotel or accommodation.

children's experiences

Allow your children to experience things in their own way. The statue may seem very impressive to you, but if your son seems to be more interested in the vendor of sticky drinks, don't think the trip is a failure and he would have been better at home. You'll be surprised at the memories children will take home, and the insights they will have of the culture and people they met. Don't devalue the things your children find exciting and wonderful or try to always turn their attention to what you feel is more important. As long as they find something exciting and wonderful the trip will be a success.

children's activities

Just about everywhere you can find things that seem to be tailor-made for children. They will be fascinated by the obvious differences from life at home – the houses, the different forms of transport, the way people dress and the local customs. Equally, there are things that adults might pass by which prove absolutely irresistible to children. Besides all the special treats and children's attractions, don't underestimate their ability to be awed, enchanted and delighted by more 'cultural' pursuits. You can also encourage them to use their imagination and develop make-believe games from what they see in their new environment.

They'll also find other children to play with, either local children or other travelling families. Initially they may need some encouragement to approach other children but they'll soon get the hang of it, particularly if they're a child travelling alone with their parents. If they develop a good friendship while travelling it may be worthwhile adjusting your plans to spend a bit longer with their friend in that place. Obviously you can't do that with every child they meet but sometimes it may be worthwhile to avoid feelings of leaving people behind and not doing the things they'd like to. Adults will often be prepared to change their plans to spend time with new acquaintances and it shouldn't be any different for children.

travel tips

Get kids to choose, write and send their own letters and postcards. It'll remind them of friends at home and help them realise they're doing something worthwhile and interesting.

Mark Lightbody, Canada

road rules

Travelling as a family will create loads of happy memories that your kids will talk about for years. On the other hand, the intensity of travelling together can also create conflict and put parenting skills to the test. While parenting on the road creates different situations to what you may be used to at home, the issues are basically the same. Encourage positive behaviour and listen to your children as much, or more, than you would at home. They will also probably need more attention than usual to feel secure in a strange environment and will need more explanation about what's going on.

create boundaries Make it clear at the start of the trip what the rules are; work them out as a family and discuss what they mean. For example, if you decide it's a rule that no-one wanders off without letting anyone know where they're going then be clear what that means. If you feel the need to change the rules along the way then discuss them together. If you have a situation where someone wants to change the fast food once a fortnight rule to once a week then have a family discussion. Be consistent in your parenting as much as possible and if there are two of you be united in your approach.

travel tips

My parents made a contract with my sister and me that we'd get one ice cream every day, guaranteed, as long as there was no nagging for anything else. It cut down on whining and we thought we'd struck gold!

Bridget Blair, Australia

misbehaviour Travelling presents lots of opportunities for children to learn to take responsibility for their actions – from deciding on what toys and books they'll take and then carrying their own pack to managing their spending money and coping if it runs out. It's easy for parents to take responsibility for their children's actions, but it's better if children learn about behavioural consequences themselves from a young age.

If your children are misbehaving despite your best efforts to calm them down, consider what they are trying to achieve by their behaviour. Is it more personal space? More of your attention? Feeling the need to compete with their sibling to fulfil their role in the family? If you can ascertain the reason for the behaviour it can help by responding to the cause not the symptoms. In some situations it may be appropriate for the family to solve the problem together so everyone has ownership of it, for example seating arrangements in the car can be decided by everyone.

If teenagers appear to be uninterested in everything you're doing, it's probably because they're at an age when they're starting to separate from their parents more and further developing their own identity. While they may say that everything their parents do is boring, they will actually appreciate that you're making an effort and are interested in them even if they don't show it. Hopefully with more time together on holidays you'll be able to get them talking about what they're feeling.

Travelling can be really stressful when you've got to make quick decisions or change plans. Even though at times you may be feeling stressed yourself, don't use anger in discipline. Discipline is meant to teach your child what is acceptable and unacceptable behaviour, not be a pressure valve to relieve your frustration. Also be careful to criticise your child's behaviour, not your child; explain that a behaviour is not appropriate and why rather than saying the child is bad or hopeless. A child told that often enough will believe it.

recording the trip

There are lots of fun and enjoyable ways that children can record their trip, depending on their interests and inclination. Below are a few ideas that might appeal:

- take a glue stick and stick into a journal things that children collect along the way: tickets, stamps, souvenirs etc
- a project book (with alternating lined and blank pages) can provide space for drawing pictures and maps, and for interesting snippets of local history or culture
- even young children can manage a camera and their perspective will usually be fascinating; a disposable camera is a cheap alternative that kids can break or lose without much worry or expense
- a tape recorder makes a good alternative to a journal for children who are too tired for writing at the end of the day; they can record their impressions as well as sounds they hear
- for toddlers you could write a poem or story about the trip highlights and illustrate it with photos or drawings
- older children and teenagers can send emails to their friends and keep copies of them to put into a book as their trip record
- families have created Web sites about their trip including stories, journal entries and photos

travel tips

Don't expect too much of your kids and make sure you feed them regularly – low blood sugar leads to short tempers.

Rosie Whitehouse, UK

places to stay

hotels

Often what was acceptable to you alone is no longer so with children. As a parent you may feel more comfortable in more expensive hotels although you won't necessarily have to spend very much more to find places that are ideal.

Travelling with young children usually means that your days start early and end early, when you have to feed them and get them to bed. So it's nice sometimes to stay in a place which has rooms near a dining area. You can feed the children early, get them to sleep and then go and eat, taking turns to check on them every 10 minutes to see that they are still asleep.

Older children can usually stay up later and accompany you to dinner, but there are occasions when they are too tired or you feel like having a more adult dinner. Depending on where you are travelling, if the restaurant is in the hotel or very close by, you could leave the children with somebody you trust to keep an eye on them and call you if necessary. Write down where you will be and make sure your children know exactly where you are.

travel tips

We make personalised storybooks so our toddler can re-live his travels. Just put snapshots and brochure images in a photo book with plastic pockets and scribble text alongside.

Robyn Jones and Leonardo Pinheiro, Australia

Before one of our trips, members of the family seemed to be at war. David and I had time and work pressures, and the children had the usual stresses of getting along together, performing at school and helping out at home. It seemed the only time I talked to my children was to hurry them up – to get to the dinner table, to do their homework, into the bathroom, into bed, to get dressed in the morning, to eat their breakfast and, finally, out to the school bus.

family dynamics

GET AWAY & GET ALONG

Lyndall Parris has travelled regularly with her husband, David, and three children, Margo, 22, Richard, 20 and Sam, 15.

Apart from the time pressures of catching planes and trains, our three months away was a pleasant respite from this rut in which we seemed to have been stuck. There seemed no reason to hurry into bed while staying on Mykonos, we only had to be up in time to get to the beach the next day. In Egypt, the pyramids weren't going anywhere and it didn't seem to matter what time we started off in the morning while touring Vermont.

We had time to really talk to each other. Having no other friends or time pressures, the family became friends. Family conversation is different as there is less need to talk about repetitive organisation and routine. We discovered that we liked each other's company and our friendships continued after we arrived home.

While travelling, the older children have a looser regime and have the time and inclination to help the younger children learn or do tasks. At home you've usually done it all!

"The big hint when travelling with a young family (perhaps with general parenting, too) is to be realistic about your goals and objectives."

Over the years we have had many family trips and holidays. Generally speaking, when we have remembered that our times together are for all the family and not just for parents, we have enjoyed harmony and fun. Occasionally, we would push the art gallery or the shopping too far and our children would gently remind us to consider their needs too.

The big hint when travelling with a young family (perhaps with general parenting, too) is to be realistic about your goals and objectives. A relaxed outdoor, nature holi-day is much easier with children than a fast-paced, city sightseeing trip. Save the cities until you are holidaying without children or when they have grown older.

settling in & sleep Your children may not like too much moving around and you may find that they have difficulty in settling into a new room. It's worthwhile making sure you are always settled into a new hotel early in the afternoon to give your children time to get used to the room. Even very young babies can be extremely sensitive to their surroundings. Try to give them time to explore the room, play in it, learn where the bathroom is, etc. It is also an idea to carry something personal which will make the room familiar. Try to have something that a baby can always have within view; a small mobile, a fluffy toy that sits on the bed.

Small children need a sleep during the day and will be extra tired when travelling. Some children may sleep quite happily on your shoulder wherever you may be, others need to be laid down on a bed, given a drink and a cuddle before they can drift off. You can sometimes make a choice: keep your children awake all afternoon, and put them to bed early (which means your day ends early too); or insist that they have an afternoon nap or rest, in the hope that you can all go out to eat at night without exhaustion making the experience a misery for all of you. It is not worth trying to force your children to 'get used to it' in this sort of situation; you will have to organise your travelling to suit them. This is where the compromise comes in – you have to, your children won't.

Older children are much easier; they usually like new hotel rooms and will run around checking out what they have to offer. Usually they have a preferred bed to sleep on within minutes of entering the room, and they also like to set out their toys and books, and make a space for themselves. If they want to move things, let them (within reason). Going to bed at night is the usual matter of getting them to settle down, but usually present few problems as the day's events will have worn them out.

privacy Teenagers probably won't have much trouble settling in and sleeping but privacy can be a big issue, especially if they are sharing a room with a sibling and their parents. They will work out their own ways of getting changed in private if that's important to them, but there are ways you can make it easier for all of you.

Whatever their age, if there are four of you it may be easier to take two rooms side by side, rather than all pile into one. You may also have the benefit of two bathrooms. It's surprising how often even pretty basic hotels have some sort of family room or suite. Getting a place where you have your space and the children have theirs can make a real difference to everybody's comfort.

With a verandah or some separate space the parents can sit and read or talk while the children sleep. Sometimes this is not possible, so you are stuck with trying to dim the room sufficiently to encourage the children to sleep but not so much that you are forced to go to bed too. As the children get older you may find that they can stay awake until reasonably late, and then you can all go to bed at the same time.

cots Expensive 'international standard' hotels can almost always supply cots and in many countries even the more reasonably priced hotels will have something for a baby or small child to sleep in. In some places you may be charged extra for a cot.

You can carry a port-a-cot or look at alternatives, including the children simply sleeping with you (although if your children are restless sleepers, that may be no fun at all). Two armchairs placed facing each other can make a fine, safe sleeping cot for a small child. Even if you don't leave them there all night it can be useful for daytime sleeps or for the first part of the evening when the baby is asleep, but the rest of you are sitting up reading. A large drawer might also prove serviceable as an improvised cot.

From 18 months old onwards children (depending on how big and confident they are) can usually sleep in a bed. You can always make sure they get a bed against the wall and put a pillow beside them if you worry about them falling out.

location If your hotel is near the main sights, or public transport, teenage children can head back to the hotel if they don't want to traipse around for the day.

bathing Bathing your children may sound very simple but depending on the age of your child, it may require some organisation, particularly if your room does not have an attached bathroom or there is no bathtub in the bathroom.

Some small children will take showers, but most of them do not like the experience of water gushing down on them. You can always use a plastic change mat, get a bucket of warmish water and wash them down with a cloth. Then you can let them splash around as much as they like and hopefully clean themselves in the process. Occasionally you will strike it lucky and find a bathroom with a tub, not just a shower.

If you're somewhere where they're swimming a lot you can dispense with a lot of bathing though they'll need salt washed out of their hair.

> **travel tips**
>
> **When bathing children in countries with non-drinkable water, don't give the children bath toys or a washer as everything ends up in their mouths.**
>
> Dave Quinn, Australia

camping

Camping means more equipment but also the joys of living simply, enjoying the outdoors and always having your accommodation with you. If you haven't camped as a family before, do a weekend practice run or two before embarking on longer trips to make sure you've mastered the basics to make it an enjoyable experience. When you're planning your trip, check the brochures for a camping ground with a swimming pool, the kids will love it.

Things you'll want to have with you include tent, sleeping bags, first aid kit, matches, cooking equipment, water filter, camera and perhaps binoculars. Half-length sleeping bags used by climbers are ideal for children to use and much better quality than the average child-size sleeping bag, although the latter are probably fine for warm-weather trekking.

If your children are older you may want to take a separate tent for them to give them some privacy. For babies and young children take some kind of mat you can use as a clean space for them to play on. Make sure you let the kids get involved as much as possible in setting and packing up camp – what is a chore at home is often great fun when you're camping. You could plan your meals before you go, have your children help choose them and then get them to help out with meal preparation as well. With children it can be useful to have a central base and do short hikes from this base in different directions, rather than pack up camp regularly. Also see the walking & trekking section in the Getting There chapter for more information or check out Mark Lightbody's experiences of hiking with a teenager in New Hampshire in the Northern America chapter.

travel tips

We would dig a hole large enough for baby's bath. Line it with a plastic ground sheet, boil water and fill bath with warm water. To empty, pull ground sheet away and lay out to dry.

Deidree Noss, Australia

apartment/house

Renting an apartment or house is an option if you're going to be staying in an area for a while. As well as being more affordable than a hotel, it provides space for you and the children to spread out, more privacy and you may also have more connection with the local community. See the Europe chapter for Morna O'Neill's experiences renting an apartment in London and a castle in Ireland. Another option is to join a home exchange agency or organise your own exchange which can include a family car and may come with a ready-made network of babysitters and other children to play with.

There are many different rental companies and home exchange organisations as well as some hospitality exchange organisations advertising on the Internet. See the Web Site Appendix for some places to start.

tour/family resort

If your time is limited there are an increasing number of companies offering family-friendly tours and resorts. Establish how suitable they will be for your children by checking out what activities they provide specifically for children, what age range they cater to, how many other children are likely to be there etc. You also need to decide whether you want a holiday with your children or one where they'll be taken off your hands, you'll usually find both on offer. Generally, resorts will provide plenty of outdoor activities to keep healthy kids busy if all you want to do is enjoy a break.

campervan/recreational vehicle

Travelling in your own self-contained vehicle means you can stop when you like and you have most things you'll need with you. Stopping at camping grounds can provide a good place to meet other travellers and there are usually other kids around as playmates. The disadvantages of living in your own vehicle are that you're all in a very cramped space and camping grounds are often not centrally located. It's a good idea to take a tent so you can stake your claim to your site if you drive off sightseeing. If you're going to be staying somewhere for a while, you might want to create a play area where the whole family can throw a Frisbee or play soccer.

When we'd made the decision to travel around the world, we immediately thought of a campervan, even though we had little experience with this kind of vehicle. The initial investment is very costly – there's the purchase of the campervan, the sea crossings from continent to continent and the bank guarantee for the Carnet de Passage en Douanes. (Some countries ask for a guarantee on arrival preventing the sale of the car. To avoid leaving money at each border, this guarantee – the value of the car – is made at the automobile club in your own country.)

campervanning AROUND the WORLD

Annie and Stéphane Marais left home on a four-year trip with their children Louise, eight, Lola, six, and Léo, three. They finance their travel with a self-published magazine.

But the campervan has many advantages. For our three children the campervan is a familiar home with their rooms, beds and play things. They really miss the campervan when it is sailing from one continent to another. It is also a protection against mosquitoes, insects and other undesirable animals. We cook in it, so we limit the risks of illness due to contaminated water and food. As soon as water looks suspect, we use water purification treatment in our tank (which has a 100 litre capacity). We have our own bathroom and the toilet is useful, especially for the kids. The campervan allows us to bring more materials, toys, books, clothes, even a computer, so it adds to our comfort. And lastly, we save money on hotels, restaurants and transport.

Our van is a mass-produced Fiat campervan, to which we have made some improvements – mosquito nets on every window and door; an additional diesel heater; and an auxiliary battery which powers lights, water pump, and computer in the passenger compartment. Air-con would be useful but it's too expensive; consider it depending on where you are travelling. The children's bunk beds are converted to seats and a table during the day so they have a nice space to play.

The children brought with them their Barbie dolls, small cars, Lego, cards and miniature parlour games. They also have pens, pencils, paints and paper for drawing. We buy new toys for birthdays or Christmas. Consider taking lots of books in your own language because they are rare and expensive in other countries. The children often use our computer for play and education.

As we are travelling for a long time, our daughters are using a correspondence course from the French education department. We pay for the courses, but when we go home, their return to school should be easy. We regularly send their work back to France; it is corrected and returned to their grandparents in France who send these notes back to us by email. Of course, you could follow the school's course more closely using supplied books but you have to be disciplined to follow the school's schedule.

When we are driving, the children are always busy. They play, read, listen to their favourite CD or look at the landscape through the window. They never bother us. Sometimes, we play games together or sing along with the CD.

For overnight stops, we rarely go to camping grounds but we always respect one principle – never be isolated. We stay free of charge in rest areas, in public squares, at petrol stations or in car parks, depending on the country we are in. Some countries are very safe and we never have a problem finding a place for the night in Scandinavia, Australia, Muslim countries, Greece and Turkey. In Vietnam, it was difficult because it is forbidden to sleep in the streets. We asked at hotels if we could stay in their car parks and we usually had to pay for this.

Cambodia and Laos were terrible because of the bad conditions of the roads, especially during the monsoon. If you are not good mechanics (we aren't), you should buy a new or slightly used campervan to avoid problems. Pakistan and Bangladesh were very tiring because when we stopped hundreds of people would surround the van! But in these countries, we were easily able to park at goverment 'rest houses', which were always free.

"They really miss the campervan when it is sailing from one continent to another. It is also a protection against mosquitoes, insects and other undesirable animals. We cook in it, so we limit the risks of illness due to contaminated water and food."

Before starting our trip, we wanted to have a meaningful thread to it. We knew of Handicap International, a French organisation looking after people wounded in wars. They received the Nobel Peace Prize in 1997 because of their work removing land mines. We met them and they liked our project. So, now, when we know they are in a country, we go and see them. They explain their work to us and they tell us a little more about each country. Because we are not ordinary tourists and we want to learn, our children are getting an education that includes open-mindedness and respect for all people. And our meetings with Handicap International are a part of this education. It is a partnership we are very happy with.

toilets

If your children are past the nappy stage, they may well be at the 'toilet-fixation' stage. You know, when they can't pass up the opportunity to use a different toilet wherever they go? If toilet facilities are not conveniently to hand any restaurant, coffee shop or hotel will let you use their bathrooms in an emergency, whether you are a patron or not. In small towns or villages, if there is an absence of public places, you can always explain the situation to a pleasant looking bystander.

In some places where toilets are usually of the squat-down rather than familiar, Western sit-up variety your children may baulk at these 'hole in the ground' affairs. Try to be patient, you probably had reservations too when you first saw them. If you show them how it's done, they'll probably come to regard it at least as an interesting novelty. You should always always go with them and help them to get organised and they will probably want to be held while they are squatting as many children are actually afraid they are about to disappear down the hole.

laundry

Unfortunately, this will probably need to be done frequently. Some hotels will offer a reasonably priced laundry service, in other places you can use a laundry – if you want to save time, money and wear and tear on your clothes, take your own pegless clothesline, wash your clothes and let them dry outside. If you need to hand wash do it every second day so it doesn't build up, and do it in the morning when you've got more energy will probably get it done more quickly and there's more drying time available.

food

breastfeeding

If you're travelling with babies it's usually much easier to breastfeed; it provides a convenient, safe, nutritious supply of nourishment as well as comfort. All the usual advice to nursing mothers applies when you are travelling. The easiest way of dealing with night feeds is to take the baby into bed with you and just let them get on with it; you don't need to become totally conscious and it's not nearly so tiring.

When sightseeing don't try to race around and see everything in a hurry. Go easy on yourself, slow down, then you will be less tired and more relaxed. Drink lots of fluid and make sure you eat properly. Help ensure your milk supply doesn't diminish by breastfeeding on demand.

travel tips

To bottlefeed a baby on the go, invest in a set of disposable bottles with pre-sterilised plastic bags inside. The teats have special carry cases that keep them sterile for 24 hours.

Rosie Whitehouse, UK

bottlefeeding

If you are bottlefeeding your baby the main issues will be clean water and sterile equipment. Formula must be made up with either bottled, purified or boiled water. Made-up formula deteriorates quickly so bottles should be made up as the baby needs them or refrigerated and used within 24 hours. The bottles and teats you use to feed the baby must be sterilised by either boiling them for 10 minutes or using sterilising tablets.

For basic bottlefeeding carry two small plastic bottles and teats, some sterilising tablets and a suitably sized container with a lid to put them in. You should sterilise bottles in boiled water each night.

self-catering

If you have access to a kitchen you'll want to minimise the time you spend in it cooking and cleaning. Keep breakfast and lunch simple and don't prepare any elaborate meals. Keep to the tried and true favourites; it will be easier and you'll know everyone will eat well.

Camping stoves can be useful. There are various types on the market, but those that use kerosene or spirit are more useful than gas as you will be able to refill them just about anywhere and you can empty them out for flights. Gas cylinders may not be widely available and you cannot carry them on planes.

snacks

Always carry snacks with you, particularly if you are going walking or travelling by bus, train or car. Even if you know there are shops around or the trip is scheduled for just an hour – remember that delays are possible and that when you arrive shops may not have anything suitable for your child to eat. So carry sultanas, raisins or nuts (for children over five), an apple or orange (bananas go mushy very quickly), some juice or milk cartons, and some bread or biscuits. Water is a necessity, for drinking and cleaning. Carry a knife for peeling and cutting fruit. If travelling with a baby, pack a few jars of baby food just in case.

loss of appetite

Try not to worry about how much your children are eating. There may be days when you think they are living on air, but they probably do that at home as well. Children eat when they are hungry, so don't start worrying that this trip will end with starved, malnourished children. You should make an effort to find things that they can eat and would ordinarily like. You should carry some children's multivitamin drops or tablets, make sure they drink a lot of water and milk, offer them plenty of fruit and remember to relax.

places to eat

Even if you have your own kitchen facilities you'll probably eat out quite a lot. In many places you will find local street stalls or restaurants that are safe, appetising and cheap but there may also be times when all that is available is an expensive hotel or restaurant, because other places look too unsavoury, the food simply doesn't appeal to young tastes or there is simply nothing else.

There will probably also be times when all your children want is familiar fast food. Most big hotels anywhere in the world can provide a suitable copy and the indulgence is sometimes worthwhile for the pleasure it will bring. To tell your children to wait until they get home in a few weeks for familiar food, is like saying in January that 'next Christmas you'll get to decorate the tree'. Children have no real concept of time, so a few weeks is a very long time. The kind of meal that they recognise can help them feel a little more secure and also reassure them that they won't have to eat 'strange food' forever.

Unfamiliar food or not, there are some great dining possibilities which children will love. Food that is colourful or arrives sizzling or with flames on it will usually appeal. While it certainly makes ordering easy you may have to dissuade your child from ordering the most luridly coloured dishes. Remind them they have to eat the meal as well as look at it.

A phrasebook or food guide can be useful for deciphering menus and older children and teenagers can use them to help work out what they want to eat as well as develop their language skills. Lonely Planet's phrasebooks include a food section or for real junior gourmets there's the World Food series.

travel tips

In restaurants look for chairs, preferably with arms, to which the baby can be attached using a stroller harness or safety reins.

Elizabeth Wear, Hong Kong

choosing a restaurant

Outdoor restaurants are worth looking out for; as are restaurants where there is plenty of space inside or something about them that might appeal to kids, eg, an aquarium or fountain. Check the menu to make sure there is something your children can eat and if they're restless take them for a short walk while you're waiting for your meal to come. You may want to take wet wipes to clean a highchair or other surfaces for babies and young children. If there isn't a highchair and you have a child on your knee, order meals you can eat with one hand. Older children and teenagers may want to eat at their favourite fast food restaurants regularly. It's best to come to some agreement about how often this should happen to avoid arguments at every mealtime.

servings

The amount of food served in restaurants is usually too much for a small child. While a sandwich may sound the right size it can sometimes come with chips (French fries), and salad which remains untouched. Entrees (appetisers) are often the right amount for children, or sharing a meal between two can work out perfectly. With older children and teenagers you could order several meals and share them between all of you. If your children aren't very adventurous eaters let them try some of your meal so they can order something similar next time if they like it.

alternatives

When you have been out all afternoon, the baby is tired and you all feel a bit strained and hungry, the last thing you want to is eat in a restaurant. At times like this a quiet meal where you're staying can be a terrific alternative to a crowded restaurant.

If you're staying in a hotel, room service is one alternative. The inflated prices and sometimes mediocre food which seem to come with room service are nothing compared to the joy of not having to set out to find a restaurant to suit everyone, find something everyone can eat, keep the children awake and happy through the process of ordering and waiting for food to arrive, and finally persuade them to eat something.

Children usually really enjoy room service and if it is kept for those special occasions, the idea may cheer them up completely. In the privacy of your room they can eat how they like, in their pyjamas perhaps, ready to go to bed as soon as they've finished eating. There will be a mess of course, so try to avoid eating on the beds.

Hotels can often send someone out to get a takeaway (takeout) for you. Alternatively one of the parents can go on a food-gathering mission to a local fast food place, a restaurant with takeaways, or even a night market or food stall.

utensils & equipment

Carry spout cups for small children to have their drinks from; this can save a lot of spills. If they are embarrassed by drinking from spout cups, teach them to drink through straws which they can usually manage from an early age. Always carry a mop-up cloth, bibs, wet wipes and other cleaning apparatus. It helps to have your own plate and spoon, so that you can organise a small portion for your child without being delayed by waiting staff or going through the sometimes frustrating task of getting them to understand that you really do just want an extra empty plate. For babies who have recently started having food, take a food grinder with you so that you can grind up food from your plate or other food to make it the right texture.

babysitters

Babysitters are a possibility in many countries. Large hotels in tourist areas can often make babysitting arrangements, but it's much nicer when the hotel you are staying in is run by a family and the daughters would just love to look after your children. You can come to some arrangement as to when and how much; usually it will be a very small financial cost.

If you are planning a long stay in one place, you can often organise someone to look after the children; inquire at your hotel or if you know someone in the area ask them to check it out for you. As you would at home, meet the babysitter, check out their level of experience, and make sure you and your children feel comfortable with them. If you are not comfortable, trust your intuition and don't leave your children with that babysitter. Ideally, you should wait to employ a babysitter until you've settled into a place, to make sure your children are likely to feel happy and secure with the babysitter. Always tell children, even very young ones, where you're going and how long you'll be gone for so they can express any concerns they have or don't wake up upset if you're not there. See the individual country profiles later in this book for more information on babysitter availability at different destinations.

At 26, I've had the opportunity to travel to many countries, and in more recent years I've been blessed by a very enthusiastic, and rather lively travel companion. This relentless little man and fervent globetrotter is my four-year-old son Sam. Travelling alone with a child is never as easy as it is to take off alone with just a backpack or with a group of friends, but the rewards are precious.

sole parenting

GOING it ALONE with KIDS

Jacqui Higgins has travelled with her son, Sam, four, since he was just over a year old. They've travelled around Portugal, Spain, Turkey, the USA and the Caribbean.

Many single parents can get hung-up on the idea that travel is impossible and in doing so they are often stopping themselves from breaking new ground. I've watched Sam pat and feed stingray; learn to swim among schools of pilot fish and speak foreign languages like a native. We've stayed with friends, in budget hotels and campsites, and on each occasion, Sam's excitement has meant double the satisfaction for me.

I've often found that Sam has forced me to interact with locals, in situations where I might otherwise have held back. With his mop of blond curls and blue eyes, it was hard to pass through villages or towns unnoticed in areas of Portugal, Spain or the Caribbean, so we succumbed to his popularity and enjoyed local life wherever we went.

Like his mother, Sam loves the beach and many hours were spent on sandy shores in sun-kissed countries. I would lie in a central spot, close enough to the water to intervene if there was a problem and watch the little skinny body flip around in the waves with local children. In the Azores, where we spent several months in a small village, Sam was speaking more Portuguese than I was. He picked up all his language within a few weeks and most of it was learnt on the seashore.

Of course, there are the difficulties. Getting to less touristed areas sometimes means multiple flights, dodgy public transport or expensive and sometimes treacherous cab rides. I learned quickly the importance of checking out transport before embarking on a trip to out-of-the-way destinations.

On our first occasion taking a crowded bus in Portugal, I suffered the wrath of the driver as I struggled onto the bus with child, stroller, bags, and fumbled in my purse for the correct change. I handed the driver a note, and watched in horror as he stopped the bus again and shouted obscenities about tourists, while searching for the correct change. After practically throwing the coins at me, he thumped his foot down, and the bus took off again, leaving me, child, buggy and bags to fall clumsily around while trying to locate a standing place in the overcrowded aisle. One lady either felt sorry for me or got sick of me pounding her foot with the buggy wheels and offered me her seat. After that experience I knew to throw the buggy in the luggage compartment, cut down on the bags, calm Sam down before boarding and always have the correct change ready.

Functioning normally in the restricted space of aeroplanes can also be a challenge. When Sam was a lap passenger I used to wait until he was asleep before I would lower the table to eat my meal. On more than one occasion I've gone without the meal, but have nearly always been offered a sandwich or some cold hand food by considerate flight attendants.

"Functioning normally in the restricted space of aeroplanes can also be a challenge. When Sam was a lap passenger I used to wait until he was asleep before I would lower the table to eat my meal. On more than one occasion I've gone without the meal, but have nearly always been offered a sandwich or some cold hand food by considerate flight attendants."

Travelling alone with a child does restrict your possible destinations. I wouldn't jump at the idea of visiting the Amazonian rainforests with Sam, for instance. I need to have the security of knowing that help is always available if we need it. Of course, taking a few simple precautions – like knowing the emergency phone numbers, carrying a phonecard, carrying a well-equipped first-aid kit and keeping family and friends aware of where we will be – is always important.

Almost everywhere we have travelled children are revered and now I wouldn't so much as raise an eyebrow if everywhere we went, people came running up to kiss my son on his head. I have on occasion found it important to acknowledge our vulnerability and take steps to keep this hidden from strangers. Harassment from sleazy men can always be remedied with the oldest line in the book; 'My husband/partner is on his way/in that shop/rather large and aggressive'. If this ploy doesn't work it's important to stay central and call on other tourists, locals, shopkeepers, police or anyone else around.

We have already planned two more excursions to foreign shores – we want to tackle Chicago and Italy before Sam starts school. Although he won't remember all the details of our trips together, I really hope that Sam will keep with him a fondness for travelling.

Travelling with a child who has special needs is not only possible – it makes for special memories and a wonderful feeling of breaking the confines of a disability. However, it requires a little extra work, flexible plans and a lot of patience.

christina's travels

ACCESS all AREAS

Tania Kutny has flown three times between Australia and Canada and had several driving holidays with her three-year-old daughter, Christina, 10-month-old son, Mykola, and husband, Roman.

Our daughter Christina was born with an extremely rare genetic disease called Fanconi's Anaemia (FA). The disease affects individuals differently in terms of physical anomalies. Christina was born with multiple anomalies: a blocked oesophagus, a stomach connected to her lungs, severe hydrocephalus (excess water on the brain), a pelvic kidney, a short and curved radius bone in one arm and a missing radius in the other, missing thumbs, severe gastrointestinal problems, an imperforate ear, scoliosis and a hole in her heart.

Her poor health, however, did not deter us from travelling. After spending her first year in hospital, we took off soon after Christina became stable enough to travel. We made our first trip driving from Ottawa to Wisconsin – a distance of some 1800kms. A trip of any great distance involving a child with a pre-existing condition can seem daunting. It's not possible to prepare for every scenario. I called countless insurance agents but only one was willing to cover our daughter, however given the price they were asking, the agent himself advised us to take the risk and go to America without insurance. We did just that.

Christina was 16 months old and dependant on two machines, an enteral pump to feed her continuously and a suction device to clear her passageway of saliva. In the past she was prone to choking on her own saliva on a daily basis; Christina slept attached to an apnoea monitor that gave off a loud shrilling siren whenever she stopped breathing. Our 10-day trip to Wisconsin went without a hitch. The experience empowered us as parents and enabled us to enjoy life as a family again. The most important thing we learnt was the importance of rest. Having children is exhausting enough in itself, add to that the weight of administering medications, dealing with behavioural difficulties and the special care of your child.

Get your doctor to supply you with extra prescriptions and purchase enough medical supplies to cover more than twice the duration of your trip. Plan for as many unforeseen circumstances as possible. Flights can get delayed, luggage can go missing, and medical assistance may not be available. Pack medical supplies in different bags so that even if a bag or two go missing you haven't lost all of your medicine. I always keep one complete supply in my baby travel bag and scatter the rest in other pieces of luggage.

We planned a month-long trip to Montreal from Australia for a special operation on Christina's hand. The trip turned into a three-month stay due to unforeseen hospital delays. When we ran out of medication we discovered that this medicine had been pulled off the North American market and we couldn't replace it. Fortunately we were able to get our family to post some from Australia by overnight courier. Make sure your child's doctors know about any impending overseas trips as they can assist in the event of such an emergency.

It is on the shorter journeys, however, when one can never become too complacent. During a visit with relatives, a five-hour drive from home, our daughter's feeding tube, which is normally permanently attached to her stomach, came out. A trip to emergency in Canada's biggest hospital became a day long event involving a lot of red tape and frustration. Emergency routine dictates that a child's history must be included during treatment. Christina's history, at age 14 months, was already complex and extensive comprising three thick volumes. By chance, another surgeon who we'd met a year ago, helped us through the system. The lesson learnt was to ask your child's specialists if they recommend a doctor at centres in your destination. It is also vital that you carry with you a brief summary of your child's medical history written by their main paediatrician or specialist.

> "Our 10-day trip to Wisconsin went without a hitch. The experience empowered us as parents and enabled us to enjoy life as a family again."

Another area to consider before making international flights is the on-board use of medical equipment. All medical equipment to be used during the flight must be pre-authorised by the airline. This can be a lengthy process. On a trip from Ottawa to Melbourne we needed to use the plane's electrical supply to re-charge Christina's feeding pump. Tests had to be carried out by electrical engineers in Sydney to ensure that the equipment did not interfere with the aeroplane's instruments. This procedure took four months and many international phone calls. We also made arrangements with staff for pre-boarding and disembarking assistance. I recommend that any arrangements with airline staff begin as soon as possible and be recorded in writing which can be helpful when confirming previous arrangements prior to departure.

Most of all don't be afraid to travel with children wherever your heart desires. Bring along a friend or relative who can help and also share the fun experience of adventure. Your journey will not only strengthen your family bond but also help quash fears about travelling with a special needs child. Best of all, you forget about the illness for a while and simply enjoy what life has to offer.

single-parent families

For widowed, divorced, separated or single, gay parents, travel with children can seem like a major challenge. Most of the information in this book applies equally to single-parent families as two-parent families but there are some different issues that arise. Travelling with one child is usually manageable, more than one child and it's worth planning for some assistance, just so you get a break, a chance to have some adult conversation or do something for yourself. Travelling with another adult with a child, other members of your extended family or staying with friends can help spread the load.

In some countries there may be an issue on arrival if you're a single parent with a child, eg, Mexico. Check with the embassy or consulate of your destination as to whether you need the consent of the other parent to take your child away, even if you're the custodial parent.

When you're flying, if you are using a stroller take it to the airline departure gate and check it in there and ask for it to be ready at the other end. If you have a child on your lap you may want to request a cold meal so that it's easier to manage; you need to book 48 hours in advance.

special needs children

Having a special needs child won't limit their travelling but it does mean you need to do more planning. Consult your medical specialist before you go and contact support organisations where people may have already had the same kind of experiences.

before you go

If your child has a health problem which may require urgent medical attention, make sure you discuss a standard medical plan with your doctor as well as an emergency plan and be sure to have lots of extra medication with you. Check out in advance where the nearest doctor and hospital emergency departments are in the places you will be staying. Make sure you have adequate insurance cover and check that it does not exclude people with a pre-existing medical condition. Also ensure that it will cover replacement or theft of any medical equipment. If you need any electrical equipment make sure you know the voltage in your destination and take an adaptor. If you're using a wheelchair, take a repair kit with you.

If you're taking a wheelchair explain the facilities that will be required when booking a hotel, eg, wheelchair access to hotel, ground floor room or lift access, room with access to the bathroom, reasonably level surroundings. Also book ahead for cars that will accommodate wheelchairs. Check with the local tourist office or a special needs organisation in the country you're visiting for details of wheelchair access.

flying

When travelling by plane keep your child's medication in hand luggage in case your other luggage is delayed or lost. Some airlines will carry respirators and most will take portable kidney machines. Using cramped toilets is an issue for many special needs kids; ask the airline what they can do to assist, eg, some have a couple of designated accessible toilets and others will provide a screen so the door can be left open to allow more space to move.

When making a flight booking provide all relevant information such as any help your child might need during the flight and special dietary requirements. Reconfirm these details 48 hours before and check in early so that you can get a seat that will suit you. Some airlines require a medical clearance form, check if your child will need one of these. If your child needs a special restraint in the car take it with you. Depending on the type of restraint and the age of your children you may also be able to use it on the plane.

If your child is in a wheelchair, give the airline as much notice as possible so they can provide assistance. They should be able to organise a wheelchair once your child has been checked in and have yours ready and waiting for you at the end of your flight. You'll need to provide instructions on how it should be reassembled and it's best to take detachable pieces such as the wheelchair cushion on the plane with you. The wheelchair is usually not included in your baggage allowance. If you have a folding wheelchair it may be possible to take that on board; some airlines have aisle wheelchairs. See the Web Site appendix for a list of useful organisations.

HEALTH

As well as the potential health risks of your destination, you should consider the age and temperament of your children, and what sort of trip you're planning. Babies are easy to feed (especially if they are exclusively breastfed) but they can quickly become dehydrated and are very sensitive to heat and sun. Toddlers are more complicated to feed, and to keep amused and safe, particularly around water. Older children and teenagers can at least tell you what their symptoms are.

before you go

doctor & dentist

It's a good idea to make sure your child is as healthy as possible before you go. Talk to your doctor about illness prevention and work out a plan of action for common problems. If your child has an ongoing condition like eczema, diabetes or asthma, be clear about what to do if the condition worsens while you're away.

It's worth making sure your children have a thorough dental checkup before going away and remember to leave enough time for any treatment to be carried out if necessary.

immunisations

Children should be up to date for all routine childhood immunisations and they'll need the same travel-related vaccines as you. Most fully immunised school-age children won't need further doses of routine immunisations, but babies and younger children who haven't completed their normal childhood immunisations may need to complete the schedules earlier than normal. Ask your doctor about immunisations when you start planning your trip. Some vaccines have age restrictions and your doctor should be able to help you with these restrictions.
For example:
diphtheria and tetanus (usually with pertussis, as DTP) – the first dose can be given at six weeks of age if necessary
polio can be given at six weeks if necessary
measles can be given at six months of age if necessary (it's normally given as part of the MMR vaccine at 15 months of age)
Travel-related vaccines your child may need include the following:

hepatitis A vaccine can be given from the age of one year (two years in the US); younger children should have immunoglobulin
typhoid vaccination isn't normally given under two years of age
hepatitis B and tuberculosis (not used in the US and some European countries) have no lower age limit

If kids are going to react to an immunisation, it will usually happen about 48 hours after the injection and can generally be settled with a dose or two of paracetamol (acetaminophen). Children can go on to have further reactions and sometimes develop rashes 10 days after the immunisation, so the earlier you get kids immunised, the better.

If you're coming from a region where yellow fever is an issue – such as South America or Africa – you may need certificates of vaccination to enter some countries. It's a good idea to keep records of vaccinations, but ask your doctor for up-to-date information about vaccination requirements. Also ask about malaria prevention, particularly if you're visiting Africa, Asia or South America. You can also check out Lonely Planet's Healthy Travel series for more information on immunisation.

medical kit & medications

It's a good idea to take a child-specific medical kit as well as your own basic medical kit. If your child takes any medications regularly (for asthma, eczema or diabetes, for example) remember to take a good supply of these medications with you. Otherwise, a basic medical kit for children should include most of the following:

- remedies for pain and fever, for example paracetamol (acetaminophen) or ibuprofen paediatric syrup
- antibiotics for common ailments like ear infections or coughs – discuss this with your doctor, but you could consider these if you are planning on going to remote areas where you may not have ready access to medical care or supplies. Suitable antibiotics include co-amoxiclav, cephalexin or clarithromycin (if your child is allergic to penicillin)
- a plentiful supply of oral rehydration salt sachets, barrier cream for nappy rash, calamine cream or aloe vera gel for heat rash and sunburn, motion sickness remedies, sunscreen, thermometer, antiseptic wipes and antiseptic liquid or spray
- sterilising tablets are a good idea for cleaning feeding utensils, or you might want to consider taking a sterilising unit with you
- plastic spoons (5mL and 2.5mL) are useful for measuring out doses of liquid medications. A plastic syringe (5mL or 10mL) can be handy for giving medicine (and fluids) to a reluctant patient

If you do need to give your child medication when you are away, remember children need a child-sized dose and not all medications are suitable for children. Follow the dosing instructions given by your doctor or on the packet. Doses are generally based on your child's weight. You should also check that your child's medication is legal at your destination.

staying healthy

Children can be very adaptable to climate and time changes but they are more susceptible to infections and accidents.

earache & flying

On flights, air pressure changes can cause ear pain in babies and young children. Give babies a drink as the swallowing reflex will clear their ears and older children can be given chewy sweets or drinks, or encouraged to blow their noses, which should help their ears to pop. Younger children and babies can be given decongestant nose drops if necessary (get these from your doctor or pharmacist before you go) as well as paracetamol (acetaminophen) syrup to ease the pain. If your child has an ear infection or a bad cold, you should postpone flying until it is better.

travel tips

We have a daughter prone to car sickness so we always pinch the airline sick bags whenever we fly and keep one in the car seat pocket.

Carol De Giorgio, Singapore

motion sickness

This is extremely common in children and can turn even a short journey into a trauma. Ginger is a good remedy and you can buy ginger capsules from many health food stores; check that the capsule dosage will be suitable for your children's weight and age. You could also use promethazine (follow the dosing guidelines, and note that it's not recommended for children under two years). Promethazine will often make your child sleepy, although the effects are very variable. A natural soothing alternative is camomile.

food, water & cleanliness

You'll probably want to avoid giving children carbonated soft drinks, but packet fruit juices and UHT milk are usually available and make safe substitutes. If you can, try to prepare any food for babies yourself, making sure that the utensils you use are sterile (take sterilising tablets with you).

Children who are crawling or just walking are particularly at risk of diseases spread via dirt. Wash their hands and faces frequently throughout the day, especially if you're travelling on public transport. Another good preventative measure is to discourage hands wandering into the mouth, eyes and nose as much as possible. A supply of wet wipes can be invaluable, especially on long journeys.

If you get sick with diarrhoea yourself, be extremely careful to wash your hands after using the toilet to avoid passing diarrhoea to your child. Be careful with nappies etc if your child has diarrhoea to prevent it passing to you.

diet & nutrition

New foods are usually met with surprise and a reflex refusal, but stress and new surroundings can distract children from eating and heat often reduces even the healthiest of appetites. Try to introduce new foods gradually, perhaps starting before you leave. Even if your child doesn't want to eat, fluids are a must, especially if it's hot.

Take children's multivitamins on trips when you can't be sure the children will be able to eat as nutritiously as they might at home.

Carol De Giorgio, Singapore

insect bites

Biting insects carry a number of serious diseases so it's extremely important to protect your child from bites. Make sure your child is covered up with clothes, socks and shoes, and use insect repellents on exposed areas – either DEET-containing repellents or the new natural repellents containing lemon eucalyptus. Permethrin-soaked mosquito nets or coils will keep the nasties away at night and during daytime naps (the mosquito that spreads dengue bites during the daytime).

Try to discourage scratching of bites if they do occur, as this often leads to infection. Keep fingernails cut short and use calamine cream or a sting-relief spray to ease irritation.

accidents & other hazards

Children are accident-prone at the best of times, but the dangers are even greater when you're travelling, so you need to be even more vigilant than normal. Many hotel rooms and restaurants are not built with children in mind and may have a nightmare-inducing lack of safety features, particularly where windows and balconies are concerned. Some precautions to think about taking:

- be on the lookout for potential risks and unsafe features
- try to be aware of what your child is doing at all times, especially if they're playing outside
- use a harness for toddlers when you're travelling or walking in crowded places
- make sure your child has some form of identification on them at all times, including details of where you are staying
- drowning is surprisingly common – be particularly vigilant around swimming pools or at the beach and remember that drowning can occur in shallow water as well as deeper water
- check new beaches for debris, discarded hypodermics, glass and tins, as well as various 'offerings' left by people and animals

cuts & scratches

In hot, humid climates these can easily become infected and it can be difficult to keep children clean, especially if they are running or crawling around. You'll need to take a bit more care of abrasions than you would normally. Wash any break in the skin carefully with soap and water or antiseptic solution (or an antiseptic wipe if you haven't got access to water) and keep it covered with a sterile, non-stick, non-fluffy dressing (a sticking plaster is fine if the wound is small). It's probably worth checking your child carefully at the end of each day for cuts, scratches and potentially problematic bites.

sun

Anyone can get sunburnt but little ones are especially vulnerable. Keep children and babies covered up (with a long-sleeved T-shirt and long trousers, skirt and hat, or an all-over sunsuit). Apply liberal amounts of the highest factor sunscreen you can find on any exposed skin and reapply it frequently. Keep your child out of the sun during the middle of the day when the sun is at its fiercest. Not only is sunburn miserably painful for your child, it's thought to be a major risk factor for skin cancer in later life.

heat

If your child is not used to a hot climate, they will need time to acclimatise. Children tend to acclimatise easily, but young children (with their greater surface area relative to their body mass) can lose fluid through sweating very rapidly, and become dehydrated and vulnerable to heatstroke. Babies and young children may not be able to tell you how hot they're feeling, so if you're feeling the heat, check to see how your child is coping, and whether they are dressed appropriately. Try to discourage mobile youngsters from rushing around in the heat of the day. Baby backpacks or slings are a handy way to carry children, but it can be easy to forget how exposed they are to the elements.

Because babies and children can become dehydrated relatively easily, they require a significant increase in their fluid intake. As a general rule you can double their fluid intake. Consider sprinkling a little salt on their food, as salt can be lost through sweating. You could also encourage them to eat lots of juicy fruit and vegetables. Keep an eye on how much urine they are passing – small amounts of dark urine or dark urine-stained nappies in babies mean you need to increase their fluid intake.

cold

Children feel the cold, as they lose heat very rapidly, especially if they are immobile in a carrier, so wrap them up well and check them regularly for signs of cold. Appropriate layers of clothes are vital for keeping kids warm, including mittens and warm hats. Give children plenty to eat and drink, as they can use up their energy reserves quickly and this makes them more vulnerable to the cold.

stings

Children seem to attract bees and wasps like the proverbial honey pot, so take plenty of insect repellent (although this is less effective against stinging insects like bees and wasps) and be prepared to apply sting relief spray and lots of sympathy. If you know your child is allergic to bee stings, discuss this with your doctor before you leave and pack adrenaline (epinephrine) in your emergency kit.

altitude

If you're planning on going to high altitude destinations remember that littlies are just as vulnerable to the effects of altitude as adults and they may not be able to tell you about their symptoms. Altitude sickness may have nonspecific symptoms

– such as nausea, headache or vomiting – which can be easily confused with other kiddy illnesses. Keep a close eye on your children and familiarise yourself with symptoms by discussing altitude sickness with your doctor, especially if you're trekking or going to be higher than 2000m above sea level. It's best to descend promptly if your children show any signs of altitude sickness. Treatment drugs such as Diamox are best avoided with young travellers. Lonely Planet's Healthy Travel series offers tips and information on safe trekking and avoiding altitude sickness.

malaria

Malaria is best avoided with a few sensible preventative measures. If you are travelling to an area where malaria is a problem – such as Asia, South America or Africa – you should be wary of mosquitoes, which can carry the malaria virus. Make sure you're well protected with mosquito nets, child-friendly insect repellent and preventative drugs. If you take children to malarial areas (which should only be done if they are old enough to take preventative drugs), make sure you're very careful about covering up at dawn and dusk. Lonely Planet's Healthy Travel series has a comprehensive discussion of preventative drugs or ask your doctor for more information.

if your child falls ill

Children are at risk of the same diseases as you are when you are away. Because children can't always tell you what's wrong and in many cases don't show typical symptoms of diseases, it's even more important to seek medical help at the earliest opportunity. Always get medical help if you have any concerns about their condition.

is my child unwell?

Children can quickly change from being well and active to becoming ill, sometimes seriously ill. In young children especially, the signs can be quite subtle and difficult to interpret, which can be a worry.

As the parent, you will know your child best of all and any change in their behaviour should be taken seriously – listen to your sixth sense. This is particularly true of young children. Babies up to six months may become quieter than usual, miserable and start crying without apparent cause. They may not want to eat or drink, or they may develop more specific signs, such as diarrhoea, coughing, vomiting or rashes.

Older babies and toddlers may just not 'perform' as well as you are used to. They may stop walking, stop sitting up, stop feeding themselves or being as developed as you are used to. Children of this age are unable to tell you what's wrong and this may be the only sign before a rash or a cough appears.

Don't rely on a child's skin temperature as an indication of whether they have a raised temperature or not. Instead you should always carry and use a thermometer (preferably a digital one or a fever strip – less accurate but easier to use). It is important to have an actual reading of the temperature. A child cold to touch may have a raging temperature and the other way round. If you have any cause for concern, check the temperature and make sure your child is taking at least enough fluids to pass urine twice a day, even if they have gone off their food.

fever

This is very common in children wherever they are and is always a cause for concern. In addition, a high temperature can sometimes cause a convulsion in babies and young children. Skin temperature is a confusing and unreliable sign – see the previous entry. If you think your child has a fever, for example if the child is flushed and irritable and obviously unwell:

- take your child's temperature and then take it again 30 minutes later as a check
- put your child to bed, removing most clothing (perhaps covering the child up with a cotton sheet) and making them comfortable (under a mosquito net if necessary)
- wipe your child's face and body with a sponge or cloth soaked in tepid (not cold) water or place in a tepid bath to help lower the temperature
- giving paracetamol (acetaminophen) syrup or tablets every four to six hours will also help to lower the temperature
- prevent dehydration by giving small amounts of fluid often – make up oral rehydration salts with bottled or boiled water, or fruit juice diluted half and half with safe water; give 5mL every 15 minutes for the first hour

Conditions like viral infections, colds, ear infections, urinary tract infections and diarrhoea are common causes of fever. If you've been travelling in malarial risk areas, you must always consider the possibility that a fever could be malaria.

Take steps to lower the temperature and seek medical help urgently in the following situations:

- if the temperature is over 37.7°C (100°F) in a baby of less than six months
- if the temperature is over 39°C (104°F) in any infant or child
- if your child has had fits in the past
- if it could be malaria; malaria should be suspected with any high fever if you are in a malarial area
- if the fever shows no sign of improving after 24 hours (take your child's temperature regularly to show you if it's going up or down)

diarrhoea

Children – especially young children and babies – are more likely than adults to get diarrhoea when they are away. They also tend to get more severe symptoms and for longer. It's partly because children are less discriminating about what they put in their mouths and it's hard to keep little hands clean, but it may also be because they have less immunity to disease-causing bugs.

Babies and children can become rapidly dehydrated through diarrhoea and vomiting, and it can be difficult to make sure they drink enough. The best fluids to give children are oral rehydration salts (ORS). You need to start giving them ORS as soon diarrhoea or vomiting appears – you can make ORS more palatable by adding flavours or look for ready-flavoured sachets of ORS. Avoid food if kids are vomiting.

You don't need to give your child ORS if you're breastfeeding, but make sure you're taking in enough fluid yourself. If your child is being fed a milk-based formula, you need to replace this with ORS until the diarrhoea is better. As the diarrhoea improves introduce diluted milk feeds then solids. For older children follow the same dietary guidelines as for adults, avoiding milk and milk-based products until your child is on the mend.

The World Health Organization gives the following guidelines for the quantity of fluid replacement:

- under two years: one quarter to one half cup per loose stool
- two to 10 years: one half to one cup per loose stool
- over 10 years: as for adults (two cups per loose stool)

If children are vomiting, allow the stomach to rest for about an hour before trying to give them fluids. Then reintroduce fluids very slowly – 5mL every 15 minutes for the first hour and build up from there. If your child is refusing to drink, try giving small amounts by teaspoon or syringe every few minutes. Seek medical help earlier rather than later, especially if you notice any of the following symptoms developing:

- prolonged vomiting and diarrhoea
- refusal to take fluids
- listlessness
- fever
- blood or mucus in the diarrhoea

In children faeces may take 10 to 14 days to return to normal (though sometimes longer). As long as the faeces are not too frequent, you shouldn't worry about slightly loose faeces in an otherwise fit and recovered child.

Note that symptomatic antidiarrhoeal medications ('stoppers') are not recommended for children and should be avoided. If your child is ill enough to need antibiotics, you should seek medical advice. If you are in a remote area away from medical assistance, co-trimoxazole is a suitable antibiotic option.

tummy ache

This is a very common complaint among children and adults. The causes are many and varied, and some may be serious. If your child is prone to tummy aches, the stress of travelling may make them more likely while you are away. Otherwise, situations when you should seek medical help include:

- any tummy ache with a fever as it could be malaria, typhoid, bladder infection etc

- severe tummy ache that is continuous for more than three hours as it could be appendicitis
- tummy ache with profuse vomiting and diarrhoea as there is a danger of dehydration
- tummy ache that's not normal for your child, especially if your child is generally unwell

colds, coughs & earache

Children are particularly likely to succumb to new germs in new places, so be prepared! Asthma (cough, wheezing) may occur for the first time while you are away and can be frightening especially if your child has never experienced it before. You should seek medical advice if your child is having difficulty breathing, especially if you notice that their ribs are being drawn in with each breath.

If you suspect an ear infection consult a doctor as antibiotics will be required for a middle ear infection. If your child does get an infection try to avoid water getting in their ear for two weeks. If they do have grommets in their ears, your doctor will generally advise that they shouldn't swim.

prickly heat & nappy rash

Prickly heat tends to be more of a problem in children than in adults. Calamine cream can soothe the irritation. You can help prevent the rash by dressing children in loose cotton clothing, bathing them often and drying them carefully, especially any skin folds and under their arms.

Nappy rash can be a lot worse in the heat. Take a good supply of barrier creams (such as petroleum jelly, zinc and castor oil cream, or Sudocrem). Wash the affected area with water after your child has a bowel movement, dry it well, apply barrier cream and try to keep the nappy off as much as possible.

If the affected area is red and painful, and the rash doesn't clear up with simple treatment, it may be due to a fungal infection. Try applying an antifungal cream twice a day (options include clotrimazole, or Canesten; or an antifungal with hydrocortisone if it is very red and painful). Check your child's mouth, as they may have a fungal infection (thrush) there as well, indicated by white patches that are difficult to remove. Treatment is with antifungal drops (such as nystatin). Remember to change rubber teats and feeding utensils as soon as treatment is started and halfway through.

after you get back

Consider getting a checkup for yourself and your children if you've been on a long trip or have been travelling rough. Make sure your doctor is aware you've been travelling and where.

NOTE that all homeopathic remedies should be prescribed by a qualified homeopath and preferably purchased before departure as it may be difficult to find a practitioner in a foreign country. Your homeopath will prescribe the proper dosage and potency according to specific criteria for your child. In homeopathic terms 'c' refers to centesimal potentising which means it must be prepared by a qualified practioner. It is important not to prepare your own homeopathic remedies as in the wrong form many ingredients (including arnica and podophyllum) can be toxic. Naturopathic remedies purchased from a health food store should have the recommended dosage on the bottle/jar. Otherwise ask your practitioner for the correct dosage. The following tips are only for guidance and should not replace medical diagnosis and treatment.

alternative health for LITTLE TRAVELLERS

Bernadette Saulenier is a naturopath and reiki practitioner who treats many babies and children.

diarrhoea A simple preventative measure is to take slippery elm capsules before each meal – the powder coats and protects the delicate lining of the bowels to prevent inflammation. Alternatively, to sterilise water use two drops of tea-tree oil in a litre of water. Let it sit overnight and use it as a mouthwash or even for drinking. A few drops of a grapefruit seed extract is also very useful for sterilising water and keeping the bowel free of parasites. In many countries it may still be necessary to stick to bottled water or use sterilising pills depending on the possible threats in local water.

If your child has symptoms of malaise, tiredness, abdominal cramps, bloating, stomach gurgles and pale, floating stools, you may assume that they have eaten contaminated food and will soon get 'the runs'. Give them a half-hourly dose of podophyllum 30c, carbo veg 30c and hepar sulph2 30c as soon as symptoms appear and for a couple of days after symptoms disappear. In the meantime you can feed them bananas, or white rice to solidify their stools. No matter what treatment is used you should keep fluid levels up.

If you notice bright red blood in their stools, they will need medical care immediately.

vomiting In case of vomiting, or indigestion, give them a dose of hepar sulph or ipecac 30c. A bit of lemon juice and honey in warm water will also help to clear the stomach and liver.

constipation There is usually nothing that some pear/prune juice or fresh figs cannot clear. A tablespoon of linseeds or psyllium husks on cereals will help as well. And remember to make them drink plenty of water.

bruising & bleeding One great remedy is arnica cream, applied on the bruised area immediately. However avoid using it on open wounds and cuts. For any bleeding whether external or internal, five drops of arnica 30c placed under the tongue every half hour for four doses is the best way to stop a haemorrhage. For anything more serious than nose bleeds and small wounds, seek the help of a medical practitioner.

motion sickness If you know your children are motion sensitive, then act before you leave steady ground or as soon as they start yawning a lot. Give kids five drops of cocculus 30c and remember that a full stomach may find it harder to turn upside down, so do not ride or fly on an empty stomach.

jetlag Gelsemium drops or tablets will alleviate the aches and pains of sore muscles and oxygen deprivation. Taking vitamin C will help your child cope with the fatigue, stress and lack of fresh air. Another natural way of helping a child's body clock to adjust is to let them play outside in the morning sunlight.

insect bites A drop of lavender oil will help soothe the itch of a mosquito bite. You can also prevent bites by putting a few drops of geranium oil on your skin. Mosquitoes hate the smell of geranium! Avoiding mosquito bites is crucial in preventing malaria and other potentially fatal diseases, so pack citronella candles or nets to keep mosquitoes out of biting range.

For anything more serious than that (such as spiders, bees, wasps and fleas) place five drops of ledum 30c under the tongue. This remedy is also great for any puncture wounds – great to help the body recover from an injection or from a close encounter with a porcupine.

cuts & scratches Use a eucalyptus or tea-tree oil spray on cuts to disinfect and some comfrey or calendula cream to speed up healing.

anaphylactic shock In case of severe allergic reaction the body goes into shock, lips turn blue, skin is moist and clammy, breathing is difficult, the brain becomes foggy and the child may lose consciousness.

A dose (five drops) of homeopathic carbolic acid 30c every 15 minutes while you wait for medical assistance will make all the difference. A few drops of Dr Bach's Rescue Remedy on the tongue, temples or wrists will also support the nervous system.

shock & stress The best treatment to carry around is Dr Bach's Rescue Remedy. A few drops under the tongue every 15 minutes will alleviate all symptoms of trauma.

insomnia Most children find it difficult to adjust to different sleep patterns and different beds. The best alternative is to give some tissue salts of magnesium phosphate (Mag Phos 6x) before bed or some camomile tea. For babies dilute 50mL normal strength camomile tea into 100mL of water; for children under five dilute half and half.

cold & flu symptoms A combination 'Q' of tissue salts will help with sinus and throat infections. A herbal tea of thyme or sage will alleviate sore throat and feverish symptoms and echinacea tablets or vitamin C will boost the immune system. The homeopathic remedy of gelsemium will get rid of muscular aches and pains and allium cepa will stop a runny nose and watery eyes.

earache To treat earache two drops of tea-tree and lavender oils in a teaspoon of carrier oil (such as almond or olive) is effective; put two drops of this mixture in each ear twice a day. Also give the child a dose of aconite/belladonna/camomile 30c every hour until better.

red, itchy eyes Bathe the eyes with a saline solution. If possible apply a warm camomile tea bag to eyelids for half an hour. Give the child some Ferrum Phos 6x tablets for inflammation.

toothaches Children should take one dose of aconite and arnica 30c every half hour and a dose of combination 'R' tissue salts whenever needed. For abscesses take one dose of aconite/belladonna every half hour and if possible gargle salt or warm water with two drops of tea-tree oil.

sun If they get sunburnt despite all protection, a few drops of hypericum oil on the burn will soothe the skin and quicken the healing. Comfrey cream is also very helpful for any kind of minor burn or skin irritation. For sunstroke, give the tissue salt of calcium sulphate (Calc. Sulph 6x) every 15 minutes until better. Also take Dr Bach's Rescue Remedy for shock and belladonna 30c for the fever/burning feeling.

nappy rash Your best friend in this case is calendula or comfrey cream or aloe vera gel.

fever Various remedies will help check a fever. Babies/children should have one dose (five drops) every hour of whichever relevant remedy until symptoms abate. For a sudden fever with agitation try aconite 30c or if the fever has chills with aches and pains use gelsemium 30c. For a red face, burning skin, and sweat treat with aconite and belladonna 30c.

homeopathic immunisations All traditional vaccines can be replaced by homeopathic immunisations. A qualified homeopath must be consulted to establish a schedule, particularly for young children travelling to exotic destinations.

PREGNANT TRAVEL

Being pregnant doesn't have to put an end to your travels. Plenty of women either choose or end up travelling while they are pregnant, without any adverse effects on mother or fetus. However, there are some important considerations if you are planning to travel while pregnant. The information included in this section is to give you an idea of the issues that are involved – you should get medical advice well before you plan to go on any trip. If you have had complicated pregnancies before or you're expecting twins, it would be best to postpone your trip until after the birth.

when

Most doctors suggest that the best time to travel in pregnancy is during the middle 12 weeks, when the risk of complications lessens, the pregnancy is relatively well established and your energy levels should be getting back to normal.

Before the 12th week, there is a relatively high risk of miscarriage (which could require surgical treatment like a scrape of the womb lining or even a blood transfusion) or tubal pregnancy, which occurs in about one in 200 pregnancies. Tubal pregnancy nearly always requires surgical treatment and is an emergency situation. In addition, many women experience morning sickness in the first three months (sometimes for longer), which could make travelling less than enjoyable. Occasionally, it can be severe enough to require treatment in hospital. More mundane, but just as incapacitating for travelling, is needing to empty your bladder more frequently as the enlarging womb takes up more room in the pelvis and presses on the bladder.

Note that most airlines prohibit flying after the 36th week of pregnancy (sometimes this can be waived if you have a doctor's certificate to say that there are no complications) – this is because they don't want to risk a woman going into premature labour during a flight, not because there's thought to be any intrinsic danger to the pregnancy.

In the last three months, major complications – such as premature labour, blood pressure problems and problems with the placenta – can all occur, so you would probably not want to risk a trip of any length during this time.

where

You need to go somewhere with a reasonable standard of medical facilities in case complications occur while you are away. For the same reason, it's probably not a good idea to plan a trip to remote areas when you are pregnant, in case you need urgent medical treatment. Some people feel absolutely fine during their pregnancy while others get very tired so a quiet time at an exotic location immersing yourself in the local culture may appeal or alternatively somewhere you've been before so you know what to expect. Hiking and cycling are still possibilities (make sure you drink lots of fluids) but scuba diving and canoeing are not advisable.

immunisations

Generally, it's best to avoid all vaccinations in the first 12 weeks of pregnancy, as there's a theoretical risk of harm to the fetus and miscarriage. In addition, 'live' vaccines ideally should be avoided at any time during pregnancy; 'live' vaccines include oral typhoid. Hepatitis A is a much more serious illness in pregnancy, so it's important to have the immunoglobulin injection or the hepatitis A vaccine as well as to take food and water precautions. An inactivated polio vaccine can be used instead of the usual oral 'live' vaccine in pregnant women if necessary. A tetanus booster can be given safely in pregnancy and tetanus protection is conferred to the newborn. Make sure you are clear on what your travel health insurance covers during pregnancy.

travel tips

I was unable to find a policy that would cover me for pregnancy-related problems after 24 weeks.

Phillipa Schultz, Australia

what to take

It's a good idea to take a well-stocked medical kit with you, with medications for common problems. (See the Health chapter for advice on a basic medical kit.) You should avoid non-essential medications when you are pregnant and don't take any medications while you are away unless you know they are safe during pregnancy (read the information leaflet or packaging carefully or ask a reliable doctor or pharmacist).

You may want to consider taking multivitamins, iron, folate or calcium tablets, and check with your doctor, naturopath or health food store as to the most appropriate.

medical considerations

Long flights or bus rides increase the risk of blood clots in the legs, so if possible try to get up and walk around, drink plenty of water and consider wearing support stockings to reduce this risk on a long journey.

Every traveller should take steps to avoid illness, but it's even more important in pregnancy, when illnesses can have more severe effects on both your health and your baby's: prevent insect bites, take food and water precautions, and avoid risk of accident.

I'd never been airsick before, so when I started feeling nauseous on the flight to Kuala Lumpur I already had my suspicions. 'One last long-haul trip before we have children,' is what we'd said. Perhaps we hadn't booked those tickets quick enough!

south-east asia PREGNANT BACKPACKING

Liz Chasseloup travelled through Malaysia and Thailand in the early stages of pregnancy.

The first thing that hits you when leave Kuala Lumpur airport is the humidity. I found it very hard to cope with the 90% humidity and found myself practically immobilised for a large part of the day. We were used to doing a lot of walking on our travels, rucksacks on our backs, but I found myself getting tired very quickly and resorting to taxis or *tuk-tuks*. They were worth paying for, but it needs to be taken into account when budgeting.

The humidity got the better of me and we decided to head up to Thailand. We booked an air-con bus to Phuket. White sand and turquoise waters seemed just what the doctor ordered although I'm sure that no sane doctor would have ordered that minibus! It was built for small Thai people and our heads banged against the ceiling regularly as we hit potholes or went suddenly from dirt track to sealed road. On long journeys my main concern was food, as I found I felt nauseous unless I ate very regularly. Luckily, there were plenty of roadside food stalls in Thailand with plenty of dishes on offer, though there were not so many in Malaysia.

I was so relieved to finally arrive on Phuket and ecstatic to see a chemist. The following day we made our way to Ko Phi Phi where the accommodation is mainly in small bungalows. Unfortunately, we arrived on a Saturday afternoon when all the cheapest accommodation had gone. We walked for miles, before ending up at square one with an expensive bungalow. Organisation is probably a good thing when you are pregnant.

Food-wise, Ko Phi Phi was paradise. There are many restaurants on Ko Phi Phi where you choose your fish or lobster before you sit down to eat. Not only is it very fresh but it is also cheap, which is just as well as I could only manage half of my lobster – pregnancy does strange things to you!

And the sarongs! All the colours of the sea or jungle, just perfect for that expanding tummy. We spent our days snorkelling, marvelling at the kaleidoscope of fish and coral beneath us. This must be the perfect way to spend your days when pregnant, particularly in the later months.

On our travels, I never once worried about hygiene. Cooking and washing facilities are simple on the islands, but there is a high turnover with the amount of people visiting, so freshness is almost guaranteed. While snorkelling you watch the fisherman catch the fish that you will be eating that evening.

After a few days we flew up to Bangkok. Travelling in Bangkok is a long haul in itself. A simple journey from one area to another can take hours, depending on the traffic. Bangkok is so crowded, hot and polluted that it is worth paying out extra for an air-con taxi. We took few buses, as they were usually crowded with standing space only. The river buses lurch violently in the water as people jump on and off, but they are a calmer, cooler way to travel and you get to see a few sights as well.

Having battled (and lost!) my way around the Grand Palace, I decided that I really couldn't cope with walking around in the heat. A quick look at the Emerald Buddha and I was out of there, heading for an ice-cream stall. Reality had to be faced and a pregnancy test bought! We went to a large shopping complex and found a chemist's counter. In large stores, the Thais speak English and even the instructions were in English. So I chased the cock-roaches out of the bathroom and went and did my test.

No more Thai whisky, no more cigarettes and no more carrying the heaviest rucksack!

"No more Thai whisky, no more cigarettes and no more carrying the heaviest rucksack!"

We decided to head back down to the east coast of Malaysia, to the Perhentian Islands. All the trains were full (I think I already mentioned that organisation is more important when you're pregnant!) so we were persuaded to take a 24-hour bus ride. We started off in a large, luxury coach, complete with TV, air-con, etc, but then changed a few hours later to a minibus – another low roof and no air-con affair. We had a giggle though when we crossed the border and saw the 'anything to declare' sign. Well actually...

It was all worth it when we arrived on the islands – more seafood and snorkelling. Cocooned in my belly, the baby was protected from the bouncing of the speedboat that took us from island to island, from beach to beach.

Our return tickets beckoned and although I could have stayed on the beach indefinitely, I was in need of a medical examination and a bit of reassurance from my doctor. I never felt that the baby or I were in danger, but I could have done without some of those long bus rides. Backpacking while pregnant is possible, with a light bag (or strong partner!) but with a bit more organisation.

During pregnancy your immunity is lower; infections, such as cystitis and chest infections, can be more severe and should be treated early with antibiotics – get medical advice. In the tropics you may be less tolerant of the heat. Rest, drink plenty of fluids and give yourself lots of time to adjust.

If you get diarrhoea, try to clear it up with rest and a bland diet. If you can't get rid of it this way use a kaolin preparation. Doctors advise against Lomotil as a therapy during pregnancy. If you want to pack something for diarrhoea check with your doctor first. Preventing diarrhoea is much better than taking medication to get rid of it when you are pregnant.

Yeast and fungal infections, such as thrush, can be a problem for the pregnant woman. Infections of the vagina are common in pregnant women anywhere, but if you are travelling in the tropics the hot climate exacerbates the problem. Cotton underwear that is not tight-fitting is absolutely essential. Don't wear tight jeans or trousers; loose cotton dresses are better. Carry an antifungal cream or appropriate oral medication.

what to eat

It's a good idea to make sure you eat a well-balanced, nutritionally sound diet during the trip, avoiding potential problem foods like raw or partially cooked eggs, peanuts and peanut products, and soft cheeses. Try not to miss meals or wait too long between meals and read up on food values and nutritional requirements so that you know which foods to eat. All the general advice about not smoking and being careful with alcohol obviously holds true.

special considerations

If this is your first pregnancy, it's a good idea to read up on it before you go so you have an idea of what to expect (such as tiredness, heartburn etc) and are familiar with any minor problems that may arise. Discuss these with your doctor or midwife, and work out strategies for coping in advance.

In the first three months, you'll be surprised how hungry you get. If you miss a meal due to travelling by train or bus or arriving late you may feel sick or even faint, so always carry something to eat with you, and snack on fruit, biscuits, anything you can find to keep you going. You do need it.

Don't try to do all the things you did before you got pregnant. Take frequent rests, particularly in the first three months when you're still adjusting to pregnancy. If you have one day of hard travel, have a day or two of rest and just plan to travel at a slower pace. Finally don't be alarmed by how often you'll need to find a toilet. You'll need to go to the toilet more often than you thought physically possible. It's wise to dress for quick and convenient toilet visits.

Also you may find that travelling on a bus or train for many hours at a stretch makes your back ache. If you are prone to motion sickness, you should consider trying to avoid it by limiting your trips on vehicles that make you sick, particularly if you actually vomit. Really, you have to take the same precautions you would if you stayed at home but you have to take more responsibility as your medical practitioner may not be a phone call away.

part 2 ...WHERE TO GO

EUROPE

Europe is a great place to travel with kids. How could you go wrong on a continent where they invented frankfurters, and fish and chips? And Santa lives there. You can take a sleigh ride to visit him in his arctic hideaway in northern Finland, if you wrap up warm. This is the home of Little Red Riding Hood, Cinderella, King Arthur and Tintin, to mention just a few local heroes. There are fairytale castles, long sandy beaches, ancient ruins and theme parks galore – just take your pick.

Europe is easy to get around with kids. The roads, trains and air services are all relatively child-friendly and making things easier for parents is high on the political agenda. Breastfeeding, if you're discreet, is acceptable nearly everywhere.

You can travel light, as everything you need is available unless you head for the remotest corners of Russia or the Balkans. The tourist industry is family orientated and there's a huge choice of accommodation to suit all pockets and tastes. Europeans may like to give the impression that style and culture are their top priorities but you'll find that if you give gourmet restaurants a wide berth you'll be welcomed wherever you go. Forget about the British stiff upper lip and German reserve, kids are not only popular they're big business too.

AUSTRIA

Austria is beautifully clean and a perfect destination with small children. Being friendly to kids is in vogue there. You can wheel your stroller onto every bus in town and you'll find your kids are greeted with smiles. That said Austrians expect good behaviour. You can't go wrong wherever you choose to stay from a tent to a five-star hotel. Guesthouses in the countryside are a good option with children. In summer many hotels and pensions in Vienna offer free B&B accommodation for up to two children, under 12, if sharing their parents' room.

Children's menus are available in some restaurants. Local tourist offices and hotels can recommend babysitters. Laundrettes and service washes are easy to find. Supermarkets close early and on Sundays but there are late night shops at railway stations and there is always a 24-hour pharmacy open.

Public transport is efficient and during school holidays in Vienna all under-15s travel free. Most of the sights in Vienna are within easy reach on foot and there are plenty of cafes serving up huge slices of chocolate cake. Kids will love Christmas in Vienna when there's ice skating in front of the City Hall and a fantastic Christmas market.

information

Look out for the tourist board booklet, *Small Guests, Big Welcome* that lists benefits and attractions for families. In Vienna, teenagers should look out for *Jugend Info* for listings of what's on.

things to see & do

wild things The zoo at the Schönbrunn Palace is the oldest in the world and has an authentic Tyrolean farmhouse. There's also a butterfly house in the palace grounds. Outside Vienna head for the Alpenzoo in Innsbruck.

interesting & educational In Vienna, there are special children's tours of the Schloss Schönbrunn, the Kuffner Sternwarte Observatory and Planetarium. Among the museums devoted to kids are the Puppen & Spielzeug Museum (Doll and Toy Museum) and ZOOM Kindermuseum in the Museumsquartier. Kids will like the displays at the Spanische Reitschule (Spanish Riding School) but book well in advance. Out of town, the splendid palace of Schloss Schallaburg in Melk is so stunning it's guaranteed to grab the kids' attention and they'll like the Salzbergwerk (salt mines) at Hallstatt, especially the gruesome rows of decorated skulls near the local church!

pure entertainment Vienna's Prater amusement park, made famous by the film *The Third Man*, is something you won't want to miss either. In bad weather try the puppets in the Marionettentheater at Schloss Schönbrunn or the IMAX cinema.

In Linz, there's a wonderful grotto where you can ride on a mini-train past hundreds of tiny gnomes and in Graz you can take a train ride past 2km of scenes from fairy tales on the longest grotto railway in Europe.

activities

On the slopes there are plenty of kids' ski schools and creches in the main resorts. There are lots of indoor and outdoor swimming pools in Vienna and under-15s don't have to pay in the summer holidays.

parks & playgrounds

There's a beautiful forest next to the Prater amusement park, which is good for picnics. Playgrounds across Austria are all of a high standard with safety always important in their design.

books & films

Rent the film *The Sound of Music* (1965) before you go and take the official 'Sound of Music tour' when you get there. Teenagers will enjoy Graham Green's *The Third Man*.

When my daughter Jessy was seven months old I was invited to present a paper at an international conference in Vienna. The thought of weaning and leaving Jessy for 10 days was unbearable so I decided to take her with me. Since our finances wouldn't stretch to include my husband I was to travel solo with Jessy. As luck would have it I found out that two friends of a friend, Andrea and Lyn, would be backpacking in Europe when I was due in Vienna and might enjoy the chance of earning some money by looking after Jessy. I arranged to meet them in Vienna.

vienna BALANCING BUSINESS & BABY

Sarah Mathews travelled to Vienna on a business trip with her baby, Jessy, seven months.

Once everything was arranged I started my 31 hours in transit from Brisbane to Vienna. I had pre-booked a bassinet seat for Jessy, which was fabulous on the flight to Vienna because I had no-one sitting next to me and Jessy was happy to sit in it for entertainment and eating. During our trip Jessy went through 18 nappies and four changes of clothes (the altitude must have played havoc on her bowels!) and I found the aeroplane change tables quite inadequate to completely wash and change an infant covered in baby poo. Luckily, my anticipation of lost luggage meant I had packed what I thought would be enough for two to three days in my hand luggage. I breastfed Jessy for comfort during the flight, and found I had to drink plenty of water and avoid alcohol to ensure I was hydrated. Lauda Air supplied baby food but no nappies or baby blankets, however the flight attendants happily entertained Jessy during the flight when time permitted.

On arrival in Vienna it was easy to share a taxi (the cheaper option) to the hotel where I was very happy to see the cot already made up in the room. Since the conference was starting in two days and I was the second to speak on the program I needed to get Jessy and myself over jetlag quickly. We went for a walk, had a snack, showered and were both asleep before 4 pm, and stayed that way until Jessy woke at 2 am ready for the day. I fed Jessy and we played quietly for an hour before going back to sleep until breakfast. Amazingly, this was all we both needed to get into the correct time zone. The next day Jessy and I explored Vienna on foot and tram, marvelling at the architecture and outdoor markets. The heart of Vienna is enjoyable to get around with a stroller. Travelling on the trams was easy enough with a stroller because the guards and passengers were keen to help. However, the trains were somewhat more difficult since there were often many steps leading down to the station and I often had to request assistance.

It was easy to find nappies, baby food and baby clothes (since most of Jessy's baby clothes were drying over the oil heater in the hotel room). Jessy was still on puréed food during our trip and I easily found both popular and gourmet baby food brands. Nappies were available in the mini-marts which are jotted throughout the Vienna city district. The shopping district in Vienna consisted mostly of boutique stores and I found some gorgeous baby clothes. European baby clothes sizes are based on the length of your child so it is very useful to know how long your baby is.

When Andrea and Lyn arrived we quickly got to know each other as we were all sharing the same hotel room. We organised a routine for Jessy and tried to get her to drink breastmilk from a bottle (I had packed my trusty breast pump) before I went out for the conference opening in the majestic Town Hall. During the next five days Jessy saw more of Vienna than me as Andrea and Lyn took her sightseeing while I attended the conference, only stopping by to let Jessy breastfeed since she refused to take anything but juice from a bottle.

"At the tourist attractions Jessy was something of a highlight. People often stopped to ask her name and age, and make sure she was rugged-up well enough in the cold September winds."

During gaps in the conference schedule we all managed to see the Prater fun park, Stephansdom (St Stephens Cathedral) and Schloss Schönbrunn together. At the tourist attractions Jessy was something of a highlight. People often stopped to ask her name and age, and make sure she was rugged-up well enough in the cold September winds. Jessy became easily frustrated when being carted around the palaces. Her favourite place was at the top of the Risenrad (a large Ferris wheel) at the Prater fun park where you can view the entire Vienna district in the comfort of a cable car. For older children there was a mini-fun park within the gardens near St Stephens Cathedral which helped parents balance the fun activities with the palaces.

The week went quickly; Jessy learnt to crawl in Vienna and the return flight consisted mainly of consoling Jessy as she cut her first teeth.

BELGIUM

Belgium is easy to travel around with kids especially by car. It's so small that no journey takes longer than a couple of hours, which cuts moaning time. The public transport system is good but most city centres are pedestrianised so pack good walking shoes and a sturdy stroller.

Belgians like kids. There's a diet of chocolate, waffles and chips so it's easy to keep the kids' blood sugar up as you do the sights. Gourmet restaurants are child-free zones, and those for tourists are expensive and usually poor quality. Opt for self-catering in one of the growing number of apartment hotels. It's easy to get a highchair, cot or extra bed.

You can buy everything in the main supermarkets but they shut early and are closed on Sunday. The Belgians give children's medicines as suppositories, so bring your own children's paracetamol (acetaminophen). Pack reins for turbo toddlers as canals and bikes are hazards. Tourist offices will put you in contact with babysitting agencies.

brussels

things to see & do

wild things The best animals in Brussels are stuffed and on show at the Musée Royal de l'Afrique Centrale in Tervuren. The Musée des Sciences Naturelles has a collection of genuine iguanodon skeletons.

interesting & educational The Surrealist paintings by Magritte at the Musées Royaux des Beaux-Arts go down well. Youngsters like the antique cars at Autoworld and the collection of planes and tanks at the Musée Royale de l'Armée et d'Histoire Militaire. The hands-on Scientastic Museum is good for all ages.

pure entertainment Kids want to see the Manneken Pis, the statue of the urinating boy and the Centre Belge de la Bande Dessinée, the cartoon museum. After this head for the Atomium, a huge exhibition centre shaped like a molecule that looks like something out of a Tintin comic.

activities

Bruparck has a water park and model village: Mini-Europe. Walibi, about 20km south-east of Brussels, is the country's biggest amusement park.

parks & playgrounds

Brussels has an especially good supply of parks. There's a handy playground opposite the Palais Royal and older kids can run off steam at the Parc de Bruxelles.

around belgium

Take a trip to the medieval city of Bruges. Don't miss the Russian submarine at Seaworld in Zeebrugge. Make time to explore the battlefield of Waterloo and the WWI battlefields around Ypres. Even babies like the view from the monument at the Butte de Lion, at Waterloo, but the graveyards and museums of WWI in Flanders are better for older kids. Check out the National Scheepvaart Museum (Maritime Museum) and zoo in Antwerp.

books

Invest in a set of Tintin books. Tintin memorabilia abounds and most shops stock some of Hergé's books in English.

BRITAIN

The British like kids and Londoners in particular are keen to be seen as child-friendly. You're no longer restricted to eating in the pizza-burger ghetto as even gourmet restaurants have started serving up designer crayons with the aperitif. Britain's a great destination with kids. There's plenty to do and most attractions have family tickets, but be warned, days out in Britain are among the most expensive in Europe.

Outside the capital things can still be a bit stuffy. Many pubs restrict children to cold, damp family rooms and many hotels won't let children in the dining room after 7 pm. Outside the main cities food can often often be poor quality and overpriced.

Twenty-four-hour shopping in London means you can buy whatever you need for the kids whenever you want it. Even in the countryside supermarkets are open on Sundays and there's usually a late-night shop but it may not stock baby products.

If you're travelling in the countryside opt for self-catering or B&Bs on farms. In London it is possible to rent apartments but there's also a growing number of apartment hotels which are a good option with a family. Cots and highchairs are usually available but changing facilities can be basic.

london

information

The monthly magazine *Kids Out* has a full listing of what's on around the capital. The listings magazine *Time Out* has a children's section. The best and cheapest books for kids are *I-Spy Books*, which are mini-guides for kids – you tick off the sights and earn points as you go.

practicalities

London's public transport system is overcrowded and crumbling. Many of the escalators on the Underground don't work properly, and strollers and double-decker buses don't mix, so with a small baby a sling is a good option. Avoid the rush hour and don't forget it's cheaper to buy a family travel card. Both Rock-a-bye Babysitters and Universal Aunts are respected agencies and cover central London.

There's driving rain and a force nine gale as we drive into Lyme Regis but nothing is going to deter my daughters. They've got an appointment with local dinosaur-hunter Steve Davies and they aren't going to miss it whatever the weather. Pulling on his waterproof jacket, Davies laughs at me when I ask him if we are still going fossil hunting. 'Of course, this is marvellous weather for fossils. Anyway, the sun will be shining by the time we get on the beach!'

dorset HUNTING DINOSAURS

Rosie Whitehouse took her daughters, Esti, nine, and Rachel, six, along with baby twins, Jacob and Eve, to Lyme Regis in Dorset on the south coast of England.

As chief palaeontologist for the multinational company BP, Davies spent months excavating the frozen oilfields of Alaska. 'Kids make great fossil hunters,' says Davies, as he guides us towards the beach. 'You've got to get as close to the ground as possible and they've got a natural advantage!' Pushing the baby twins in the double pram, I have to run to keep up. Davies found his first fossil here on a school outing and now runs Dinosaurland, the local museum.

By the time we reach the seafront the sun is shining and the waves are lapping quietly on the rocks. Davies is bubbling over with enthusiasm. Esti and Rachel are entranced. With eyes wide they listen to Davies as he tells them that we're standing at the bottom of what was once the Tethys Sea. 'Two hundred million years ago this place was paradise on earth. It was bursting with marine life. There were ichthyosaurs, plesiosaurs, and heaps of ammonites and belemnites. When they died they sank to the bottom and were covered in mud.'

The girls immediately identify with the 12-year-old, Mary Anning, who found the first complete ichthyosaur, a kind of Jurassic dolphin, here in 1811. Mary used to gather shells and fossils to sell to visitors. The tongue twister 'She sells sea shells by the sea shore' is all about her. Davies' 13-year-old son, Christopher, is helping out on this walk along the beach. He's a natural-born fossil hunter too. When he was just 11, he found the head of a baby ichthyosaur lying at his feet.

The girls follow Davies like the Pied Piper. Their bucket is soon bursting with flint and pebbles. Shells prove a major distraction but one boy who's with us finds an ammonite the size of a small coin!

I'm left dragging the double buggy back over the rocks. You can only get to the fossils at low tide and it's very easy to get cut off, I can't see us getting out of here in a hurry. I've never been here before or seen the film *The French Lieutenant's Woman*, which made Lyme Regis really famous, but the tiny painted cottages look familiar. Esti is certain she's seen them in a storybook at home. She's right.

Beatrix Potter immortalised Lyme in *The Tale of Little Pig Robinson*. So did Whistler and Jane Austen but they're not in the same league.

Coming back empty handed is a bonus as now we can spend an hour or two cruising the souvenir shops. There's an ichthyosaur for a small fortune but thankfully Esti and Rachel settle on a tiny box of fossilised shark teeth, a couple of pencils and a purple teddy bear keyring.

Behind Lyme Regis is some of the most beautiful countryside in England. Steep green valleys, thatched cottages and ancient woodlands. The girls love it when we find the road blocked by cows on their way home for milking. The twins sleep off the excitement as we drive along the coast to Abbotsbury. The view from the cliff edge is spectacular. There's a double rainbow. The girls have their cameras out and are snapping.

Abbotsbury is a real Miss Marple village but it's deserted. It's famous for its swans and there are hundreds gliding in and out of the reeds in the estuary. We feel like bit players in *The Ugly Duckling*. Eve baulks as she comes eye to eye with a three-foot hissing swan.

It's time to head for civilisation and I've booked the cottage in a hurry forgetting to read the small print. As we arrive back in Stoke Abbot the mobile phone cuts out. It's a real chocolate-box village, just like it said in the brochure, but like Abbotsbury it's deserted. Our cottage is literally dug into the edge of a graveyard that looks as if it's stepped right out of a horror movie! The graves rise up from the kitchen window and when you turn on the tumble dryer the whole kitchen smells earthy and damp.

Alone with four children, I almost turn tail and run, but you can't tell them you're scared of ghosts can you? The next day, as we drive back to London across the moors, Dorset looks sinister in the grey light. Thomas Hardy wouldn't recognise it. I ask Esti if she'd noticed anything about the house. She did but had decided it was wiser to keep quiet.

"'Kids make great fossil hunters,' says Davies, as he guides us towards the beach. 'You've got to get as close to the ground as possible and they've got a natural advantage!'"

things to see & do

wild things London Zoo is one of the best in the world. Don't miss the London Aquarium by Westminster Bridge.

interesting & educational Older children will like the British Museum. It's just been renovated and you can see Karl Marx's seat in the Old Library. The Tower of London is always a favourite as kids love gawping at the crown jewels and the chopping block. You can't go wrong with the Natural History Museum, especially the dinosaurs and earthquake galleries. The Science Museum has plenty of hands-on activities. Older children like the Planetarium. Often overlooked but excellent is the National Army Museum, which is free. Toddlers will love the London Transport Museum.

pure entertainment It's cool to be seen at the IMAX Cinema at Waterloo and kids usually find Madame Tussaud's wax works entertaining.

activities

Take a sightseeing trip on a topless bus and a trip down the river to Greenwich. Watch the Changing of the Guard outside Buckingham Palace. Kids love a ride on the London Eye, a giant Ferris wheel with capsules to ride in. When it comes to the shops they'll want to check out Hamleys – the biggest toy shop in the world – but beware, the mark-up is just as big.

Have a rest in an art cafe while the kids decorate pots and plates but remember it usually takes three or four days to fire their masterpieces. There are art cafes in Portobello and Maida Vale. Try brass rubbing in St Martin-in-the-Fields.

parks & playgrounds

London has plenty of parks that make for ideal picnic spots. Hire a boat on the Serpentine. Visit the giant glasshouses at Kew Gardens. Meet the deer in Richmond Park and don't miss the statue of Peter Pan in Kensington Gardens.

festivals

Kids will like the Lord Mayor's Show in November and Chinese New Year Parade in January. They won't like the Notting Hill Carnival – crowded, difficult to see anything and full of lurching, drunk or stoned adults.

around britain

Top of the kids' list will be a visit to Legoland at Windsor. Kids will enjoy a day trip to Brighton to walk on the pier. Hampton Court Palace is supposed to be haunted by one of Henry VIII's wives. Stonehenge is a two-hour drive from London. To get a quick feel for England head for Kent and Sussex where there are Roman villas, Norman castles and Tudor mansions. Further afield kids love the rocky coves in Cornwall, Snowdonia National Park and the castles along the North Wales Coast. Northumberland has Hadrian's Wall, some of the best beaches in Britain and you can watch seals and puffins on a boat trip to the Farne Islands. Take the night train to Edinburgh and check out the castle and museums. Edinburgh is a very small, child-friendly city and a sharp contrast to London.

books

Look out for history books in the Ladybird series. British kids love Terry Deary's series *Horrible Histories* and *Top Ten Tales from Dickens*. Pack a copy of *Peter Pan* by JM Barrie. Teenagers will enjoy the futuristic view of London in Aldous Huxley's *Brave New World*.

DENMARK

Not surprisingly, Denmark – the home of Lego and Hans Christian Andersen – is a family-oriented place. There's plenty for kids to see and they'll love all the Viking remains. You'll appreciate the fact that Denmark isn't as pricey as the rest of Scandinavia and the weather is milder. There are good discounts for children on trains but a car is probably easier for touring. Highchairs and cots are both readily available.

Like the rest of Scandinavia, it's clean and efficient. There are plenty of family rooms in all types of hotels and it is possible to rent cottages. Camping is always a good option in the summer and sites usually have a playground. Staff at local tourist offices can provide useful information on babysitting services. Laundrettes are usually plentiful and easy to find.

things to see & do

wild things Copenhagen has a huge zoo, Zoologisk Have. To see fish, turtles and sharks head for the excellent Danmarks Akvarium at the northern side of the city.

interesting & educational Once they've gawped at the statue of the Little Mermaid in Copenhagen, for the name alone the kids will want to check the 2000-year-old bodies of the 'bog people' in Silkeborg. Then it's on to the Viking ships at Roskilde, the Viking museum at Århus and the Viking fortresses of Trelleborg. One of the best castles is Rosenborg Slot in Copenhagen.

Even the stuffiest of museums will have a hands-on section for the kids. Statens Museum for Kunst (state art museum) has a new children's gallery and at Louisiana, the modern art museum in Humlebæk, budding artists can even let the paint hit the canvas.

pure entertainment Top of the kids' list of attractions are the 45 million Lego bricks that make up Legoland but there are also two big amusement parks in Copenhagen. There's a marvellous puppet theatre in the grounds of Rosenborg castle. The kids will also enjoy the variety of strange attractions at Ripley's Believe It or Not Museum, Guinness World of Records Museum or Louis Tussard's Wax Museum.

activities

Denmark has some wonderful sandy beaches and fantastic flat cycling. In Copenhagen kids will love a canal boat tour.

parks & playgrounds

There are plenty of parks to run off steam and playgrounds are safe and clean.

books

Pack a collection of Hans Christian Andersen's fairy tales and to find out more about this famous Dane the kids can read Andrew Langley's mini-biography *Hans Christian Andersen*. Henry Treece's Viking adventure *Horned Helmet* is on audiotape and will entertain them in the car between sights. The *Eyewitness Guide: Viking* is a an excellent beginner's history.

FRANCE

You'll find a warm welcome everywhere in France and there's an abundance of things for children to do. When it comes to eating out remember French children have immaculate table manners and know how to behave – if yours don't, avoid classy restaurants. Head for the outdoor cafes in summer.

The range of baby products on offer in French supermarkets is the best in Europe but 24-hour shopping has yet to arrive in France, so stock up for the weekend.

In France, although the breastfeeding rates are low (50% at birth), nursing a young baby in public is completely acceptable. Nursing an older baby or child is not common, but there are no legal restrictions.

There's plenty of opportunities for self-catering. If you're touring opt for B&Bs, or *chambres d'hôte*. They'll have swings and see-saws and many do excellent evening meals. An apartment hotel is a good option in Paris.

French trains are fast and efficient and have good discounts for children. Cots and highchairs should be booked in advance. Tourist offices have lists of babysitting services and creches and it's easy to find a launderette or service wash.

paris

information

If you like walking, look out for the guides *Les Sentiers d'Emilie* which will give easy walks suitable for children. There's a children's section in the listings magazine *Pariscope*.

practicalities

The tourist office can put you in contact with babysitting agencies. Paris has an excellent bus service, which is more child-friendly than the Metro which can be crowded and stuffy. All the buses are stroller-friendly.

things to see & do

wild things Jardin des Plantesis has the Ménagerie which is smaller and more accessible than the Parc Zoologique de Paris and home to an extraordinary collection of giant turtles, goats, cows and camels.

interesting & educational Make the Eiffel Tower your first stop, so the kids can get an idea of what there is to see. Then it's down to Musée Les Égouts de Paris to see and smell the 1.2 million cubic metres of sewage that flows under the city!

Older kids will enjoy exploring the Egyptian galleries in the Louvre. Little ones will prefer hands-on art at the Musée en Herbe in the Bois de Boulogne. The magic shows at the Musée de la Curiosité et Magie are great fun. The waxworks at Musée Grévin are a good bet but the queues are horrible. The Cité des Enfants is good for older children. Tiny tots will like the rat run, at the quainter Palais de la Découverte, just off the Champs Élysées.

pure entertainment Whatever you do, don't miss the French version of Punch and Judy in the Théâtre du Luxembourg. There's a mini amusement park in the Bois de Boulogne – the Jardin d'Acclimatation. Disneyland Paris is hard to miss with the kids in tow. You should visit out of season or plan to stay late to dodge the queues. Avoid the hotels. Parc Astérix is a good European alternative. You can find the cartoon Gaul and his pals just 30km north of Paris.

activities

Children always like a boat trip along the Seine or a ride on the giant Ferris wheel. You can hire bikes with baby seats in the Bois de Boulogne.

parks & playgrounds

Paris has an abundance of parks but the Jardin du Luxembourg is the one to see. There are pony rides and even a carousel where you can test out your jousting skills.

around france

Among the top sites in the north that kids like are: the mysterious island of Mont St Michel and the Bayeux Tapestry. Monet's home in Giverny usually appeals. In central France, the boat ride along the underground river through caves – the Gouffre du Padirac near Rocamadour – is a winner. In the south, children like the fortified town of Carcassonne. The 3D cinemas at the Futuroscope theme park near Poitiers are considered cool.

To avoid the heat in summer head for the Pyrenees. Kids will love the wildlife, waterfalls and watching the cyclists trying to get to the top of the highest peaks. Older children like exploring the battlefields of the Somme and the ancient tunnels below Arras. The dormant volcanoes of the Parc Naturel Régional des Volcans d'Auvergne are a hit. If you want to explore the Côte d'Azur, base yourself in Villefranche-sur-Mer. The best beaches with toddlers are in Normandy and southern Corsica.

books & films

Pack the adventures of *Madeline* by Ludwig Bemelmans for the under-eights. Asterix gives a good insight into French culture, especially *Asterix in Corsica*. Watch either Disney's *The Hunchback of Notre Dame* or the older 1939 version. *Le Ballon Rouge* (1956) is a classic and perfect for creating the atmosphere.

Last summer, I cobbled together enough money for two plane tickets to Paris – one for me, the other for my daughter. I had lived in Paris during the 1980s, so I emailed my French friends and said to be on the lookout for us. We boarded the plane without plan or itinerary.

paris EIFFEL or MOUTHFUL

Stephanie Levin-Gervasi spent a week in Paris with her eight-year-old daughter, Camille.

This isn't to say I didn't have a maternal portrait percolating in my brain. I fancied a kind of storybook vacation with my eight-year-old. Camille and I were excited to be in Paris, but we had entirely different agendas. A Francophile and a French 'foodie', I longed to sashay, arm-in-arm with my daughter through one of the city's oldest markets, Rue Mouffetard. The open-air food market – stuffed with culinary counsellors hawking cheeses, oysters and sumptuous produce – is the most colourful market in Paris. Camille's *raison d'être* – the Eiffel Tower and a ride on the Ferris wheel, the one she had seen on television during the millennium celebrations.

Food was our biggest challenge. In a city where food is an art, Camille lived on sliced ham and baguettes. She had a litany of complaints about French food: the dollop of crème fraîche crowning the ice cream didn't taste like American whipped cream, the cheeses smelled like stinky feet and the mustard was the wrong colour yellow. We frequented *boulangeries*, corner stores, pizza places and discovered a plethora of Chinese restaurants in the 13th arrondissement (Place d'Italie). Each morning we ferreted out croissants, hot chocolate and *café au lait* at corner cafes. We didn't starve.

Once we solved the food conundrum, we tackled the nasty lines snaking around every monument or museum. I hate standing in line, ditto for my daughter. Thankfully, I had the foresight before leaving the States to contact Rail Europe in New York for French Rail Passes. The pass allowed us to bypass long lines at the train stations. That was our only reprieve from lines. The queue curling around the Louvre looked like a line for a sold-out Stones concert.

'Forget the Louvre,' I said. We took the metro to the Eiffel Tower. 'I knew we should have come early in the day,' I groaned, checking out the four-hour line for the two elevators. 'That's OK, mom, we can wait in the short line and walk up,' suggested Camille good naturedly. An hour later we shelled out our 15 francs and started up the mighty monument. Actually, Camille bolted up the steps while I huffed and puffed. Thankfully, we could only go to the third tier by foot. Because

I avoid lines, this was my first trip to the Eiffel Tower. And, like every other tourist, I oohed and aahed at the high-rise views of Paris, the architectural feat of the last century. We bought postcards, posted them from the Eiffel Tower post office and headed down.

Get an early start, and you're less likely to stand in lines in Paris during the summer. We never got started before 10 am and our days sorely lacked structure. We needed to mend our ways. Our casual approach to Paris was whittling away precious days. We hatched a plan. Since the French do not eat on the run, we decided not to either. We packed picnic lunches – baguettes, cheese, ham and fruit, then ate in different parks around the city. Camille got to ride the Ferris wheel after our picnic in the Tuilleries. In the park behind Cathédrale de Notre Dame de Paris, we munched our sandwiches under the watchful eye of gargoyles, then strolled across the Seine and boarded the *Bateau Mouche*. The big *bateau* glides down the Seine, past the Palais de Justice, Île Saint Louis and the Statue of Liberty in less than an hour.

"A Francophile and a French 'foodie', I longed to sashay, arm-in-arm with my daughter through one of the city's oldest markets, Rue Mouffetard."

Paris is stunning after dark and it stays light until around 10.30 pm in the summer. The Left Bank is the hot spot at night and the square in front of Cathédrale de Notre Dame de Paris always has something going on. Forget Quasimodo's bell tower, Camille was dazzled by the daredevil skateboard competition in the square. A tin can toss from the Notre Dame sits Shakespeare & Company – the English language bookstore crammed with literary treasures and reading alcoves. We purchased the English version of Harry Potter.

We put a lot of mileage on our feet peeking into store windows, soaking in the street theatre and stopping for sugar crepes on the street. Sometimes our feet got sore and our tempers frazzled, but we remedied this by riding the Metro.

Every Metro station has a gigantic map with colourful buttons that lead to different Metro lines. I let Camille pick a point, within reason, and we would ride to that destination. In Bois de Vincennes we discovered a little zoo, and in Place Des Vosges, Camille found kids to play with.

We spent a brilliant day at La Vilette – the city of science that proved to be an ingenious marvel. Every hands-on scientific secret is here to explore. The cavernous halls are designed for various ages and tickets sold in hourly chunks so that the exhibit halls and geodesic dome IMAX theatre don't overcrowd.

Our week in Paris was coming to an end. It was time to move on to our next adventure, a train ride to see our friends in a tiny village near La Rochelle. But that's another story.

FINLAND

Finland is one of the most child-friendly countries around. So it should be – Father Christmas lives here! It's clean, safe and a tranquil place to enjoy a family holiday. Most hotels and hostels have family rooms. Finns love camping and it's a good option for families in the countryside but come prepared for mosquitoes.

Supermarkets stock everything you'll need and many trains and ferries have special children's play areas. The best time to visit is summer. The Finns take to their country cottages and the place is about as sleepy as you can get. This is essentially an outdoor country, where winter is harsh. The best way to get about is by car. The roads are empty and you'll never be held up by roadworks. Highchairs and cots should be booked in advance.

things to see & do

wild things Helsinki has a lovely island zoo and kids will enjoy taking the ferry to get there. Spotting elk isn't a problem; they have to fence the motorway out of Helsinki to keep them off the road. There's a marvellous nature reserve at Ähtari in the east and plenty of reindeer in Lapland but don't visit in summer because of the mosquitoes.

interesting & educational If the kids like castles they'll love picnicking at Soumenlinna, Helsinki's island fortress and Olavinlinna Castle in Savonlinna in the east.

pure entertainment You may find the trip a bit tacky but the children will want to visit Santa Claus in Rovaniemi in Lapland. The post office here receives over a million letters a year for St Nick alone. Kids will like having their photo taken at the Arctic Circle marker and there are tours of the local reindeer farm. There's an amusement park called Santapark as well. There's good skiing in winter if you want to escape the elves.

Moomin World in Naantali is a wonderful amusement park based on the characters of the children's story. Finnish kids love it but you need to read the book before you go. Linnanmäki amusement park in Helsinki is also a good diversion.

activities

In Helsinki take a ferry boat tour and rent a bike. There's a large water park at Espoo west of the capital. The lakes around Savonlinna are the best places for walking in the woods, canoeing and swimming. The beaches are sandy, shallow and toddler-friendly.

parks & playgrounds

You can easily wear them out in the mass of small parks and playgrounds in Helsinki.

books

Pack the classic *Tales from Moominvalley* by Tove Jansson for under-10s.

GERMANY

Your children may not receive the rapturous reception they get in Italy but you'll find that Germany is efficient, clean and family orientated. Children's discounts are widely available for everything from museum admissions to bus fares and hotel rooms. Public transport is family-friendly and if you do rent a car there's no problem getting a car safety seat.

Hotels are of a high standard but can be pricey. Most large hotels offer a babysitting service. Hostels, however, aren't usually family orientated. Guesthouses are a better budget option with a family. German families are keen on self-catering accommodation especially on farms in Bavaria. Book cots and highchairs in advance.

Kids are welcome in casual restaurants and bars, but give gourmet joints a wide berth. You can buy everything you need for babies and children in supermarkets but remember they close early. The rule is: stock up for the weekend. There are plenty of laundrettes and good nappy changing facilities.

Breastfeeding a young baby in public is completely acceptable. Nursing an older baby or child is not common but generally accepted.

information

The Munich tourist office publishes a free booklet, *Hits for Kids*. In Berlin the tourist office will give you details of special children's tours of the city.

berlin

practicalities

The babysitting agency KidsCare is geared specifically towards travellers. Sitters come to your hotel or home, lugging a bag of supplies customised to your child's age.

things to see & do

wild things Berlin has two zoos, which is a hangover from when there were two Germanys. The Zoologischer Garten is home to 15,000 animals so tots should find at least one they like.

interesting & educational If you take time to explain to children the history of the city, they'll enjoy the main sites. Berlin is a better destination with older children, who'll find the remains of the Berlin Wall, the Reichstag and the 1936 Olympic Stadium particularly interesting.

To give them an idea of the city climb the Fernsehturm in Alexanderplatz. Berlin's main museums, like Pergamon Museum, are bound to interest older children but beware, the city's museums are not particularly kid-friendly. Even sucking on a bottle is out of the question in most places and don't even think about letting your tots run around – their movement may set off the highly sensitive alarms.

The little ones will find that the medieval village at the Museumsdorf Düppel (Düppel Museum Village) or the farm museum, Dahlem Museum, are more their style. The Puppentheater-Museum Berlin is a good bet and dinosaur fans will like the Museum für Naturkunde (Museum of Natural History).

The Museum für Volkerkunde (Museum of Ethnology) has a special children's tour once a month. The Kindheit & Jugend Museum (Museum of Childhood & Adolescence) and Spectrum! at Deutsches Technikmuseum (German Technical Museum), which has loads of hands-on experiments, are both good. The Allierton-Museum (Allied Museum) is worth the trip, as there's an old guard tower and cabin from Checkpoint Charlie.

pure entertainment Kids can let their hair down at the Britzer Garten adventure park where there's a water playground, theme garden, outdoor laboratory and animal enclosure. The stunts and special effects at the Babelsberg film studios go down well with youngsters.

activities

A trip to Blub Badeparadies leisure pool with its wave pools, waterfalls and giant slide should wear them out. There's a separate pool for toddlers.

parks & playgrounds

Berlin must be one of the easiest cities to visit in summer as it's surrounded by parks, forests and lakes, where you can swim, picnic, cycle or simply unwind. Wherever you head, they're all lovely – the Wannsee Lake and Grunewald forest are especially good. Don't miss the grounds of the Schloss Charlottenburg and the Tiergarten.

festivals

Christmas is a great time to visit Germany with fairs and markets across the country. Berlin's Weihnachtsmärkt (Christmas fair) is the biggest in Europe.

around germany

There are plenty of theme parks, water parks and national parks scattered across the country. In Munich kids will enjoy the Olympic Experience where they can try their hands at a virtual Olympic games. A trip to the fairy-tale castle of Neuschwanstein is a must – it looks just like Sleeping Beauty's Castle. It's touristy so visit out of season to get the magic.

The best place for a family holiday is in Bavaria, where there's everything from theme parks to the wilds of the Berchtesgaden National Park. Steam train fanatics should ride the rails in eastern Hartz or take the train in eastern Saxony near Dresden. It's Christmas all year round in the medieval town of Rothenburg ob der Tauber where there's a permanent Christmas market.

books

If it's Christmas pack a copy of *The Nutcracker*. Follow little Emil's adventures in Berlin in Erich Kastner's classic *Emil and the Detectives*. If you want to get them speaking the language, try *My First Oxford German Words* to get them started. Judith Kerr's story *When Hitler Stole Pink Rabbit* is a good introduction to the period for 10-year-olds.

IRELAND

Ireland is child-friendly and relaxed. The charm of Ireland is its wild remote countryside and coast; slow down and take time to soak up the atmosphere and just enjoy being with the kids. The best way to see the countryside is to hire a car, then when you come across that strange round tower or fantastic beach, you can just pull over and explore.

Kids will get a warm welcome in hotels and B&Bs but it's a good idea to reserve a cot. This is the place to enjoy that stone cottage in the middle of nowhere; self-catering is a good option as finding a restaurant can often be a problem. Children are allowed in pubs until 7 or 8 pm but in smaller towns this restriction is treated with customary Irish flexibility. There's usually a family ticket for attractions and family passes are available on public transport.

It's easy to find anything you need for babies and children but shops close early in the countryside. Rain will be your biggest problem so come prepared. Ask the tourist office for local babysitters. You won't see a lot of women breastfeeding in Ireland as breastfeeding rates are low by European standards but discreet breastfeeding in public places is not a problem.

dublin

information

The Irish Tourist Board, Bord Fáilte, publish a useful booklet, *The Family Fun in Dublin Guide*.

things to see & do

wild things Dublin Zoo is where the lion that roars at the start of the MGM movies was born. Don't miss the crazy chickens with pink hairdos at Newbridge Demesne Traditional Farm. The dinosaur-mad will like the National Museum's geological section.

interesting & educational Start at the Dublin Experience, an audiovisual introduction to the city. Then move on to Dublin's Viking Adventure where you can ride on a Viking ship and walk through a Viking village. A trip to Dublin Castle is usually a hit and Kilmainham Jail will appeal to their gruesome side while they learn a little about Ireland's struggle for independence.

Older kids will like looking at the *Book of Kells*, an illuminated manuscript and one of the oldest books in the world, in Trinity College. Kids who like stranger relics will like the curiously mummified cat and mouse in the crypt of Christ Church Cathedral.

Renting a castle in Ireland for C$15,000 a week doesn't exactly sound like budget travel, but divide that number between 30 friends and suddenly it begins to look not only possible, it looks like a real bargain.

ireland & london LIVING like KINGS

Morna O'Neill vacationed in Ireland and London with her partner, Geoff, and children, Emily, eight, and Noah, four.

One warm summer night, my aunt and I were sharing a bottle of wine, when we started daydreaming about Millennium New Year plans. The further into the wine we got, the more fanciful the plans became, until I said, 'What about a castle in Ireland?' That brought the conversation to a halt. An Irish castle. It had just the right ring to it.

I didn't think much would come of it, but regardless over the next couple of weeks I started scouring the Web for Irish castles that were available to rent. I eventually found a company that rents manors and castles throughout Ireland. They had a castle called Belle Isle, in Enniskillen, Northern Ireland. It seemed to fit our developing plan perfectly. Our approach was simple enough we thought; give people enough incentive and time (three years notice!) and they will come. With this in mind I started to put together plans to spend a week at Belle Isle with my kids Noah and Emily, my partner Geoff and 25 willing or easily coerced friends.

We also wanted to spend Christmas in London, so I began to look for accommodation and found all the rumours to be true – London prices are exorbitant! The problem with B&B and hostel prices is that the rates are per person, with very little discount for kids. Twenty-five pounds per night is not bad for a solo traveller but four times that per night for a family with little more than a bedroom didn't seem like it would work and we wanted something that was more like home than a hostel. I began looking at self-catering apartments online at around the two- or three-star level. I found a company that specialised in luxury flats but did list a couple of places that were two-star. I felt confident that a company with a focus on high-end flats would not list places that were dives. I hoped. They looked simple and clean and, at £58 a night, just what we were looking for.

The flat turned out to be a great place: one bedroom, full kitchen and foldout bed in the main room. It was located two blocks from Marble Arch and two minutes from Oxford Street. We walked to all the major sights and London began to feel like a big neighbourhood. In the evenings we would wander and take in the lights on Regent Street or stop for dinner in a small, steamy pub.

After spending 10 days in London, we were ready to leave for Ireland. We took the train to Holyhead, caught a ferry to Dublin, rented a car and drove north to Enniskillen, all in a day.

As we drove onto the property, we couldn't believe our luck. It was beautiful, more than we could have hoped. The estate sat on 400 acres surrounded by the waterways of Lough Erne and included a working dairy farm as well as cottages connected by narrow twisting roads that wove through the soft green hills that define Ireland. The estate was so picturesque, it bordered on cliche. The castle itself comprised the caretaker's quarters and the Hamilton Wing, which we used. There was a formal dining room with minstrels' gallery, seating for up to 40 and a bright entrance room with a 9m double-vaulted ceiling and arched windows.

There were other places for people to stay on the property as the castle could only sleep up to 22. The four of us stayed in a recently converted coach house, a stone's throw from the castle. Across from us were converted stables that could accommodate up to 60 guests. We had worked out a C$100 cost per person per day which included dinner every night in the dining room, cooked by a chef and personal friend whose accommodation was paid for by the group in exchange for a fabulous dinner every night. We arranged Irish grocers to deliver fresh food from neighbouring farms and markets daily. The arrangement worked out well for everyone; the chef was happy and the meals were outstanding.

"In the evenings we would wander and take in the lights on Regent Street or stop for dinner in a small, steamy pub."

Our days were spent wandering the estate, exploring old ruins nearby and visiting nearby towns such as Derry, Omagh, Sligo and Donegal. We always made sure that there was some sort of hook for the kids in all the places that we went. A stop at a park, £5 to spend any way they wanted, or even a trip to McDonalds (where the woman who asked, 'Would you like yer burgers dressed or plain?' has given us one of our favourite lines of all time) were essential to keeping it fun for all. These type of perks were key to keeping them interested on days when another ruin is about as interesting as, well, another ruin.

The advantages of planning stays of a week or more are numerous – the rates are cheaper, you can cook for yourself and you have more of a home (or castle) than a hostel. But the most significant thing we found was that you become familiar with your surroundings and have a momentary glimpse into the lives of the local people.

In the Dublin Writers' Museum in Parnell Square there's a whole room devoted to modern children's authors, including a giant Magus the Lollipop Man, the eponymous hero of Michael Mullen's book, and Tara's Palace, an outsize doll's house. There's another huge doll's house in the ramshackle Museum of Childhood.

Train fanatics won't want to miss the Fry Model Railway Exhibition at Malahide Castle. It's the world's largest display of model narrow-gauge trains, trams, boats and vehicles. There's also an excellent playground. Stop off at The Ark in Eustace St for some hands-on science and environmental activities.

pure entertainment The National Wax Museum is filled with models with the best in the Children's World of Fairytale & Fantasy section.

activities

Head for Premier Indoor Karting where you'll find kids as young as three strapped into karts and let loose on the 350-metre course. If the weather's good try the assault course at Fort Lucan, just north-west of Dublin. The slides, trampolines, mazes and suspension bridges should wear them out. If you're feeling tired rest your feet at the Lambert Puppet Theatre and Museum.

parks & playgrounds

Run off steam in Phoenix Park – one of the largest city parks in the world. It's easy to get out of Dublin by train and enjoy the beach.

around ireland

The kids are here for the ultimate countryside experience; Donegal has some of the remotest countryside in the Republic and the most beautiful beaches. Just south of Dublin are the lovely Wicklow Mountains.

Don't let political problems in Northern Ireland put you off. It's actually relatively safe and the Troubles will only make it more interesting for older kids. Ride down the Catholic Falls Road in a taxi where kids will find the murals and painted pavements fascinating. Hire a car and drive up the Antrim coast. Carrickfergus Castle and the Giant's Causeway will be a hit with kids.

festivals

Kids will like the St Patrick's Day Parade on 17 March, which is at its best in Dublin.

books

Curl up in bed with *Tales from Old Ireland* by Malachy Doyle and Niamh Sharkey. Ann Pilling's *Black Harvest* is a classic set in the Irish Potato Famine. For older readers, pack Joan Lingard's series of stories about a young couple trying to overcome the religious divide: the first book is called *The Twelfth Day of July* and is also available on audiocassette. Younger children will love Michael Mullen's *Magus the Lollipop Man*, while parents will delight in the fun illustrations.

ITALY

With all that pizza, pasta and ice cream you can't go wrong. Italians love children and it's a marvellous place to travel with kids. Hotels usually have the best facilities for kids and most restaurants can provide highchairs and children's portions.

There's so much to see there's a danger of overdoing it. Remember that soaking up the atmosphere is half the fun. Avoid cities in the heat of the summer and remember Rome is very crowded at Easter.

All city transport is free for children under a metre tall. Most museums, galleries and archaeological sites are free for under-18s. Discounts are available for children under 12 on public transport but the best way to get around the country is by car.

You can buy everything you need for babies in the supermarket but you'll have to go to a chemist to buy baby formula. If you run out of fresh milk while seeing the sights most cafes will happily offer a refill. Late night shopping has yet to arrive and many shops will close for an hour or so around lunchtime. Most supermarkets are open on Sunday morning but close on religious and public holidays so have enough stocks to tide you over the first few days. Most hotels provide a babysitter but in Italy you don't really need one as most people take their kids out with them in the evening.

rome

information

There are children's listings in *Trovaroma*, the Thursday supplement to the Italian-language *La Repubblica*. If you're in Florence get hold of *Florence for Kids*.

things to see & do

wild things The Bioparco at Villa Borghese is a good place to run off steam but some of the best animals in Rome are in stone. Kids will like statues and mosaics of animals in the Vatican and Bernini's marble elephant near Piazza della Minerva.

interesting & educational Among the ancient ruins, there's more for kids to see at the Colosseo, the remains of the Foro Romano (Roman Forum) and the nearby port of Ostia Antica. Wear them out by climbing to the top of the dome of Basilica di San Pietro for a spectacular view of the city. Then go underground into the catacombs. Pasta fans will enjoy the Museo Nazionale delle Paste Alimentari (Pasta Museum).

pure entertainment At Villa Sciarra in Monteverde Vecchio there's a permanent funfair. There are cartoons at the mini-cinema in the Villa Borghese. In the outer suburbs of there is an old-fashioned amusement park, LUNEUR, that still has appeal.

We arrived in Genoa early in the morning and immediately found a large, quiet hotel room near the train station. Zach was by now a seasoned traveller but this was Ben's first overseas adventure. With two kids we had taken double the usual requirements – clothes, nappies, toys and, of course, two strollers. Subsequently our focus this trip was exploring at a slower pace than usual. So we set ourselves the target of visiting Genoa and Milan, and spending most of our time on Liguria's beaches.

italy SEASIDE SIESTAS

Crispin Walker travelled to Italy for two weeks with his fiancée, Yvette, two-and-a-half-year-old Zach and two-month-old Benjamin.

Genoa was compact and a pleasure to explore – both boys loved the Acquario in the old port area and shopping for picnic goodies in the local market. Zach especially enjoyed the lions outside the magnificent San Lorenzo cathedral. Although we mistakenly stumbled into the red-light district, the city's winding alleyways were great fun.

The civilised Italian habit of siesta incorporated well into our routine, as it presented a convenient time in the heat of the day for us to rest back in our rooms and let the kids nap while we recovered. Genoa was a nice introduction – but nothing could have prepared us for Milan.

Milan might be the fashion and financial capital of Italy, but we found it pretty much the most child-unfriendly city we have visited. We all loved the magnificent Duomo and there are some tremendous sights but the city is designed for adults. Maybe we were unlucky but we witnessed numerous pickpocketing incidents, Zach got knocked over by a businesswoman who didn't even stop to see if he was OK and the poor kid got chased by an unsupervised dog in a park. The city's narrow pavements weren't fun to navigate with kids. To top it all off we had little or no sleep in the YHA hostel, as we were surrounded by school kids causing havoc till all hours.

After a nice day trip to Lago di Como we headed south to Savona and stayed in an amazing hostel situated atop the town's fortress. Getting up took some stamina but once up we had a great time exploring the fort and relaxing in the hostel common rooms with the very friendly staff. Savona and other Riviera di Ponente resorts aren't on the main tourist trail, and because of this we found them perfect for travel with kids. We uncovered some gems like the stunning Borgio Verezzi caves and Italy's best *gelato* at Alassio. The locals were friendly, the prices reasonable and the beaches uncrowded. We stayed mostly in beachfront hotels as they proved cost-effective and gave us our own bathroom and balcony.

We met mainly vacationing Italian families and were welcomed in all restaurants. Zach's appetite was more than satisfied with pasta while we enjoyed some excellent pizzas. We also indulged in some cheap and succulent seafood, and found fresh milk easy to locate. Most cafes were more than happy to provide warm milk for Zach's bottle (often for free) and Ben was easily catered for as he was breastfed throughout.

Each evening we happily fell into the pattern of eating alfresco early – usually in the town square or boulevard. Then it was onto a *gelaterie* for an incredibly delicious dessert and then perhaps the best thing about holidaying in Italy – the playground. Italy is overflowing with playgrounds and suprisingly between 8 and 11 pm, they are very busy with kids.

Everyone knows Italian society revolves around family and everyone – aunts, uncles and grandparents – takes turns to look after the kids. We learnt that most grandparents take the kids of an evening so that the parents can enjoy a lingering meal or have time to themselves – an ideal situation. Zach loved playing after dinner and of course it was great for us as he got to associate with the locals who welcomed him to their arena, and he was usually worn out by bedtime.

"The civilised Italian habit of siesta incorporated well into our routine, as it presented a convenient time in the heat of the day for us to rest back in our rooms and let the kids nap while we recovered."

At first we were worried how well Ben would travel as we had only taken Zach away after he had turned one. But Ben was really good – sleeping through most of the journey in his stroller or baby carrier. Both kids loved playing in the mini-dome tent we took, which proved invaluable on the beach as it provided shade and a cubby house. Ben was also content using a child's blow-up boat as his cot! The gentle Mediterranean surf suited Zach just fine and pebbly beaches provided ammunition for him to toss into the sea.

In comparison the coastal route to the French border, the Riviera di Levante that heads towards Tuscany with such great spots as Portofino and Cinque Terre, wasn't good for kid travel. We travelled almost exclusively by train – which was great as Italy's train network is cheap and efficient. The only problem was the narrowness of the corridors which could accommodate strollers but needed skilful manoeuvring. It turned out to be a good holiday, and demonstrated that a gentle pace and relaxed attitude means a nice time when you have more than one kiddy.

activities

Adventurous kids can explore the ancient Via Appia Antica on bike. Unwind at the Villa Borghese, where you can also rent bikes or take a pony ride pony or just enjoy the fun of the mini-train.

parks & playgrounds

The Gianicolo hill, between the Basilica di San Pietro and Trastevere, has a panoramic view of Rome and is a good place to take the kids if they need a break. At the top of the hill there is a permanent merry-go-round, pony rides and puppet shows on Sundays. Villa Doria Pamphili is the largest park in Rome and a lovely quiet spot for a picnic.

festivals

At Christmas, Piazza Navona is transformed into a festive market place. Most churches set up nativity scenes, which will fascinate kids with their attention to detail.

around italy

For antiquities head south; kids will like Pompeii and Greek ruins at Metaponto. Top of their list of things to see will probably be the volcanoes of Mt Vesuvio and Mt Etna. They'll also enjoy taking a boat to Sicily, where they can see a more traditional Italian culture or just soak up the sun.

If you're travelling in northern Italy, stop at Gardaland, the amusement park in Lombardy. To get a taste of the lakes without coach loads of grannies getting in the way, head for the beautiful Lago d'Orta, north of Milan. Further west, older kids will enjoy exploring the rugged mountain wilderness of the Parco Nazionale del Gran Paradiso. In Genoa they'll find the house where Christopher Columbus was born interesting and the giant aquarium around the port is a fantastic treat for all ages.

Older children will like the collection at the Museo Stibbert in Florence but little children will find the crowds stifling. They'll enjoy the Leaning Tower of Pisa more.

In the east, check out Italia in Miniatura near Rimini. Don't miss Venice with its canals and gondola rides.

books

Peter Connolly's *Ancient Rome* is an excellent first history with fantastic illustrations that will bring the ancient sites to life. For under-10s pack Geraldine McCaughrean's *Roman Myths* and to get them interested in the renaissance *The Genius of Leonardo* by Visconti and Landmann. If you want something lighter, pack *The Lost Diary of Leonardo's Paint Mixer* found by Alex Parsons. There's also a new, clever whodunit set in Ostia Antica, *The Thieves of Ostia* by Caroline Lawrence. If you want them to be able to read the menu and chat up old ladies pack *Italian for Beginners*.

MALTA

Malta is a good destination for a family holiday. So it should be: they make Playmobil here, those tiny plastic figures that seven-year-olds love. Children are welcome everywhere and there are plenty of fantastic activities to keep them occupied.

Eating out is a relaxed child-friendly affair with lots of pasta and pizza. The sea is beautifully clean and the sun shines nearly all year round. The best beaches for children are in the north of the island and are cleaned every day so hygeine is never an issue.

It's easy to get a package deal which cuts the hassle factor in half. Self-catering apartments abound and are the easiest option with children. Big hotels will have a babysitting service.

Car hire is relatively cheap, but public transport is a better bet. It's cheap and efficient and the longest bus journey you're ever likely to make in Malta is around 50 minutes.

Pharmacies are well stocked with baby products and there's always one open on Sundays, so travel light. There are big supermarkets in Sliema. Most shops close for lunch but there are plenty of late night shops. Tap water is safe to drink and all milk is pasteurised. The laundry service in Valletta is one of the few outside hotels.

things to see & do

wild things Mediterraneo Marine Park has an extraordinary collection of everything from dolphins to wallabies. You can book private swimming sessions with dolphins for over-eights.

interesting & educational Older kids will like exploring Malta's rich archaeological sites and the fortress of Mdina, especially the dungeons. Before you set out, take them to the audiovisual history, the Malta Experience, in Valletta. Whatever your kids' age they'll enjoy a trip on a glass-bottomed boat to check out the local underwater life. If you're feeling flush opt for a helicopter sightseeing tour.

pure entertainment Top of the agenda will be a visit to see where they make those tiny plastic figures – the Playmobil factory which also has a free Fun Park. There are re-enactments of historical military parades every Sunday throughout the year in Valletta. Popeye Village is built on the set where they made the 1980 film and is always popular with younger children, even if they've never heard of Popeye.

activities

It's easy to hire boats, pedal boats, snorkelling gear, canoes and dinghies at most tourist resorts. The Splash & Fun Park is good for all ages. Older kids can sign up for sailing lessons or try their hand at go-karting.

THE NETHERLANDS

If you're feeling nervous about travelling with kids, the Netherlands is a good place to start. It's a small country with fantastic public transport, so you'll manage to cover the ground easily without going to the expense of hiring a car. You can rent bikes with baby seats at nearly all railway stations. The place is as flat as a pancake so even little people can manage to cover some distance on two wheels.

The Dutch are relaxed and friendly but some hotels have a no-children policy – check before you book. Base yourself in Amsterdam. Choose a mid-price hotel as budget hotels and hostels tend to be a bit druggy, and often don't take reservations. Most hotels offer a babysitting service. Agencies use both male and female sitters. Most restaurants have highchairs and children's menus with children allowed in most pubs. The Dutch eat early so you won't feel out of place.

You can buy everything you need for babies in the Netherlands, so travel light. Be sure to pack a set of reins to stop toddlers from falling in the water. Laundrettes are also in short supply outside Amsterdam.

amsterdam

information

Look out for the monthly English-language *What's On In Amsterdam*.

practicalities

For babysitters in Amsterdam try Oppas-Centrale Kriterion in Roetersstraat, which seems to be consistently reliable or Oppascentrale De Peuterette, which has also had good reports.

Amsterdam is famous for its red-light district – don't let that put you off. Although there are a lot of sex shops about, little kids don't usually even notice and when it comes to older kids they're charmingly prudish about it.

things to see & do

wild things The Artis Zoo has a great aquarium and you can come face-to-face with a bison at the children's farm in Amsterdamse Bos in the south of the city.

interesting & educational Start with a canal cruise. Then climb to the top of the steeple of the Westerkerk – that's the church with the crazy imperial crown teetering on the top. Then visit the Anne Frankhuis, where the Jewish Frank family hid from the Nazis and young Anne wrote her famous diary.

Kids also like the Van Gough Museum, but don't forget to tell the story of how he cut off his ear. Buy time at the Museum Het Rembrandt with a visit to the Holland Experience next door. The film is a bit tacky but kids like being sprinkled with water when the dam breaks.

The new Metropolis Science & Technology Centre is hands-on and usually a hit with kids. At the Scheepvaartmuseum (Maritime Museum) even little ones will like climbing around the replica of the *Amsterdam* that was wrecked in 1748.

After that pretend to fly a plane at the National Luchtuaartmuseum, the national aviation museum. Round the day off riding on a historic tram at the Tram Museum Amsterdam. If they're still not exhausted try a harbour cruise or hire a bike to explore the canals.

pure entertainment Kids love the Madame Tussaud Scenerama on the corner of Dam Square and don't care if they can't recognise all the waxworks. Over Christmas there's usually a circus in the Koninklijk Theater Carré.

activities

Wear them out in the swimming pools at De Mirandabad in the south of the city where there's a beach and wave machine. Chill out on the ice at Jaap Edenbaan in the eastern suburbs where there's both an indoor and outdoor ice skating rink.

parks & playgrounds

The best place for picnics is Vondelpark. There's plenty of ducks and a good children's playground. And the beach at Zandvoort is only a short train ride away and well worth the trip.

festivals

Koninginnedag (Queen's Day) on 30 April is a wonderful party for kids as much as grown-ups. In November Santa Claus arrives in Amsterdam accompanied by Black Peters who throw sweets to passing kids. Santa arrives by boat from Spain, a hangover from the days when this was a Spanish colony.

around the netherlands

Start south of Amsterdam at Oudewater where they used to weigh witches. If you were too heavy you couldn't ride a broomstick and got a certificate to prove it. Then it's on to Kinderdijk to check out the windmills, where there are 19 spread along the canal. Round off the Dutch experience by a bike ride along the dikes at Zeeland.

To the North, kids will enjoy the open air museum, Zuiderzee Museum at Enkhuizen which is re-creation of a 19th-century village. The people in the traditional costumes actually live here. Then spend a day on bikes exploring the sand dunes on Texel Island, which is famous for its shipwrecks. Stop off at the Maritime and Beachcombers Museum to explore some extraordinary junk recovered from the bottom of the sea.

books & films

Pack a copy of *The Diary of Anne Frank* and Carol Ann Lee's *Anne Frank's Story*. Older kids will enjoy the film *A Bridge Too Far* (1977) about the WWII Battle of Arnhem and Aidan Chambers *Postcards from No Man's Land*, which tells the tale of a young boy's first trip alone to Amsterdam and his father's experiences on the battlefields of Arnhem. For little ones lookout for *The Cow Who Fell in the Canal* by Phyllis Krasilovsky but if you're under three there's only one Dutch character who counts – that's Dick Bruna's little rabbit Miffy.

NORWAY

Kids like Norway. It's all about the great outdoors and there's plenty of Viking stuff to get them interested. And it's full of reindeer. Add to that the fact that most Norwegian towns have attractions specifically for youngsters and that many places have children's corners with toys and activities; and it's fair to say this is kids' country.

Admission is usually free for under-sixes and half-price for under-16s. There are plenty of family rooms in hotels and hostels which cost about the same as a regular double. Hostels usually have kitchens. Cutting costs is often an issue as Norway is horrendously expensive. You can buy whatever you need for children but remember supermarkets shut early and late night shops are pricey. It pays to bring as many supplies with you as you can.

Trains and buses are the best way to travel around. They offer children's and family discounts and long distance buses have toilets. Car journeys can be taxing because of the mountains and having to break the journey to catch ferries across the fjords.

Car seats, cots and highchairs should be booked in advance. Laundrettes are rare and costly, so be prepared to hand wash. The best time to visit is early summer but pack warm clothes.

things to see & do

wild things The best place to spot reindeer is in the north or catch the Easter reindeer races at Karasjok and Kautokeino.

interesting & educational This is Viking country. Take them to see the Viking longboats on Bygdøy Peninsula near Oslo, where there's also an excellent open-air folk museum.

pure entertainment One of the best places for kids is Dyrepark in Kristiansand, which has a zoo, pirate ship battles and family accommodation in a fantasy town.

activities

Kids will love the train ride from Oslo to Bergen and taking a boat trip through the fjords. Older kids will find no shortage of places to ski in the country that claims to have invented the sport or for a real Norwegian outing try dog-sledding.

parks & playgrounds

Most of Norway is a vast wilderness so running off steam isn't likely to be an issue. In Oslo you can get a glimpse of what the town is like and wear them out by climbing up the observation tower at Tryvannstårnet. Then head for the grounds of Akershus Slott and Vigeland Park, where you can admire the sculptures while they feed the ducks. There are good beaches on the Bygdøy Peninsula.

festivals

Kids will enjoy the big parades of people in traditional dress on Constitution Day (17 May) in Oslo and the bonfires on the beaches on *Jonsok* (Midsummer's Eve) which is celebrated throughout the country.

books

For older kids pack Henrietta Branford's powerful novel about one young girl's fight for survival in Viking Norway, *The Fated Sky*. There's plenty of drama and action in Barbara Leonie Picard's *Tales of the Norse Gods*, which should whet younger appetites for Norse siteseeing.

PORTUGAL

It's difficult to find a more child-friendly destination than Portugal. The Portuguese love children even when they are naughty and noisy. All but the stuffiest restaurants tolerate kids and happily serve child-sized portions at child-sized prices.

You'll get a warm welcome wherever you choose to stay and most places will have a cot handy. Children under eight are entitled to a 50% discount in hotels and *pensões* (guesthouses) if they share their parents' room. Lower-end places may charge nothing extra at all. Self-catering flats are a good bet with kids, as many restaurants don't open until after seven at night. If you're touring around, stay in *pensões*, which are nearly all family-friendly. Camping is also a good option and in Lisbon the youth hostel has private rooms.

Children between four and 12 years old get 50% off tickets on Portuguese Railways, and those under four years travel for free.

Basic supplies are no problem, unless you head right off the beaten track. Most shops and pharmacies sell Portuguese and imported brands of tinned baby food and disposable nappies. Many shops close for lunch and on Sunday.

Tourist offices can recommend babysitters. Local papers in the Algarve and Lisbon often advertise babysitting services too. Many resorts, self-catering apartment complexes and larger hotels have their own childcare facilities staffed by trained nursery personnel. Several UK-based tour operators have special kids' clubs in the Algarve resorts. Some day nurseries may be willing to take in little tourists during the summer months – the local tourist office will be able to advise you.

On the beach beware of the midday sun, the Atlantic Ocean's undertow and serious pollution around Sines and Porto.

lisbon

information

The Saturday edition of the newspaper *Publico* lists children's activities for the week ahead and you can find babysitters in the small ads.

practicalities

Lisbon is relatively safe and easy to get around with kids. Pre-school children usually get into museums and other sights free.

things to see & do

wild things Kids will enjoy the aquarium, Oceanário at Parque das Nações. It's home to 25,000 birds, fish and mammals. The Jardim Zoologico is a bit depressing, with most of the animals in small, uninspiring cages but kids will like the dolphin shows.

interesting & educational Kids like exploring the Núcleo Arqueológico – a web of tunnels that used to be a Roman spa and the castle, Castelo de São Jorge. The Museu da Marioneta has more puppets than you have ever seen. Catch the puppet shows at the weekend. Toy soldier fanatics will like the huge collection of artillery at the Museu Militar. The Gulbenkian has a special hands-on kids' section.

Computer fanatics will enjoy Pailhão do Conhecimento with its hands-on exhibits and cybercafe. Toddlers will like riding the funiculars and taking the tram to Belém where there's a great naval museum, Museu de Marinha, and a host of other museums that kids will enjoy.

pure entertainment The school of circus arts, Chapitô, has regular performances or classes and the Teatro Infantil de Lisboa (Lisbon Children's Theatre) at the Teatro Maria Matos has special performances for children. Feira Popular is a good old-fashioned fairground with roller coasters, big Ferris wheels and all kinds of stalls.

activities

Around Lisbon there are lots of lovely beaches for kids to build sandcastles on. Cascais is the liveliest resort but the beach just north at Praia do Guincho is cleaner. Don't miss Costa da Caparica where a train runs along the edge of the beach in summer. Paria Grande is good for budding beach bums and has some of the best surf in Europe.

parks & playgrounds

Portuguese playgrounds can be a hazard. Many are bashed up and rusty. Run off steam at Jardim da Estrela and on the riverfront at Viana do Castelo.

around portugal

For a day trip out of Lisbon head for Sintra, where there are horse and cart rides. Further afield, kids love the Algarve with its warm, calm beaches, water sports and horse riding. Rent a bike to explore the coast. Don't miss the dolphin and seals at the marine park Zoomarine, near Albufeira. The night-time theme park Planeta Aventura near Quarteira is a sure hit. There are no fewer than three huge water parks along the main highway. Older kids will love exploring the Parque Nacional da Peneda-Gerês.

Visit the Museo do Carro Eléctrico (Tram Museum) in Porto and take a boat ride up the river. Coimbra may be the Oxford of Portugal but the kids will be more interested in Portugal dos Pequenitos – where you can explore Portugal and its empire in miniature. The full size castles of Óbidos, Marvão, Castelo de Vide, Valença and Elvas are great for letting the young imagination run wild but watch out for toddlers as the larger battlements might create some problems with balance.

books

Older readers will enjoy reading the adventures of the explorer Vasco da Gama in Joan Elizabeth Goodman's beautifully illustrated book *A Long and Uncertain Journey: The 27,000 Mile Voyage of Vasco da Gama.*

SPAIN

You won't find many activities and places set aside for children in Spain. That doesn't mean it's a no-go area for kids – quite the opposite. Parking children in a special play area goes against the Spanish way of thinking, with Spanish kids included in everything their parents do. That makes babysitters a bit of an irrelevance as you can take your children nearly everywhere you go. That said Spain has one of the lowest birth rates in Europe, which may explain why highchairs are such a rarity in restaurants.

Kids are welcome at all kinds of accommodation, and in virtually every cafe, bar and restaurant. Spanish children stay up late. Visiting kids like this idea too but can't cope with it quite so readily. A siesta is crucial. You'll need to escape the heat in summer. If you can't get them to sleep at least encourage them to rest by packing plenty of books and audiocassettes.

Spanish supermarkets carry everything you could need for babies, so travel light. Shops are shut on Sunday. Coin washes are rare but there are plenty of service washes. Reserve cots and car seats in advance. Children benefit from cut-price or free entry at many sights and museums. Under-fours travel free on Spanish trains and from four to 11 they pay 60% of the adult fare.

It is becoming more common to see women breastfeeding in public. If you are discreet, breastfeeding should attract little attention.

madrid

practicalities

The best way to get around is on foot but public transport is cheap and efficient. Apartment hotels are a good option with a family. If you're going in the summer it's worth splurging on a hotel with a pool, which unfortunately are in short supply.

things to see & do

wild things The zoo has an excellent parrot show, but it's worth the trip out of town to Safari de Madrid, the park is home to elephants, lions and monkeys. There's a pool to cool off in during summer.

interesting & educational Get the kids orientated with a trip up the Faro observation tower. Don't hesitate to take them to Centro de Arte Reina Sofía, as the Picassos and Dalis are usually a hit. Kids like the Sunday morning flea market at El Rastro and the sheer size of the Palacio Real will impress them.

Gruesome kids will like the Museo de Cera (Wax Museum) where there's a re-creation of the Inquisition. In Alcobendas, just north-east of Madrid, is Cosmocaixa, a real hands-on science museum with a special area for tiny tots. Unfortunately shows at the Planetario are in Spanish only. Other museums worth visiting are: the Museo Arqueológico Nacional where kids will enjoy the cave paintings of Altamira and the Museo del Ejército – a military museum stuffed with flags, uniforms and weapons that is bound to appeal to little generals.

pure entertainment You can wear them out at the amusement park Parque de Atracciones. There's children's theatre at the Sala San Pol but it's only in Spanish; the open-air puppet shows in Teatro Municipal de Títeres del Retiro are a better bet. There's the predictable IMAX 3D cinema.

activities

The best public swimming pool is in Casa de Campo but there are plenty of water parks. Aquópolis is one of the biggest in Europe. Alternatively, you can take to the ice at Sport Hielo.

parks & playgrounds

There are plenty of playgrounds. Parque del Buen Retiro has a boating lake, while Parque Juan Carlos I has an artificial river with catamaran rides and a mini-train.

festivals

Spanish children get their Christmas presents at Epiphany, when the Three Kings arrive. They fly into Madrid by helicopter on 6 January then take to the parade floats and throw sweets to the kids in the crowd.

around spain

Spain has some excellent amusement parks, especially Seville's Isla Mágica, Tivoli World on the Costa del Sol and the home of the spaghetti western, Mini-Hollywood in the Almeria desert.

Barcelona is a good bet with kids because it's got beaches, a funicular, a balloon ride and one of the best aquariums around. They'll like Gaudí's crazy buildings and the Museu Picasso. Many of Barcelona's museums are kid-orientated especially the Museu Marítim and the Museu d'Història de Catalunya.

The Moorish grandeur of Seville is also something that gets the kids' imagination going. Seville is also the best place to see Flamenco dancing. Take a drive through the remote Picos de Europa, in the north – kids love exploring this wilderness. If you're driving on to France, take the road through the centre of the Spanish Pyrenees to Arreau, where even the most cynical teenager will be impressed by the Grand Canyon–style scenery. The best beaches for toddlers are in Benidorm, on the Costa Blanca and near Cádiz.

The huge rock of Gibraltar is one of Britain's last colonies. For this quirky fact alone kids will enjoy a visit. Take the cable car to visit the apes and a boat trip to see the dolphins.

books

Pack a children's version of the tales of Don Quixote. Teenagers will enjoy Laurie Lee's tales of '30s Spain *As I Walked Out One Midsummer Morning*. Watch the epic adventures of the Spanish warrior *El Cid* (1961). If you want them to pick up a bit of the language pack *My First Oxford Spanish Words*.

SWEDEN

The Swedes pride themselves on being child-friendly. Parents get the best deal in Europe when it comes to maternity and paternity rights with Swedish parents expecting plenty of facilities for kids. Long-distance ferries, trains, hotels and even some restaurants have play areas for children. Most attractions allow free admission for under-sevens and half-price admission for under-16s.

The only problem in Sweden is the weather. Travelling in the winter with kids is difficult. Go in early summer when they'll enjoy the novelty of the white nights. You'll still need to pack some warm clothes, boots and a baby mosquito net.

Hotels usually have family rooms for little more than the price of a regular double and there are plenty of family-friendly camping grounds and hostels. It's easy to find chalets and mountain cabins to rent. There are plenty of cots and highchairs. The motorways are excellent but trains are a good option with kids but like everything else in Sweden they're expensive.

There's everything you need for babies in supermarkets but laundrettes are nonexistent and laundry services are slow and expensive so be prepared to hand wash. Twenty-four hour shopping in Stockholm means you can buy what you need for the kids whenever you want it. Even in the countryside supermarkets are open on Sundays and there's usually a late night shop but it may not stock baby products.

information

The Swedish tourist office publishes an excellent booklet *Sweden for Children*.

things to see & do

wild things The kids will want to head north to the Arctic Circle to see the reindeer. Abisko National Park in Norrland is the easiest place for walking but little legs will probably find it too tough to explore.

interesting & educational Most museums cater for kids. They'll especially enjoy the Vasamuseet, home to the only 17th-century ship left in the world and the open-air museum in Sansen. Near Gothenburg there's fairy-tale castles and Sweden's two largest lakes near Vänern and Vättern.

pure entertainment To let your hair down head for Liseburg amusement park in Gothenburg.

activities

It's easy to hire boats, bikes and skates in the main tourist resorts. Kids like taking a ride on a steamer on the islands all along the coast.

parks & playgrounds

A holiday in Sweden is all about the great outdoors; even in Stockholm it's never far away. There's an abundance of parks and playgrounds, all of them clean and very safe.

festivals

There are children's parades on Luciadagen (St Lucia's Day) on 13 December, when girls dress up to sing carols.

books

Buy *The Wonderful Adventures of Nils* by Selma Lagerlövis, Sweden's best-loved children's writer. It's a story of a little boy who flies across the country on the back of a magic goose.

SWITZERLAND

The best way to see Switzerland is by car. Kids will lap up the scenery. They'll want to stop to admire the view, run in the meadows and look at the cows with their tinkling bells. Public transport, however, is top notch and there are good discounts for families, if you buy a family card. If you want to do without a car, kids will love the train journeys through the mountains.

Whatever kind of accommodation you choose will be clean and of a high standard, so it's a good place to travel with babies. Hostels and hotels have family rooms, and most hostels have kitchens. When touring in the mountains in summer it pays to book ahead as many hotels and guesthouses are closed making rooms in short supply. Remember to pack something dry and warm to wear, as it can be wet and chilly in the mountains even in summer. If you want to walk, pack a sling or backpack for babies – you can't push a stroller up the alps! There's no shortage of laundrettes and hotels can often supply well-trained babysitters.

Travel light and buy everything you need when you arrive. Cots and highchairs are at hand. That said, Switzerland is expensive and if you're near a border it pays to do your shopping on the other side. You should have no problem breastfeeding in public in Switzerland. It isn't uncommon to see babies and toddlers of all ages breastfeeding in public places, on various forms of public transport or elsewhere.

things to see & do

interesting & educational High on the list of must sees is the Heidihouse at Maienfeld. It wouldn't be Switzerland without chocolate, so round off your trip with a visit to the Lindt factory in Zürich or a ride on the chocolate train to the Nestlé factory at Montreux.

pure entertainment Add a boat trip on Lake Lugano to your itinerary and stop off at Swissminiatur, the model village.

activities

Remember, resorts favoured by tour companies are more likely to have diversions off the slopes. The best place for kids to ski is Bernese Oberland. If you can't ski take a trip up the Jungfraujoch by train and visit the ice palace.

parks & playgrounds

All playgrounds are of the highest standard. Geneva has some lovely parks but the place to go is Jardin Botanique where there are llamas and an aviary.

books

Don't leave home without a copy of *Heidi* by Johanna Spyri *or* an audio version for the car. Older readers should get their teeth into Gaye Hiçylmaz's novel about how a young Turkish girl adjusts to a new life in Switzerland, *The Frozen Waterfall*.

EUROPE

THE BALKANS

Albania, Bulgaria, Croatia, Macedonia, Romania, Slovenia and Yugoslavia represent the only corner of Europe that offers any serious challenge to parents. Kids will like it here because you'll find it's the wackiest part of Europe where you never know what's going to happen next.

In capital cities and resorts, you'll find the basic supplies you need for children but in small towns and rural areas things can be tricky. That said, this is one of the truly child-friendly parts of Europe. There may be not be many theme parks but you'll find hotels that are happy to cook for your child even if the restaurant is shut. There are plenty of family rooms and extra beds.

Outside Albania, families are small and kids tend to go everywhere with their parents. Finding a babysitter may be difficult as this is hands-on granny country. Some big hotels may have a babysitting service. There are laundry services in hotels but be prepared to hand wash.

You can approach a holiday in Bulgaria, Croatia and Slovenia as you would a holiday in other parts of Europe. There are well-developed facilities for tourists and there's a wide range of accommodation choices for families. You can buy everything you need for tiny tots. Ferries are the best way to travel along the Dalmatian coast. It pays to rent a car with kids, as it gives you independence and flexibility. You must book your car seat in advance.

For trips elsewhere in the Balkans, you need to pack children's paracetamol, ready-made baby food and formula milk. Always make sure you have enough supplies to tide you over and stock up when you see the things you need for sale. Be careful when buying fresh milk as some of it needs to be boiled before it is drunk. It's better to stick to UHT to be sure. Ask your doctor to give you a course of antibiotics in powdered form that you can mix up if needed. The antibiotics available locally for children taste terrible. If you're heading out of the capital cities, you're better off getting the best hotel you can afford and if you're planning a long trip invest in a camper stove.

Plan journeys carefully. If you're driving from Belgrade to Bucharest you'll only find a handful of hotels along the route that you would consider staying in. Make sure you have plenty to entertain the kids. Flying is expensive but an efficient way of capital hopping and getting to the coast. The normal reductions for children apply. Trains are a good option everywhere but Albania. The trains usually have restaurants but make sure you carry supplies of food and drink and book a sleeping car with a lock. Economic problems have left some parts of Albania little more than bandit country and for safety, it's probably better just to visit the capital.

In Bosnia-Hercegovina and Kosovo, mines are a big problem in former conflict areas. Don't let children play in ruined buildings and stick to asphalt roads. If in doubt always ask locals for advice.

information

You need to take the troubles in the former Yugoslavia into account. The situation changes quickly and it's advisable to keep an eye on developments when planning your trip. Your own government may offer advice to travellers in the region.

things to see & do

wild things Farmhouses in Slovenia organise programs for children that include horse riding, caving, skiing, learning traditional crafts or just messing around with farm animals. The best zoo is in Belgrade and the best national parks for children are Durmitor in Montenegro and Plitvice Lakes in Croatia.

interesting & educational Balkan museums are deserted but that doesn't mean they're no good. Don't miss the Military Museum in Kalemegdan Citadel in Belgrade. It's packed with fascinating bits and pieces including a copy of the gruesome wall of skulls from Nis – find out more if you dare! Kids will appreciate the sheer folly of Ceausescu's Palace of Parliament in Bucharest. There are lots of fantastic castles but watch out, safety precautions aren't high on the list of priorities here. Kids will like Dracula's Castle at Bran in Romania. Sarajevo is interesting not just because of the recent conflict. Kids will want to see where the shot that started WWI was fired. The ancient fortified city of Dubrovnik is a big hit with kids, especially as you can cool off on the beach between museums.

activities

In Croatia, the kids will love swimming in the Plitvice Lakes. In Macedonia a good destination with children is Lake Ohrid. The beaches are good for toddlers and the hotels relatively family-orientated, as this was once a top package tour destination. In Sofia, take a trip to the top of Mt Vitosha. Montenegro has white-water rafting and beautiful beaches for children.

parks & playgrounds

In Bucharest head for Herastra Park and don't miss the Village Museum – kids love the collection of old houses. In Belgrade there's a permanent amusement park in Kalemegdan. There are lovely parks right across the region but watch out for playgrounds, some are a bit old and rusty.

books & films

In Hergé's *King Ottokar's Sceptre*, Tintin has a Balkan adventure set in the imaginary kingdom of Syldavia. *Zlata's Diary* by Zlata Filipovic is a little girl's story of life under siege in Sarajevo. Gaye Hiçyilmaz's novel *Smiling for Strangers* is a story of one girl's escape from the former Yugoslavia in the back of an aid truck. To catch the spirit of the Balkans, watch *The Game* (1951).

cultural issues

Remember that the wars of the last decade have left deep scars. Make sure your children understand that and that they don't go telling Albanians how much they like Belgrade.

CZECH REPUBLIC & SLOVAKIA

Czechs and Slovaks are generally family-oriented but you may find you get a chilly reception in Prague. Restaurants aren't very child-friendly, so self-catering is a good option. In Prague you can easily find apartments that are rented on a nightly basis. City centres are small and public transport is good but for touring the easiest way to get about is by car.

In the capitals you can buy everything you need for babies and children in supermarkets. Late night shopping has yet to arrive and most shops are closed on Sunday. There are laundrettes in Prague, elsewhere there are service washes and dry-cleaners. Big hotels will be able to supply babysitters.

information

The English language *Prague Post* has a good listing and practical information section as does the Bratislava-based the *Slovak Spectator*.

things to see & do

wild things Although there's a zoo in Prague, the best wildlife is free. Slovakia's five national parks are home to bears, deer, lynx and eagles.

interesting & educational In Prague kids will like walking across Charles Bridge, exploring Josefov, the old Jewish ghetto or Prague Castle, where there's the Museum of Toys. Then check out the National Technology Museum, where there's a huge hall full of trains, cars and aeroplanes. Also within easy reach of Prague are a selection of fairy-tale castles which kids are bound to enjoy, especially Karlštejn.

In Bratislava, tire them out climbing the Michael Tower and exploring the castle. Then walk across Nový Most.

pure entertainment There are puppet shows in all the big towns and often you'll find there's a circus too.

activities
In summer, in both Prague and Bratislava, kids will enjoy a sightseeing trip along the river. Try rafting down the Dunajec Gorge, in eastern Slovakia.

parks & playgrounds
In Bratislava take the trolleybus to the Little Carpathian Mountains where you'll find a TV tower with a revolving cafe. In Prague, Petrín Hill is the place to let the kids run off steam. Take the funicular up the hill to the mirror maze.

festivals
Kids love the Ghost Festival in Bojnice Chateau in Slovakia at the end of April and the spring fair in Prague in March.

books
Older kids will enjoy James Watson's thriller *Ticket to Prague*.

GREECE

Greece is an easy place to travel with children. There are many all-inclusive package deals and many big hotels have excellent facilities for children. There are plenty of self-catering apartments and villas. Finding a hotel at the beach can be hard though, if you're touring, as most hotels cater for the package industry. Camping, however, is a feasible option with kids. When planning the trip remember the summer is very hot. The best time to visit with kids is in the spring and autumn.

Hotels and restaurants are very accommodating when it comes to meeting the needs of children. Service in restaurants is normally very quick, which is great when you've got hungry children on your hands.

You can travel light, as everything you need is on sale in Greek supermarkets. In Athens, Thessaloniki and other big resorts there are 24-hour shops. Fresh milk, however, can be difficult to find on the smaller islands. There are laundrettes in big cities and resorts.

Don't be afraid to take children to the ancient sites. Young imaginations go into overdrive when let loose somewhere like the labyrinth at Knossos. Kids don't mind tacky souvenir shops but they do turn their noses up at crowds. Try visiting big sites early in the morning or late in the evening. Don't forget if you hire a car and follow the signs to archaeological sites you'll find some wonderful deserted ruins.

Strollers aren't much use in Greece. They're hopeless on rough stone paths and up steps, and a curse when getting on or off buses and ferries. Backpacks or slings are best. Lists of babysitters are available from what the Greeks call the 'tourist police' – they're actually a branch of the police but are basically a tourist information service.

I arrived in Prague with only one preconception. All the guidebooks said it wasn't a city for kids. They're wrong. The city centre is small and pedestrianised, so it's good for toddlers. It's a huge open-air museum, so you can enjoy it without having to go inside. Most importantly it's stunning. Kids can be quite cynical and hard to please, so you need something that's going to impress them.

prague FINDING BOHEMIA

Rosie Whitehouse and husband, Tim, took their children Ben, 12, Esti, nine, Rachel, six, and twins Jacob and Eve, 18 months, to Prague for a holiday.

The sparkling stars on the spires of the Church of Our Lady before Týn are better than Disneyland and when the Old Town Hall clock chimes the hour a skeleton pulls a rope and the 12 apostles appear from the window above. Puppets are big in Prague – they sell them everywhere. This isn't Punch and Judy but culture on strings. A miniature production of *Orpheus* had the babies transfixed.

Although every town from Warsaw to Belgrade must have been designed by the same architects, Prague is really a cut above the rest. Ben said the town planners must have travelled around Central Europe taking the best bit from every town they visited and then came up with their own masterpiece, the Charles Bridge. In the summer, tourists have to queue to get on this architectural masterpiece, but on a misty winter's evening we were able to enjoy one of the most beautiful bridges in Europe almost alone.

A steep hill leads up to Prague Castle. A Tintin fan, Ben recognised it straight away from the cover of *King Ottokar's Sceptre*. Hergé based his character on the real King Ottokar II, who lived here. When his tomb was opened during restoration work, years after Hergé's death, it was discovered that he really had been buried with his sceptre!

It was the old Jewish quarter – Josefov, they found especially interesting. Being Jewish, the children found it rather odd to visit a synagogue as if it were a museum. They were fascinated by the tales of one of the great heroes of the ghetto, Rabbi Löw, who made a living man out of clay, called the golem, to protect the Jews.

The Nazis decided to turn the ghetto into a 'Museum of Jewry', so Prague's Jewish monuments survived the war even if most of its Jewish people didn't. The walls of the Pinkas Synagogue are inscribed with the names of 77,297 Jews killed by the Nazis. Upstairs is an exhibition of drawings and poems by the children held at the Terezín concentration camp. It looks like a school project. Esti stopped to look at every picture. Her great-grandmother died in Auschwitz and coming to terms with the darker side of history is easier if you can identify with the children who experienced it first hand.

The national trait for brushing everything under the carpet means the museums are a bit disappointing. Only the National Museum is of interest because it's a museum of museums. This is where you bring your children to see what museums used to be like – stuffed animals and things in jars of formaldehyde in wooden display cases.

Travelling with a big family can make you feel at home anywhere. We soon settled down in a rented apartment that was the height of '70s Eastern European chic. The food in Prague is nothing to write home about, so we soon found ourselves in the local supermarket getting to grips with Czech-language labels.

Parks are a good place to get under a country's skin. We took the funicular up Peotrin Hill. You get about twenty seconds to jump on or off and the babies were almost crushed by doors. Nobody did a thing to help us, the Czechs give you the feeling they don't like children, especially if they're tourists.

Half the fun of travelling is the highs and lows. That evening we joined a friend for dinner. After Eve smashed the flower display on the table, I decided to take the babies home early. I waited for the tram in some anticipation. I wasn't sure how I was going to get the double buggy up the steep steps that greet you when the doors open. Not many tourists are catching trams to suburbs on snowy evenings in February. I needn't have worried when the tram arrived there was a carfuffle of excitement and cooing old ladies. We were whisked into the tram and off again by smiling young men with briefcases. At last, thanks to the babies, I had a glimpse of the real Prague.

"A steep hill leads up to Prague Castle. A Tintin fan, Ben recognised it straight away from the cover of *King Ottokar's Sceptre*. Hergé based his character on the real King Ottokar II, who lived here. When his tomb was opened during restoration work, years after Hergé's death, it was discovered that he really had been buried with his sceptre!"

Travel on ferries and buses is free for children under four. They pay half fare up to the age of 10 (ferries) and 12 (buses). When travelling between islands opt for the hydrofoil or catamaran rather than the ferry as journey times are shorter. Buses are the main source of public transport but for getting to and from the big sites with kids; tourist coaches are an easier option.

athens

practicalities

Stay near to the Plaka and ask for a room that doesn't look onto the street to avoid the noise. Avoid campsites, hostels and cheap hotels which are not very family-friendly.

things to see & do

interesting & educational The kids will enjoy the same things that you're here to see. When it comes to the Acropolis, remember little people get tired so you may have to visit twice in order to see everything. Avoid the crowds by visiting early or just before closing. Kids will like exploring the souvenir shops in the Plaka, where there's a hands-on Children's Museum. The National Archaeological Museum is good for older kids.

pure entertainment Try painting at the Museum of Children's Art in the Plaka.

parks & playgrounds

The National Gardens is the nearest park to the main sites. Near the National Archaeological Museum is Aeros Park, where littlies can run off steam in its leafy avenues. Getting out of the city to swim is the best way to cool off. Pack a picnic and watch the sunset at Cape Sounion.

festivals

Kids will adore Easter in Greece if they can manage to stay awake for the beautiful midnight torchlight processions.

around greece

The big archaeological sites to see that will interest children are Delphi, where the oracle used to be, and the site of the first Olympic Games at Olympia. Mt Olympus is fun to see even if you don't climb up. They'll also like the Corinth Canal. The best beaches for children on the mainland are at Halkidiki in the north.

Crete has to be one of the best islands with children. Many of the hotels have special facilities, and there's plenty to see at Knossos, home of the mythical Minotaur. The best beaches for children are in the north of the island. Other places with good beaches include eastern Corfu and the west coasts of the Ionian Islands.

books

Robin Lister's retelling of *The Odyssey* is aimed at children aged 10 to 12, but makes compelling listening for younger children when read aloud. The Greek publisher Malliaris-Paedia puts out a good series on the myths, retold in English for young readers by Aristides Kesopoulos.

Rosemary Sutcliff's retelling of *The Wanderings of Odysseus* is beautifully illustrated but an audiocassette version is handy to while away the time on tourist buses. If it's too hot to think opt for Terry Deary's light-hearted approach in *The Groovy Greeks* and *Top Ten Greek Legends*. Computer fanatics will like *Shadow of the Minotaur* by Alan Gibbons, where myths meet computer games.

Peter Connolly's *Ancient Greece* is a good first history with some lovely illustrations that will bring the ancient sites to life for under-10s. For something completely different try *My Life and Other Animals* by Gerald Durrell which is the story of his childhood in Corfu that will appeal to older kids.

HUNGARY

In Hungary, you'll find much of the excitement and attractions of Western Europe at half the cost. Kids will like the feeling that this is somewhere a bit different. The attractions are not the same as what you'll find to the west but come with plenty of old-fashioned charm, especially outside the capital.

Hungarian supermarkets stock everything you need for babies but most shops shut by 7 pm. If you're in a tight spot, there's always a night chemist, which will sell infant formula and nappies. The milk on sale in shops is pasteurised but it's advisable to boil it in very hot weather.

There are no family tickets for attractions but both public transport and museums are reasonably priced. Public transport is the best option in Budapest. Trains are a good way of getting about especially in winter and there are plenty of cruises on the Danube.

If you're on a budget, camping is a possibility around Lake Balaton but for the best facilities for children head for a hotel with two stars or more. Big hotels will offer a babysitting service. There's a shortage of laundrettes, so expect some hand washing. Hungarian food may not go down well with the kids but there are plenty of pizza restaurants especially in big towns.

things to see & do

wild things The kids will like the zoo in Budapest and you'll like the Art-Nouveau animal houses. They'll love watching bareback riding in the summer shows at Kiskunság National Park.

interesting & educational Start by exploring Castle Hill in Buda, especially the caves. Don't miss the scale models in the Museum of Military History. The Hungarian Open-Air Ethnographic Museum at Szentendre just outside the capital is fun. In Szeged, it's worth popping into the Ferenc Móra Museum to see the exhibition on the Avars, who conquered the area in the 5th century.

pure entertainment There's a permanent circus in Budapest near the City Park. Kids will also enjoy the shows at the Budapest Puppet Theatre.

We arrived in Athens mid-afternoon and, although the airport bus took nearly two hours to get into the city centre, we had a great first night. Having booked a hostel in the city's ancient heart – the Plaka – we enjoyed an early candlelit dinner in the main pedestrian square, where the waiters fed Zach for free and gave us a complimentary bottle of retsina. We strolled to the Acropolis to admire the city lights and stumbled on a musical performance in a magnificent amphitheatre. The three of us sat on rocks overlooking the show and the city lights, enamoured with the ancient capital.

greece DAYS in the SUN

Crispin Walker travelled to Greece for two weeks with his son, Zach, 21 months, and fiancée, Yvette, visiting Athens and the Greek islands.

Zach, who used to nocturnally sneak into our bed at home, was happy with the cramped quarters at the cheap hostel and loved the enclosed courtyard where we had a leisurely breakfast. Later that morning we headed to Piraeus to jump the first ferry to the Cyclades islands, but had a bad public transport experience. Thieves attempted to pickpocket me three times in a 20-minute period! We were sure that being laden down with a kid and backpacks made us seem a slow, easy target. What made the experience memorable was the comical ineptitude of the thieves who were easily dissuaded by my shouting.

Eager to leave the mainland we managed to get on a boat to Paros within four hours on a cheap family ticket (which I'm sure was the student discount) sold to us by a ferry operative keen to undercut his opposition. Zach found the ferry very exciting and watched fascinated as Athens drifted away behind us. We had stocked up on fruit, chips and drinks at a Piraeus supermarket before boarding, and Yvette and I took it in turns to look after our baggage whilst the other took Zach exploring around the boat – a pastime he enjoyed throughout the trip.

On arrival in Paros we were met by a scrum of hotel touts shouting and waving fliers. We had decided on a cheap hostel in the island's capital Parikia, but finding the reception unoccupied we headed back to the port and went with local landlord Costa to view his self-catering villa. The villa was great with a bedroom, living room, kitchen, bathroom and balcony all at the same price as the hostel! It proved perfect for us and a nice retreat during the midday heat.

We spent five days exploring Paros by bus, which proved to be an excellent way to meet locals as our dark-haired boy got lots of loving glances and strokes from Greek grannies. Our trip to the lovely port of Naoussa and then on to the secluded Kolimvythres beach proved a family favourite. Mainly because Zach was able to splash happily in shallow pools with dad, while mum worked on her tan and ploughed through her latest novel.

We got into the regular habit of wandering the backstreets of Parikia town in the cool afternoons before adjourning to the waterfront to watch the beautiful sunsets. Zach was always happy to munch on a Greek kebab (combining lamb, chips and salad), while cafe or bar owners would chat to us animatedly about their Sydney and Melbourne relatives on learning that I was an Aussie.

We jumped another late ferry to Naxos – only one hour away – and had a bad first night, after a hotel owner lied outright to us about her available accommodation. We spent a night cramped in a single room with a second mattress on the floor, but an early morning visit to the information centre found us in another great little apartment near Naxos town centre. We spent every day at a different beach and Zach appreciated being able to paddle in the gentle waves of the Mediterranean.

We dined at a few nice restaurants in Naxos town's harbour and Zach was welcomed everywhere we went. As always he was an adventurous eater trying out fish and lamb stews and really enjoyed the traditional Greek tomato and cucumber salads. After dinner we usually went for a cocktail or drink in the town square, which, being pedestrianised, allowed Zach to run about with the local kids while we got a rest. It was at these moments when we found Greeks the most warm and welcoming hosts. Family is of such high importance that visiting families seem to be afforded the best, quickest and friendliest service. The only downside we found was the almost pathological chain-smoking – and a rather messy vomiting episode from our little darling!

"Family is of such high importance that visiting families seem to be afforded the best, quickest and friendliest service. The only downside we found was the almost pathological chain-smoking – and a rather messy vomiting episode from our little darling!"

We ventured lastly to Mykonos on the fast ferry. When it roared into action Zach became quite excited. Mykonos town was quite dynamic and although considered the gay capital of the island, we felt right at home. Again we rented an apartment in the town centre and journeyed across the island by bus. Two notable trips we went on were to the Waterworld Fun Park, with a great kiddy section and massive water slides that kept us all happy. The other was our superb trip to the ancient archaeological island of Delos. We went first thing in the morning to avoid the crowds and heat. Zach found his niche chasing geckos, while we took some great photos of the virtually empty ruins.

On our last night in Mykonos we sat near Little Venice sipping Mai Tai cocktails watching the blood red sun disappear over the horizon, with Zach happily playing yards away with pebbles on the beach. Holidays in the sun don't get much better than this.

activities

You can tour the Buda Hills all year round on the Children's Railway. If it's hot, cool off in the outdoor swimming pools on Budapest's Margaret Island. For the great outdoors head for Lake Balaton, where you can exhaust them swimming, boating and cycling.

parks & playgrounds

Budapest has plenty of playgrounds and parks. The best park is the City Park where there's a funfair.

POLAND & BALTIC STATES

Not many foreigners travel here with children but that doesn't mean you won't get a warm welcome. If you've got a big family you might even find yourself being applauded as you walk down the street!

You can find the basics in big city supermarkets. Chemists are the best place to find formula and nappies; there's usually an all night chemist in big cities. You'll need to carry enough basic supplies to tide you over weekends. Pack children's paracetamol and ready-to-drink formula milk for journeys. Be prepared for mosquitoes in the Baltics in summer. The tourist industry is still cranking into action, so pack a sense of humour along with the sterilising tablets.

Children enjoy privileges on local transport, accommodation and entertainment but don't assume this is a cheap option for a family holiday. Restaurants in Warsaw are surprisingly pricey and to get the facilities and service you need with children you'll be better off heading for the best hotel you can afford. Laundrettes are few and far between even in big cities. However, it is possible to find good family-oriented guesthouses in Zakopane and rent cottages in Latvia. Take the train from Warsaw to Krakow and Gdansk but make sure to reserve a compartment with a lock.

information

In Poland, look out for *What, Where, When* in Warsaw and Krakow.

things to see & do

wild things The wildest thing to do is see the wild bison in the Bialowezia Forest, Poland.

interesting & educational In Warsaw, Kids love the view from the top of the giant Stalinist Palace of Culture & Science. The Warsaw Ghetto Monument and the Pawiak Prison Museum will interest older children. In Krakow, they'll enjoy exploring the vast Wawel Castle. Don't miss the incredible salt mines at Wieliczka just outside Krakow – a cavernous underworld of ballrooms and chapels where even the chandeliers are made of salt.

In Gdansk, older kids will find a trip to Westerplatte interesting, where the first shots of WWII were fired. Out of town visit Hitler's wartime headquarters, the Wolf's Lair, at Gizycko, or the world's largest brick castle at Malbork, once home to the Teutonic Knights. When it comes to castles, Sigulda in Latvia is well worth a trip.

Tallin in Estonia is the most child-friendly capital in the Baltics. Kids will like exploring the old town that has a real fairy-tale atmosphere. They'll enjoy a trip to the Open Air Museum which is full of wooden farm houses that look as if they're straight out of a children's book.

pure entertainment Riga in Latvia has the only permanent circus in the Baltics. Puppets are the thing in Warsaw, see them at the Lalka theatre in the Palace of Culture.

activities

For the outdoor life in Poland head for Zakopane in the Tatra Mountains. There are plenty of funiculars and cable cars to ride on. It's a lovely place to picnic and explore the woods in summer. Don't miss the boat ride along the rapids in the Dunajec Gorge. In Latvia, there are plenty of outdoor activities in the Gauja Valley.

parks & playgrounds

Warsaw has some beautiful parks around Wilanów and Lazienki, where there's a boating lake in front of a palace and a good outdoor restaurant in summer.

festivals

Kids will enjoy the colourful pageant held seven days after Corpus Christi (May/June) in Krakow. It's headed by a Tartar on a hobby horse.

books

The Silver Sword by Ian Serraillier tells the tale of four starving children's escape from Poland during WWII. It's also available on audiocassette.

cultural issues

In Poland it's impossible to shield kids from the horrors of the Nazi past. Take time to explain and be prepared to answer difficult questions if you take them to Auschwitz or the old Warsaw ghetto.

RUSSIA

Travelling in Russia with children can be fun as long as you come well prepared and pack a sense of humour. Russians love kids; that said, there's little on offer for tiny tots and top restaurants sometimes turn parents away. The simple rule is the more you pay the better service and facilities you'll enjoy so opt for mid-range hotels upwards, which will have a laundry service and babysitters. Hostels, self-catering and camping aren't sensible options with kids.

Jeremy's grandparents came to visit us in Moscow, where we had been living for five years, and we decided that their trip to Russia would not be complete without a side excursion to the stunning former capital, St Petersburg, the city built by Peter the Great.

st petersburg BABUSHKAS & BABIES

Tanya Seaward travelled with her son, Jeremy, 11 months, husband, Bern, and grandparents Clem and Theresa, to St Petersburg.

I insisted that we take the overnight train from Moscow; I thought it would be a more romantic way to travel. Bern was hesitant, concerned about dragging Jeremy out of bed in the middle of the night, but in the end agreed. We left from the Leningrad station – an architecturally beautiful building, but, as most train stations are, predictably seedy and grotty once you're inside. The fact that it was midnight on a Friday night didn't do much to improve the ambience.

We had booked two 1st-class compartments, each with two sleeping berths. They were quiet, comfortable and clean, once you got used to the heavily starched and ironed-stiff bedding. Jeremy and I shared one berth; he was pushed against the wall and I perched precariously on the edge of the bunk. The rocking of the train soon lulled him to sleep and he was up at dawn – none the worse for his overnight adventure. I, on the other hand, needed a strong hot cup of tea to wake up and recover from the whole romantic experience.

Luckily, we were able to check into our hotel room early, as the train arrived at 8 am. We chose an upscale hotel close to both Nevsky Prospekt (the main street) and the State Hermitage Museum. As we were able to walk to most of the tourist sights, the convenience of the hotel almost made up for the exorbitant price. Because we were only in St Petersburg for three days, our days were very full. We brought Jeremy's reclining stroller with the sun/rain visor, so he could nap while we were out, rather than having to return to the hotel.

The weather in St Petersburg can be quite unpredictable, even in the summer months. We made sure to bring enough clothes for hot, cold and rainy weather. Our experiences in Moscow warned us that if Jeremy was not dressed appropriately (more than appropriately in our opinion), we would be chastised by every *babushka* (grandmother) that we met.

I had just weaned Jeremy a few weeks before our trip, but he wasn't completely on table food yet. We brought baby cereal, small cartons of UHT milk and a few jars of baby food with us. We were easily able to supplement his meals from our plates. I usually also helped myself to a few extra pieces of bread, fruit or yogurt from the breakfast buffet at the hotel.

Nappy changing also presented a few challenges. I was yet to find a baby-changing station in Moscow and St Petersburg was the same. So it was nice to have Theresa as an extra pair of hands in the bathrooms and we often resorted to changing him in the reclined stroller. Except for walks and trips to the park, it is not common for Russian people to take young children (under two) out.

We spent most of the first day at the State Hermitage Museum, which houses an amazingly diverse and immense collection. The building itself, the Tsar's Winter Palace, is spectacular and the courtyard was the setting of the 1917 revolution. Typically, you wouldn't expect to be able to spend a day at a museum with a child, but the Hermitage has so many beautiful rooms, varied displays of paintings, sculpture and tapestries, that it provided a lot of variety. Additionally, the Russian people love to take their older children (dressed to the nines in frilly dresses, bows, suits and neckties) to museums, so there were plenty of diversions. A well-timed morning nap also helped pass the time.

The next day we took a high speed boat to Petrodvoret, just outside of St Petersburg. Petrodvoret was the Tsar's summer residence and apart from the main palace, the great attraction is the beautiful fountains. Petrodvoret is a great place for children – they love the fountains and water, and there's lots of space to run and roam.

> "Our experiences in Moscow warned us that if Jeremy was not dressed appropriately (more than appropriately in our opinion), we would be chastised by every *babushka* (grandmother) that we met."

Another one of the tourist highlights was a boat trip through the city's many canals. The weather was cooler and overcast that day, so it was nice to stay below with Jeremy and have a warm drink and a snack, while the rest of our group sat on the upper deck. There was also a little piano on board, probably for the rowdier evening cruises, and Jeremy had a great time picking away at the keys.

Then it was *das vidaniya* (goodbye) to St Petersburg. We took the afternoon train back to Moscow, so our guests could see the picturesque Russian countryside. The train was very full and the six-person compartment was at maximum capacity with an overstimulated, under-napped toddler crawling over everyone for the better part of five hours. Although the two other foreigners sharing our compartment were fairly understanding, in hindsight, we should have bought tickets for all six seats.

Despite our hectic itinerary we all had a great time, although I doubt that Jeremy will remember much about this trip to St Petersburg.

If you're off to St Petersburg, come prepared for mosquitoes in summer and stick to bottled water, the stuff from the tap contains intestinal parasites. Take extra care with babies.

Russian roads are terrible and with the exception of the Moscow-St Petersburg Express; so are the trains. Pack plenty of food, drinks and entertainment for the ride. Both Moscow and St Petersburg have a good metro that's relatively stroller-friendly and you can generally buy everything you need for babies in both cities.

things to see & do

wild things There are animals performing tricks everywhere in Moscow, there's even a cat theatre and a dolphin circus. Moscow Zoo has been done up and is a good afternoon out for little ones. The fish at Aquarium World are good for calming down toddlers.

interesting & educational In St Petersburg both the Peter & Paul Fortress and the Planetarium have special programs for kids. They'll enjoy a trip to Vasilevsky Island. The museums here are the kind that kids will like. There's the huge Central Naval Museum and the Museum of Anthropology and Ethnography will definitely appeal with its gruesome curiosities.

Moscow has the excellent Armoury as well as all the other sights in the Kremlin, which kids usually like. Don't try to see it all in a day or you'll wipe them out. If you've got older kids it's worth hiring a car and taking a trip out of town to the ancient cities of Novgorod and Vladimir. It's here you get a real feeling of Russian history.

pure entertainment Older kids might enjoy a ballet performance at the Kirov or Bolshoi but remember the theatres close in summer.

activities

Kids like the row boats near the Peter & Paul Fortress in St Petersburg.

parks & playgrounds

St Petersburg has a full-scale amusement park behind the Peter & Paul Fortress and a smaller one in the Tauride Gardens. Watch out though, some equipment in playgrounds can be dangerous. Moscow's Gorky Park also has an amusement park.

books

Older children will enjoy the story of *Natasha's Will* by Joan Lingard, that's set in both modern-day and revolutionary St Petersburg. Rent the 1980s film *Reds* to give them a flavour of 1917.

TURKEY

Turks love children and everyone will want to kiss the baby. You'll get a warm reception wherever you go. Kids will love the exotic scents of Istanbul's markets and the beautiful beaches along the coast.

This isn't easy stroller country, so pack a backpack or sling. You can buy basic supplies for babies. The market for children's products and services is not as elaborately developed as it is in Western Europe. However Turks are handy at improvising anything, which may be needed for a child's safety, health or enjoyment.

Pasteurised milk is sold everywhere but ready-made baby food is a new thing in Turkey. Hotel and restaurant staff will make up special dishes for small children.

European-style campsites are rare. With children self-catering apartments at the beach are a good option otherwise opt for upwards of a two-star hotel. The larger hotels and resorts can arrange babysitting services. There are laundrettes in bigger cities. The easiest way to get about is to fly.

things to see & do

Children of all ages will enjoy a cruise on the Bosphorus and the Archaeological and Military Museums. Outside of Istanbul head for Ephesus, Troy and Gallipoli. Do your homework and tell history as an entertaining story. Kids will appreciate a visit to Bosphorus Zoo, 48kms out of Istanbul.

Wandering in the covered bazaar in Istanbul will make them feel like bit players in the Ali Baba tales.

activities

Indoor playgrounds have just arrived in Turkey. In Istanbul try the Play Barn or head for Cosmic Bowling.

parks & playgrounds

Big seaside resorts have extensive facilities for children. Public parks sometimes have basic play equipment. In Istanbul head for Yildiz Park or the fair in Maçka Luna Park.

books & films

Rent the film *Gallipoli* (1982) and for the over-eights pack Adèle Geras's powerful novel *Troy*. Barbara Leonie Picard retells Homer's classic tale in *The Iliad* and for long journeys get hold of the audiocassette version of Rosemary Sutcliff's *Black Ships Before Troy*. For something more up-to-date, over-10s will enjoy Gaye Hiçylmaz's novel *Against the Storm*, which is a story of one boy's fight against poverty in the slums of Ankara.

cultural issues

If you take children to a mosque remember to dress them appropriately and tell them to behave as if they are in a church.

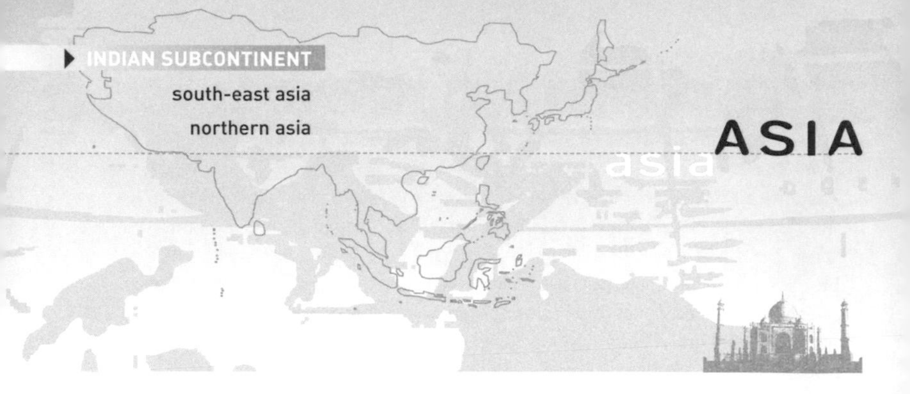

It's easier to travel in Asia these days than ever before. Having children along will give you common ground with local families, but also create the usual challenges like finding a familiar meal in Tashkent or Seoul. Whether you and the kids are walking the Great Wall in China, watching wild elephants in Sri Lanka or kicking back on a sandy beach in Thailand, flexibility and patience should be factored into everything.

Asia is incredibly affordable overall. Places like Japan and Singapore can bust a family budget in a hurry, but discounts are available. And countries such as Laos or the Philippines tend to be so cheap that you might consider the occasional splurge at a top-end hotel with a pool where you can chill out with the kids before heading off on the next adventure.

Accommodation across Asia varies greatly – from small Japanese *ryokan* (traditional inns) where you'll roll up your own futons in the morning, to exotic houseboats in southern India. Finding healthy food that your children will eat is always an initial concern. Many travellers' restaurants cater to Western tastes and finding hearty porridge, banana pancakes or fruit smoothies is easy. Though food may not be familiar, it isn't necessarily spicy and you can always ask about less spicy alternatives.

With transportation, safety is an issue. In much of Central and South-East Asia, car seats or infant restraints are hard to come by, so bring your own. Never take transport that you haven't checked out. If you hire a car, be sure the seat belts are in working order. Remember, too, that small kids will not always find a night bus in Vietnam or a crowded Indian train a rich cultural experience. Spending a couple of dollars more here and there on safe transport may save your holiday.

If you're travelling with infants or toddlers, bring all necessary medications and decide if you'll need a stroller, sling or backpack. Most Asian capitals have adequate supplies of nappies, infant formula and baby food, but be ready for sweetened varieties. Malaria and dengue fever are always a risk in southern Asia, especially in remote or mountainous areas, so consider bringing a lightweight mosquito net for the kids. See the Health chapter for more information or check out Lonely Planet's *Healthy Travel Asia & India* for more thorough discussion of possible medical concerns.

BANGLADESH

For children, the fascination of Bangladesh lies in observing the life going on around them. The country doesn't have a lot of conventional tourist sites, so plan on taking a rickshaw ride, a boat trip or visiting a village.

practicalities

The urban mayhem of Dhaka can be overwhelming, and the pollution is especially unhealthy for little lungs. Seeing mothers nurse in public is a rare sight. It would be advisable to cover with a shawl and still be prepared for stares, which all visitors receive no matter what.

things to see & do

In Dhaka, explore the Buriganga River on a cruise for a fascinating panorama of river life. For a slightly bumpier look at city life, take children for a ride in one of the capital's 600,000 rickshaws, each colourfully painted.

Outside Dhaka, cycle around the tea estates of Srimangal, where kids will see workers their own age in the fields. In the west, board a Rocket (steamer) to glide through the vast watery forest of the Sundarbans National Park, home to the Bengal tiger.

cultural issues

Physical affection is considered unacceptable in public and modesty in dress is the norm for men and women.

BHUTAN

Despite long mountain drives and no television, children seem to travel remarkably well in the Himalayan kingdom of Bhutan, where they are readily accepted by the gracious Bhutanese.

Part of Bhutan's uniqueness is its effort to protect its ancient culture, deeply Buddhist way of life and natural resources by limiting tourism. At the time of writing, the government insists visitors have a pre-planned itinerary and pay a tariff of US$200 a day that includes accommodation, food, guides and pack horses. Children under six years old are free; ages six to 12 receive a 50% discount.

things to see & do

wild things Autumn visitors can glimpse the endangered black-necked crane, which inspires Bhutanese songs and folklore. In winter the cranes can be spotted in the Phobjikha valley.

Like most mothers, my concerns for my children are monumental. I contemplate their education, their health and their futures on a daily basis. These concerns became the focus of many a debate when my husband and I decided to take our two boys on a five-week journey to India and Nepal. Almost everyone questioned our sanity, our doctor told us we were nuts and suggested we go to Disneyworld instead.

india & nepal

RICKSHAW BOY

Sharon McRae and her husband, Don, travelled to India with their sons, Roddy, 11, and Liam, nine.

Heading off to a developing country with your children is not an easy undertaking; I was overwhelmed with anxiety as we approached India. The most astounding outcome of the journey was that my fears were, for the most part, unfounded. Perhaps as adults we become too comfortable or wary of differences, whereas children thrive on novelty. The boys adapted to the tempo of life with rapt curiosity, not fear. One objective of the trip was the boys' education, but I believe they were the teachers.

The fact that we were travelling on stand-by tickets led to delays on both ends of the trip. The boys were amazingly unperturbed by the change of plans. Our unscheduled two days in London, and our week-long delay returning to Canada, were viewed as an opportunity to explore. Their enthusiasm was contagious.

Arriving at Indira Gandhi airport in the wee hours after a lengthy flight can be a daunting experience for the most jaded traveller and I will forever be astounded at the easy acceptance our boys displayed. The bureaucratic nightmare of immigration, the shouting hoard of taxi-wallahs vying for our trade, the apocalyptic drive into the pitch black depths of Delhi, were all met with quiet, albeit wide-eyed acceptance.

Our accommodation throughout the trip was definitely rudimentary; we usually slept four to a bed, hot water was a luxury and the toilets were an experience in themselves. This style of travel immersed us in the culture; the boys loved the bucket showers!

The traffic was one of my concerns with the children, but they seemed to adapt well. Traffic in India involves cows, trucks, cars, motorcycles, rickshaws, bicycles and people – the right of way being granted in that order, followed by dogs, goats, pigs and chickens. There is method to the madness and as a pedestrian you need only leap left at the sound of a horn or bicycle bell to avoid being hit. It makes even a mundane stroll an adventure; the boys approached this game with gusto and expertise! There were the odd collisions with cows, but the only traffic incident involved Liam driving a rickshaw in Delhi, successfully! This dubious opportunity arose when Liam called our daily chauffeur's rickshaw a 'cool machine' and explained his prowess at riding a dirtbike. Liam omitted the fact that he had only ever driven in wide open fields. Perhaps avoiding groundhogs takes more talent than I'd imagined, as he manoeuvred the three-wheeled demon around Paharganj with ease.

We left Delhi and explored Rajasthan, the heart of India. We rode camels into the desert, saw the sun set over the Taj Mahal, climbed to hillside fortresses on the back of an elephant, and ate a wide variety of new foods. The boys seemed to thrive on the differences.

Our journey included a long train ride, in the cattle car confines of a third class carriage (after we ended up on a train without a second class sleeper), and a two-day bus ride from India to Nepal. I do not claim to understand the boys' placid acceptance of these long confinements, but perhaps what was going on around them was activity enough, like being on the set of a Hollywood thriller. These long trips were interspersed with many trying moments, but the boys managed to see the humour in every small calamity. When a sad, elderly bus attendant repeatedly exposed himself to Roddy, he nicknamed him 'Penis Boy' amid fits of giggles; the whole bus joined in the laughter. The children's unique and cheerful view of each small event enriched the trip immeasurably.

"Traffic in India involves cows, trucks, cars, motorcycles, rickshaws, bicycles and people – the right of way being granted in that order, followed by dogs, goats, pigs and chickens."

Nepal brought its own unique challenges. When I was incarcerated at the border under armed guard (a long story!), the boys were only curious about the size of the guns. We trekked on the Annapurna route, where Roddy almost fell off a cliff while trying to catch a rooster for dinner. We took a white-water rafting trip, which took Liam's adventurous personality to new heights. He decided to kayak, solo, through the turbulent waters of the Himalayan runoff. I was left little choice but to acquiesce to his enthusiasm, how many more chances would he encounter to realise this dream? I was left with only a few more grey hairs; the boys have these memories for a lifetime.

activities

With children, an ideal trek is from Paro Town to the Jhomolhari Base Camp, which visits highland villages and yak pastures, and avoids the challenging high passes and the risk of altitude sickness.

One of the delights of Bhutan is the national passion for *datse* (archery). It's easy to watch a session and competitions are a riot of colour and excitement, complete with cheerleading and playful taunts to the honoured opposition.

festivals

Festivals occur throughout the year, but especially in autumn and spring when the weather is fair. These offer a first-hand glimpse of Bhutanese life, often providing the only opportunity to see inside the extraordinary *dzongs* (fort-monasteries).

books

Peter Steele's *Two and Two Halves in Bhutan* describes the joys of travelling through Bhutan with children.

cultural issues

Respect for the monarchy and modesty in public will always win respect for the visitor.

INDIA

Children are an integral part of Indian society and travelling with kids only enhances personal encounters. Offers of help are common and often welcome in a country that can overwhelm you with its size, clamour and diversity.

On most public buses and trains, children under 12 pay half fare and under-fives are free. You should avoid urban traffic – often a chaotic mix of transport and livestock. If you do find yourself in the thick of traffic, you'll need to be especially careful with younger children and be aware that strollers are often difficult to manoeuvre in crowds.

Nappies are available in most chemists and supermarkets. Strollers are nearly useless in dense urban areas as they put babies too close to trash and exhaust. In cities, nursing mothers should cover with a shawl and still be prepared for stares; in villages, prepare to be congratulated.

delhi

things to see & do

interesting & educational Kids often find the exotic collection of railway engines at the Rail Transport Museum fascinating, including a working 1855 steam engine and the skull of an elephant that charged a mail train in 1894.

The open-air Crafts Museum contains a collection of traditional Indian crafts: textiles, metal, wood and ceramics. The museum is part of the 'village life' complex which offers a fascinating introduction to rural life and it's all free.

Bal Bhawan is a creative centre where workshops are regularly held on music, painting and theatre. The Science Park and the National Children's Museum are also here and there's a mini-railway.

pure entertainment Appu Ghar amusement park features rides like and yet unlike those that foreigners may be familiar with. The dodgem cars are a scream and probably the only place in the country you're likely to see safety belts in the whole country.

activities

India has more than its share of great forts and at Delhi's Red Fort families can glimpse the remnants of Mughal power, while dodging would-be guides who leap forth as soon as you enter.

parks & playgrounds

India Gate Children's Park is popular with both Indian and visiting families, featuring a garden with swings, monkey bars and other play equipment.

mumbai (bombay)

practicalities

Most hotels in Mumbai have family rooms or provide extra beds and most top-end hotels provide babysitting.

things to see & do

Weekends at Juhu Beach have a carnival atmosphere, as crowds of locals and tourists paddle in the sea, play cricket and enjoy the fresh air – everything, that is, but swim or sunbathe. There are heaps of snack stands and fruit vendors, fairground rides and fortune tellers.

Western-style kiddy fun is the theme at Water Kingdom and Fantasy Land. There are pony rides for small children at the Breach Candy Club, along with a large pool in the shape of India, a toddlers' pool and a water slide.

parks & playgrounds

There are children's playgrounds at Horniman Circle, August Kranti Maidan and Kamala Nehru Park, the last of which has a giant old shoe that's a big hit with littlies.

around india

Kolkata (Calcutta) – long acknowledged as the cultural capital of India – has scenes of rare beauty amid its dense population of 12 million. The Botanical Gardens are home to the 200-year-old banyan tree, renowned as the second largest canopy in the world. At the Birla Planetarium kids will get a much better view of the stars of the subcontinent than in the polluted atmosphere outside.

The rigours of travel in the Indian Himalaya can be tiring for kids, but there are great hiking trails around the hill stations of Shimla and Dalhousie. In between is McLeod Ganj – home to the Dalai Lama and the Tibetan Government in exile. There are a number of family-friendly walking trails in the area suitable for short hikes.

Adventurous families will be tempted to visit Ladakh – the land of high passes – which marks the boundary between the peaks of the western Himalaya and the vast Tibetan plateau. The region offers everything from day hikes to serious trekking, rafting and mountain biking.

Life in the South Indian state of Kerala moves at a slower pace than elsewhere in India. The beaches of Kovalam and Varkala are inviting, though over-development is coming. Nevertheless, several small resorts offer good deals for visiting families.

Periyar Wildlife Sanctuary is home to antelopes, sambar, monkeys, over 700 elephants and 35 tigers. There are two-hour boat trips on the lake, easy jungle walks and spice tours which are fun with kids.

Winding far inland from Varkala is a network of canals and shallow palm-fringed lakes where you can see backwater villages in an open work boat called a *kettuvallam*.

festivals

The highlight of the year at Mumbai's Chowpatty Beach is the Ganesh Chaturthi festival (August/September) when kids will watch with confusion and amazement as images of the elephant god, Ganesh, are paraded through the city streets and immersed in the sea.

books & films

Teenagers might be able to handle Mira Nair's *Salaam Bombay*, a 1989 film about the plight of Mumbai's street children, but for younger, more sensitive viewers you could try *City of Joy* (1992).

Pack some of Rudyard Kipling's classics – *The Jungle Book* or *Just So Stories* are usually pretty good for all ages. A great collection of traditional stories is *Folktales of India: A Selection of Oral Tales from Twenty-Two Languages* edited by AK Ramanujan. Older children will enjoy Vikram Seth's *Beastly Tales from Here and There*, a collection of poems that includes stories of India, China, Greece and the fictional land of Gup.

cultural issues

In photogenic India junior photographers and adults should be sensitive about taking photos of people, especially women. Of course, in a country with so many customs and sub-cultures, you're not expected to get everything right. But take particular care when visiting a religious temple or shrine.

Many travellers are startled by the number of beggars in India and you should prepare children of any age for likely encounters with intense poverty – especially when they discover it on the faces of other children.

NEPAL

Surprisingly few people travel with children in Nepal, yet with a bit of planning it is remarkably hassle free. As always, children bring out local hospitality and friendliness. Kids may also surprise you with their trekking stamina. Adults often reach a village to find their children already playing with Nepali youngsters.

There is a wide range of accommodation in both Kathmandu and Pokhara and most hotel rooms come with three or four beds – ideal for families with young children. Garden space is at a premium in congested Kathmandu, but many hotels have roof gardens which may be safe play areas for kids.

Food in city restaurants is generally quite safe, but hygiene in mountain villages varies. Fresh fruit should be peeled and ice cream from street vendors is suspect. Most importantly, avoid untreated or unboiled tap water in Nepal and be careful of ice. You might bring a good water filter, but a reliable method is to use iodine tablets combined with vitamin C, which neutralises both the colour and taste of the iodine – a much easier sell to young children.

Diesel-fed pollution is hard on little lungs, and walking the congested and narrow streets of Kathmandu can be a hassle with toddlers unless you get them up off the ground, so bring a backpack.

Disposable nappies are available but pricey in Kathmandu and Pokhara. In mountain villages, however, they are anything but disposable and you need to choose between carrying them out, or using cloth ones. Bring essential medications on any trek.

kathmandu valley

Strolling around the terraced temples of Kathmandu's Durbar Square is a wonderful way for kids to get a feel for this traveller-friendly city.

To the valley's east, families can explore easy-going Bhaktapur on bicycle.

activities

Nepal's stretch of the Himalaya includes eight peaks over 8000m, including majestic Mt Everest. Families, however, can set their sites happily lower. There are several superb treks available that avoid the higher passes which risk altitude sickness. See the Health chapter for more information on altitude sickness if you're considering higher altitudes.

Treks in Nepal generally begin either in the Kathmandu Valley or around Pokhara. The popular Helambu Trek begins north of the Kathmandu Valley and is reasonably short (about seven days), sticks to moderate elevations and best of all, is never too busy.

Pokhara's lazy lakeside ambience and its proximity to the mountains makes it a favourite starting point for some of Nepal's best-known trekking circuits. There are also plenty of short walks and day trips around the valley, all suitable for children or even weary hikers.

The moment we stepped out of the car and into the streets of Kathmandu, I could immediately tell that this trip was going to be a little different to our usual holidays. In a few days my family would be trekking alone and unaccompanied in the Annapurna Ranges. But my first aim was to relish the few days of 'real civilisation' in Kathmandu that I had. Unfortunately, we would be carrying everything we bought in Kathmandu on the trek, so I had to restrict my shopping to things like paper lanterns.

nepal TREKKING TEENS

Megha Singh, 17, spent 13 days in Nepal and spent nine of them trekking with her family.

Kathmandu was unlike any city that I had ever been to. Firstly there was the notable absence of junk food, which was not missed much as the restaurants in the city centre were so good. During the day, most tourists walked through the small streets, making their way through the maze of traffic and street sellers on the road. There were many historical places to visit, but for my sister and I the greatest attraction was the numerous bargains that were available to us. The locals would follow us around trying to sell whatever they had, which was usually tiger balm. It's lucky that we gave in and finally bought some because it did come in handy later to relieve our pain after a hard day of trekking. We had luck with bargains because we're Indians and the Nepalese usually didn't notice that we were from overseas, so they usually gave us a good price. Tourists would walk away from stalls smiling having bargained a wooden elephant from 600 rupees to 300 rupees, when the initial price for us was only 200 rupees.

After Kathmandu we took a flight to Pokhara, which was a very laid-back place and great for preparing ourselves for the trek. The locals were genuinely friendly and instead of selling tiger balm they often engaged in table tennis and Hacky Sack with tourists. To the dismay of my sister and myself, Dad insisted that we walk everywhere as training for the climb that lay ahead. Every time we complained he used the same old line, 'Are you complaining about walking a few kilometres? What are you going to do on the trek when you have to walk much further and uphill, too?'

Before we knew it the first day of trekking had arrived. Just as we started we met a Nepalese family who were heading off on a pilgrimage. They were going to the same places we were going and even better, one of the men was a Sherpa. Suddenly the idea of going trekking without a porter or guide seemed less daunting.

Our first day trekking was long and hard because we didn't know what to expect. We made many stops and went quite slowly. Tired, we just stopped at the first hotel we came across which was the luxurious Hilton, no sorry, the Hillton.

Most of our evenings were spent by candlelight or in darkness, as we had no electricity for some time. However this was easy to get accustomed to, but the food was not. We didn't get sick many times, but the oodles of spices they used did cause us some problems. It was also here on our first night that we met an American couple on their honeymoon, Robyn and Eric, who became our unofficial travel companions. They had a porter who knew the best places to eat and stay, and my sister found them especially fun because during the trek they would tell the best jokes.

As the days went on the walking got easier and were helped along by our never-ending supply of chocolate. My sister was happy most of the time, but she would sometimes complain about the 'bag of air' that was strapped to her back; it was only a sleeping bag. One particularly difficult day my sister was complaining because her 10-year-old feet had had enough. As soon as Dad told her she could get a pony ride on the way down the mountain, she bounded up the mountain for the next hour.

"Unfortunately, we would be carrying everything we bought in Kathmandu on the trek, so I had to restrict my shopping to things like paper lanterns."

My funniest experience was being mistaken for a local Nepalese. Some tourists approached me cautiously and asked me, using simple English, 'Do you speak English? How far to next town?' They sure got a shock when they discovered I had no idea how far the next town was, that I could speak perfect English and I came from the very city that they came from – Melbourne!

While the endless views of mountains were great, kids have a short attention span and can get bored easily (speaking from experience!). Visits to a Buddhist monastery, dips in hot springs and socialising with locals and tourists from all over the world helped add variety to our trip and made it a truly unforgettable experience.

The last day of trekking was one that was eagerly anticipated but it was also met with a great deal of sadness. We had to say goodbye to new friends and a very unique experience. But it wasn't all that bad; at least we could catch a taxi back to Pokhara instead of walking there ourselves.

Beginning a few kilometres east of Pokhara, the three or four day Annapurna Skyline Trek is a camping trek and a fine one to do with children. It doesn't reach any great altitudes, doesn't entail any particularly long walking days and there are fine views of the Annapurnas.

The Jomson Trek, which begins in Pokhara and emerges to the north on the dry Tibetan plateau, is among the most popular with families. There is superb scenery along the way and the best trailside accommodation in the country. Highlights include staying in tea houses, where your kids might happily disappear into the candle-lit kitchen, only to emerge with a treat from a gracious Nepali cook. It takes a week to reach the pilgrimage centre near Jomson. Walking back takes another week or you can fly for US$50.

around nepal

While many people come to Nepal just for trekking in the Himalaya, there is a great deal more to the country, including river rafting and mountain biking. The Terai, a lowland strip which runs the breadth of the country, is often overlooked by visitors. At Royal Chitwan National Park wow kids with an incredible variety of bird and animal life on elephant and jeep safaris, jungle walks or dug-out canoe rides.

Every morning during the clear dry-season months, mountain flights offer panoramic dawn views of the Himalaya without too much effort for kids or parents.

festivals

Nepal's colourful holidays and festivals occur virtually year round, especially in Kathmandu Valley towards the end of the monsoons of August and September.

books

For an insight into Nepali culture pack *From the Mango Tree and Other Folktales* as told to Sarah Lamstein.

cultural issues

Younger trekkers should take care to respect Nepali culture, even on a hot day in the mountains. Girls should dress modestly and boys should never be shirtless.

PAKISTAN

As in many regions in the subcontinent, travelling with children in Pakistan is challenging. Sightseeing aside, most kids are fascinated to learn how their counterparts live from day to day. Normal precautions must be taken with food and water, but a good children's diet is always available. Breastfeeding is a rare public sight in Pakistan and covering with a shawl is recommended.

Karachi is the largest city, but it's little more than a transit stop for most visitors, who generally head north to Lahore, Islamabad and Peshawar, gateway to the North-West Frontier Province. Infant supplies are generally available in Karachi and Lahore, but are limited elsewhere.

things to see & do

There is wonderful hiking throughout Pakistan. The valleys around Ziarat and Chitral offer great walks ranging from easy to moderate. Families keen to trek in the challenging Hindukush and Karakoram ranges, however, should hire guides and porters. The stunning views along the Karakoram Highway are only matched by the winding terrain – and the possibility of children becoming car sick. For more great panoramas Pakistan International Airlines runs an amazing two-hour air safari loop from Islamabad up near K2 and back.

cultural issues

Most Pakistanis dress modestly. Long, loose, non-revealing garments are a simple expression of respect. Young female travellers who wear a light scarf in conservative company or in a mosque will win warm approval.

Local opinions vary about Islam's political grip on Pakistan, but Christians and Jews are generally respected as *ahi-l-kitab* (people of the book) and any interest in Islam will bring an enthusiastic response.

SRI LANKA

Sri Lanka is a very family-oriented society, and places to stay and eat cater to children as a matter of course. Hotels and guesthouses often have triple rooms, and extra beds are routinely supplied on request. Passionate cricket matches aside, Colombo holds less of obvious interest than other parts of Sri Lanka.

Infant supplies are available, if expensive, in Colombo. Tap water is unsafe to drink anywhere, but bottled water is available across the island and kids usually love to sip from a fresh king coconut.

Travelling on public transport is safer on trains than overcrowded buses. Alternatively, hire a car and driver for both flexibility and comfort.

Ethnic violence has rocked the north and eastern sections of the island since the 1980s. Families should confine visits to the south and west and check with embassies before finalising plans.

things to see & do

wild things Colombo's Dehiwala Zoo has a fine collection of tropical birds and a conventional trunk-to-tail elephant show, but it's nothing compared to Yala West National Park with its populations of wild elephants, leopards, bears, crocodiles and monkeys. Take a guided jeep safari around the park, then spend the night in a jungle bungalow.

Pam and I had done a fair bit of wandering about Europe, Asia and Africa in our pre-parenting days, and so it came as no surprise when our daughter Tashi was born that instead of a gift of roses and chocolates for the new mother she received a copy of Lonely Planet's *Travel with Children*. However, the plan was to travel with two children and so it was not until the arrival of Mitchell, 19 months later, that we sat down to formulate a definite route.

karakoram highway

BIKER BABIES

Pam and Dave Quinn travelled the Karakoram Highway with Tashi, two, and Mitchell, 11 months.

The destination was not difficult – we had fallen in love with the rugged isolation of the mountains of northern Pakistan during an earlier visit. We were comfortable with our level of knowledge of the region and this became an important factor for our first trip with two children. We wanted some familiarity in location, because we knew that travelling with the children would be sufficient challenge without the addition of unfamiliar culture, towns and customs. Although we did 'enhance' the challenge by adding bicycles. We still can't work out how we dreamed up that idea!

Our plan was to fly to Rawalpindi, then on to Gilgit, from where we would make our way north along the Karakoram Highway, by bus, to Kashgar in China. This part of the journey was to be relatively fast because we would then retrace our steps, somewhat more slowly, on bicycles purchased in Kashgar. Upon reaching Gilgit we would head west into Chitral; however, this stage was cancelled due to the unanticipated arrival of US cruise missiles into that part of Pakistan (and neighbouring Afghanistan) following some US embassy bombings.

Wherever we went we were treated extremely well on account of the children and welcomed into people's homes. In truth, we had little in common with most of the people we met, though we always had parenting in common. With long blonde curly hair Tashi was the centre of attention everywhere, never failing to be in the midst of a group of local children and our passport to places and experiences we would otherwise have missed.

For example, crossing the border into China, the bus was stopped at a remote checkpost, unloaded, and intensively searched – except for our gear: the officials were too busy being photographed by their colleagues holding our kids, who were dressed up in Chinese border guard uniforms. They then fed us lunch.

Mitchell was still breastfed and Pakistan was perfect for children's food. They lived on a diet of porridge and/or eggs for breakfast, and rice and dhal with vegetables for main meals, supplemented by ubiquitous chips and occasional meat dishes. In China we had a little more trouble with Tashi, getting her to eat stir-fried vegetables with interesting flavours. After a few days, however, she got used to the new cuisine and, combined with noodles, rice, pancakes and eggs, she did not go hungry. Safe-to-eat yogurt was available in all the main towns. The children used their own fork and spoon which we were careful to keep clean. If we were staying in a town for more than a day, then once we found a restaurant with which we were comfortable, we would return. Familiarity was a comfort to the children, and they quickly made friends with locals at that restaurant.

The cycling aspect of our journey was certainly interesting! From seeking bicycles in Kashgar to dealing with broken axles, poor quality components, and less-than-reassuring brakes, not to mention the occasional largish mountain or 4000m pass, there was never a dull moment.

"We did 'enhance' the challenge by adding bicycles."

The first day of our journey involved bussing it from Kashgar up a rough steep canyon to Karakul Lake (hey, we're not completely insane!) where we cycled to a local yurt and stayed with a nomad family. A somewhat exotic location for Mitchell's first birthday!

We never suffered any ill effects from altitude. The highest point of our journey was the Pakistan/China border – the Khunjerab Pass – at 4830m, but we did not sleep any higher than 4000m. We made the climb to such heights gradually over a number of days with frequent rest days giving us plenty of time to acclimatise, particularly on the northbound leg of our journey. We were always ready to make a dash to lower altitude, if necessary, and that would have been quite simple given the layout of the terrain. Our experience was that the kids had no problems with altitude.

We were equipped for camping along the road but as it turned out we never had to pull out our tent – there was always some other shelter available. Apart from village guesthouses, these included Pakistani army barracks (the occupants were kicked out to make way for us) and an abandoned building on the slopes of a 7000m mountain.

While at first thought it may seem that cycling would have created excessive additional hassle, in fact it let us travel at our own pace, to suit both the children and us. Tashi and Mitchell often slept in their bike seats or enjoyed the passing scenery. We were able to stop to attend to baby Mitchell at any time, or have extended breaks beside a creek. This is a freedom we miss when we are travelling to bus schedules.

The experiences we shared on this trip were very different to those of travelling childless. Tashi in particular obtained an amazing awareness of the world she lives in – not from a book, but by actually holding a chunk of glacier, watching a group of wild camels strolling across the road in front of her or playing with local children who look, speak and dress differently to her. The experience has only served to whet our appetite for more. We're about to head for Nepal, India and Pakistan.

Nearby Bundala National Park is home to thousands of flamingos standing side by side in the glistening lagoons and wetlands. Set up as a sanctuary for abandoned wild elephants, Pinnewala Elephant Orphanage allows young elephants to roam freely. The regular feeding and bathing sessions for the babies are a huge favourite with kids.

activities

The small and charming town of Kandy is the starting point for excursions into the cool hill country, a major draw in steamy Sri Lanka. The Horton Plains feature good walking trails, and the ancient cities of Anuradhapura and Sigiriya are easily explored by bicycle.

Check out the string of beautiful white-sand beaches running south from Colombo all the way around the coast. For junior submariners there's good snorkelling at Hikkaduwa and Unawatuna.

In Tangalla you can see endangered turtles come up to the beach at night to lay their eggs. Kids (and parents) are invited to volunteer as nest protectors while baby hatchlings scamper to the safety of the sea.

festivals

Held on the full moon around the end of July, the Kandy Esala Perahera climaxes a 10-day celebration in honour of the Sacred Tooth Relic of Kandy. This great procession features dancers, drummers and over 50 magnificently decorated elephants.

books

For teenagers Michael Ondaatje's *Running in the Family* is an insightful look at Sri Lankan culture by the author of *The English Patient*.

cultural issues

Sri Lanka is a multicultural society and visitors are generally accorded great tolerance though women who dress modestly will attract less unwanted attention.

Buddhism is the creed of the Sinhalese ethnic majority, followed by Hinduism as practiced by ethnic Tamils, so visiting kids should treat both belief systems with respect.

CAMBODIA

Although Cambodians will be delighted that you've brought the children along, be aware that just getting around is a challenge. The road and rail systems of Cambodia are now considered generally safe – after years of war and strife – but check with your embassy before travelling beyond Angkor and Phnom Penh. You should be careful not to let kids leave marked paths in the wilderness as there may be undetonated mines in the area.

things to see & do

Scattered throughout the jungle, the celebrated temples of Angkor are natural mysteries to children and adults alike. Over 100 temples dot the shady landscape, with crumbling walls and sculpted figures that leave lasting impressions.

Although tourists come to the National Museum in Phnom Penh for the masterpieces of Khmer art dating from the 4th century, many children may be more interested in the massive bat colony streaming out of the roof at sunset.

Take a *cyclo* (rickshaw) with the children to English Street near the National Museum and strike up conversations with Cambodian youngsters studying English.

festivals

Pirogue (canoe) races are held in Phnom Penh during the Water Festival (October–November) when the Tonlé Sap River reverses its flow to empty into the Mekong.

books

Younger readers will enjoy *Angkat: The Cambodian Cinderella* retold by Jewell Reinhart Coburn – a great picture book based on a Khmer legend. Or for an insight into the life of a street flower-seller find a copy of Frederick Lipp's *The Caged Birds of Phnom Penh*.

'You're going to do what? You must be mad!' We probably were, but we did it anyway. We took two pre-schoolers on an epic backpacking journey around South-East Asia.

south-east asia

TOURING ASIA

Tracy Berno and Kevin Cummins travelled with their daughters, Zoe, three, and Vienna, two, for five months throughout South-East Asia .

It was almost inevitable that it was going to happen. I had hauled my rapidly expanding body, pregnant with our first child, around Southern Africa. A few months later, off we went to Canada with a four-month-old baby and another one already on the way. A few months later, we were off to Australia then the Cook Islands with both our baby daughters, Zoe and Vienna, then aged 14 months and six weeks, respectively. An auspicious start to their young lives and one which fulfilled our pre-children declaration that having a family would not curtail our travels. Inspired by our success travelling with a young crew, we set a far more ambitious goal – backpacking around Asia.

I teach at a university (in tourism studies funnily enough) and the time had come for me to take my long-awaited sabbatical. An invitation to teach in Thailand, along with research projects in Malaysia, Singapore and the Cook Islands, provided the perfect opportunity to take an extended family sojourn overseas. It didn't seem to matter that when we started talking, dreaming and planning neither of the girls was out of nappies, only one of them could walk and their food preferences were soft or bland.

We knew that we were going to be doing a fair amount of walking on our trip – more than our children were normally used to. Several months before the trip, we would go on fun family walks with a hidden purpose – training for the trip. Each child got to put a few special things in their backpack to take along on the walk and we gradually increased the distances we went. By the time we left, they were used to walking good distances with their loaded packs on.

Part of our preparation included introducing meals (of increasing 'heat') from the regions to which we were going to travel. By the time we got to Asia, our children were familiar with the food. In a pinch, they were always happy to eat rice or noodles.

After a stay of two months in the Cook Islands, we flew to Hong Kong and went overland to Singapore, with a side trip to Sarawak. Other than a flight to Kuching and a short hop by plane between Hanoi and Vientiane (due to the monsoons), we did the whole trip overland – buses, trains, mountain bikes, rickshaws, ferries, long boats, cars, 4WDs, on foot – you name it, we used it.

Everywhere we went, the presence of the girls created opportunities for us that we would not have had otherwise. Usually mistaken for twins, our two little blonde toddlers with the purple backpacks were a constant focus of locals' attention. We were welcomed into the homes of strangers, into the kitchens of restaurants, stared at, photographed, offered food, followed, touched and included like local family in festivals and celebrations. Riding on the backs of mountain bikes through rural China; watching water puppets in Vietnam; swimming in an artesian spring in a rainforest in Laos; sea kayaking in Thailand; observing the ritual self-mortifications during the Vegetarian Festival in Phuket; spotting monitor lizards in Melaka; visiting longhouses in Sarawak – Zoe and Vienna participated in it all.

We stayed in great hostels, grotty hostels and the occasional 'real' hotel when we felt worn down or needed an indulgence. We ate at street stalls, bought food in the markets and made the inevitable trips to fast-food restaurants for treats. Before we'd left home we'd visited a travel medicine specialist several times to discuss our trip and got appropriate immunisations and medications. Other than the girls having a rather 'explosive' reaction to too many rambutans eaten on a long boat trip, we all remained healthy throughout.

"We knew that we were going to be doing a fair amount of walking on our trip – more than our children were normally used to. Several months before the trip, we would go on fun family walks with a hidden purpose – training for the trip."

They were so good at keeping pace with the adventure, that sometimes we forgot we were travelling with children who were little more than babies. Sometimes we demanded too much from them. This created tension for all of us. Throughout it all, their wonder at the world around them and their unsullied appreciation of the diversity of cultures and environments they experienced made the struggles and frustration of backpacking with pre-schoolers worth it.

People thought we were crazy when we told them what we were going to do, but we did it. Would we do anything differently? Yes, try to take more money (our average daily budget was US$50 for the four of us). Would we do it again? You bet and we will!

cultural issues

In pagodas dress modestly (no tank tops or shorts) and never allow your feet to point toward images of the Buddha. You should be prepared to explain the activities of the Khmer Rouge to older children.

INDONESIA

The islands of the Indonesian archipelago offer an extraordinary mixture of people, cultures and the arts. You'll find Indonesians down-to-earth, good-hearted and delighted that you've brought the children along.

The usual health precautions apply in much of Indonesia. Tap water and ice should be avoided. Packaged milk, fruit juice and bottled drinking water are available everywhere but the most remote islands. Infant formula, baby food and nappies are easily found in larger towns. For nursing mothers, modesty is appreciated in mostly Muslim Indonesia.

Prices for accommodation vary widely, but are still among the cheapest in Asia. In Jakarta and Yogyakarta, competition keeps prices low. You'll pay a bit more in Bali, but it's generally good value and many hotels and *losmen* (guesthouses) have inviting gardens and huge breakfasts.

jakarta

things to see & do

wild things At Jakarta's impressive Ragunan Zoo you can spend a couple of hours wandering around the rainforest grounds glimpsing the country's famous wildlife, which includes orang-utans, Sumatran tigers and Komodo dragons.

interesting & educational Taman Mini Indonesia Idah is a 'whole country in one park' exhibit, featuring traditional houses, regional handicrafts and indigenous clothing, and a large lagoon where kids can row around the islands of the archipelago.

pure entertainment Taman Impian Jaya Ancol is a rambling recreation park along the bay front with a bit of everything for kids, including an aquarium and swimming pool complex, but forget polluted Ancol Beach with kids. The biggest drawcard at Ancol, however, is Dunia Fantasi, where the resemblance to Disneyland starts at the 'main street' entrance. It's well done and features the usual fun rides to wear out parents' wits and wallets.

bali

practicalities

Children are part of the community, and sometimes a small child will be whisked off to be pampered and fed. A few resort-style hotels offer special programs for kids and most can arrange a babysitter. But in small, family-style *losmen* you'll always find someone to look after your children for a few hours – often the owners' daughters, sisters or nieces.

things to see & do

Ubud in Bali's central mountains is the centre for traditional Balinese art and culture. A favourite with both kids and adults is the stylised dance between Barong and Rangda, strange and mischievous creatures who personify good and evil.

At the Monkey Forest near Sangeh, the monkeys are considered sacred, which apparently entitles them to think nothing of jumping all over you if they suspect you're hiding a few peanuts or, worse yet, a banana in your kid's daypack.

Bali beaches at Kuta, Legian, Nusa Dua, Lovina and Candidasa have great facilities for families, excellent surfing and even boogie boarding.

around indonesia

Yogyakarta (or Yogya) provides a rich sampling of Javanese culture, from traditional batik and silver factories to a sultan's palace with costumed guards and daily dance rehearsals. *Wayang orang* is the classical Javanese theatre, but kids often favour the livelier shadow puppet performances known as *wayang kulit.* Abridged afternoon *wayang* performances are held at the Agastya Art Institute, and nightly at the Sono-Budoyo Museum. Yogya is also a good base to explore the magnificent Buddhist monument at Borobudur and the towering Hindu temple of Prambanan.

Most of the tourist traffic drops off once you leave Java and Bali. Reliable ferry services connect the major island groups, but you may want to fly to the furthest islands. The island of Komodo is home to the world's largest lizard, the Komodo dragon.

In Sumatra, the well-managed Orang-utan Rehabilitation Centre at Bukit Lawang is justly world famous for helping primates readjust to the wild.

For older kids and trekking families, check out Baliem Valley in Irian Jaya. In seldom-visited Kalimantan, hardy families can explore river life along the Sungai Mahakam.

festivals

With such a diversity of people in the archipelago, you'll never be far from a festival or celebration – from Tana Toraja's unique funeral ceremonies in Sulawesi to the Javanese festival honouring Dewi Sri, the rice goddess.

books & films

Give the kids a fright with Peter Sis' *Komodo!* – the story of a young boy's fascination with dragons that takes him to the Indonesian island.

LAOS

Known in antiquity as Lan Xang (Million Elephants), Laos is the least developed of the three former French Indochinese states. Although the travel infrastructure is poor, the Lao will shower attention on your children, who will readily find playmates among their peers.

There is a small international community in the capital of Vientiane, but it's best to bring everything you might need for infants and small children – from nappies to infant formula. While breastfeeding is common in Thailand, in Laos modesty is expected as this is a devoutly Buddhist nation.

things to see & do

In Vientiane, the sacred 16th-century monument Pha That Luang always inspires curiosity when children spot worshippers sticking rice balls to the walls in respect for the spirit of King Setthathirat.

Graceful Luang Prabang is where the Mekong and Khan Rivers meet and a great place to explore with kids. The Royal Palace Museum (Haw Kham) and a handful of historic temples and faded French mansions are always within easy walking distance. You can take a river taxi to the Pak Ou caves, which are filled with Buddha images, stopping along the way at small riverbank villages.

The Plain of Jars is the enigmatic home to huge stone jars which are scattered across the meadows near Phonsavan where you can entertain the kids with the mysterious tales of their origin.

books

Sara Gogol's *Vatsana's Lucky New Year* is the story of an American-Lao girl coming to terms with both cultures for younger readers.

cultural issues

At the Royal Palace Museum and Buddhist temples, foreigners must not wear shorts, T-shirts or sundresses.

MALAYSIA

Travel with children in Malaysia is the easiest in South-East Asia and the remarkable mixture of Malay, Chinese and Indian peoples creates an energetic culture.

Accommodation is varied and plentiful. Many east coast beach resorts have family bungalows. Traditional Chinese hotels are a good bargain as they charge by the room rather than number of people. Bus and train transport is comfortable and convenient, but long-distance share taxis make travel between cities easier.

Malaysian food is a treat with Malay, Chinese and Indian touches that give children lots of choices. Baby supplies are widely available, but pack essentials before heading to remote destinations or islands.

kuala lumpur

things to see & do

KL (as it's usually called) blends modern and traditional. A few blocks from old Chinatown, the thriving riverside Central Market is great for a family meal or a smoothie.

KL's Lake Gardens form the city's green belt. Highlights for kids include a spectacular butterfly park and the National Planetarium. The Petronas Science Centre has hands-on activities related to energy exploration, including a virtual helicopter ride out to an oil rig. Visit Sunway Lagoon – a rambling water park perfect for cooling off in hot KL. Outside KL, the Forestry Research Institute offers young visitors a chance to inspect the rainforest canopy from a walkway.

around malaysia

To beat the heat of KL, head for the cool and quaint hill stations of the Cameron Highlands or Fraser's Hill.

Take the 14-hour Jungle Railway between Gemas to Kota Bharu or break the journey at Jerantut and explore impressive Taman Negara National Park which includes one of the world's oldest rainforests.

Head for Rantau Abang on the east coast to spot the great leatherback turtles during the egg-laying season (May to August). The small islands near Terengganu are popular family destinations with pristine beaches, short boat rides, beach huts and easy snorkelling.

For trips off the beaten path, pack your gear for the Borneo states of Sarawak or Sabah for exotic river treks out of Kuching or day hikes around the base of Mt Kinabalu.

books

Kampung Boy by Malaysia's beloved cartoonist, Lat, provides a whimsical introduction to Malay ways.

cultural issues

KL is a city with both a Hard Rock Cafe and strolling religious police looking for violators of Islamic law so make sure kids are respectful and well behaved.

MYANMAR (BURMA)

Despite on-going political tension, there is much to experience in Myanmar with children, who will find playmates at practically every stop.

One of the best ways to see Myanmar is to hire a car and driver. For safety reasons, avoid flying on the government airline. For humanitarian reasons, stay at locally owned hotels and guesthouses, and buy handicrafts directly from artisans.

practicalities

Yangon and Mandalay pharmacies are well-stocked, but basic infant supplies can be scarce. As in much of South-East Asia, malaria and dengue fever are a risk in remote areas.

Kelly and I are teachers in Vientiane, Laos, and we came to Laos with our three children so we could all experience a different culture. When Kelly decided to take part in a 10-day writing course in Kuala Lumpur, Malaysia, I had mixed feelings – excitement about visiting a new country and city and nervousness about having to entertain our children for 10 days while living in a hotel. Few toys and lots of time on our hands could have been the recipe for a disastrous vacation. However, instead of disaster the 10 days we spent visiting Kuala Lumpur is remembered as one of the biggest vacations we have had as a family. The 'biggest' vacation because, as we found out, Kuala Lumpur is full of some of the biggest attractions in the world and best of all many are free or very inexpensive.

kuala lumpur THE BIGGEST VACATION

Jeff and Kelly Barrons visited Kuala Lumpur, Malaysia, for 10 days with their children, Genevieve, 10, Zachary, eight, and Jacob, six.

One of the few things that I did know about Kuala Lumpur prior to our visit was that it was home to the tallest buildings in the world, Petronas Towers. In the city or its surroundings you can also find: the tallest flag pole; the longest driverless electric train system; the largest wave pool; the longest pedestrian suspension bridge; one of the world's tallest towers; what has to be the world's largest playground; the busiest and fastest cable cars (at the Genting Highlands); and the world's largest aviary.

After spending our first day getting acquainted with the layout of the city we decided to check out the Petronas Towers. But as we soon discovered, many museums and attractions, including the towers, are closed on Monday. So on Tuesday we travelled back to the towers and managed to secure spots on a free tour. The tour doesn't take you all the way to the top but it does deliver you to the glass enclosed walkway between the towers on the 42nd floor. The view of the city is spectacular, as is the view back down to earth. The first thing Genevieve, Zachary and Jacob noticed as they looked out over the city was the large playground at the base of the towers. Of course any playground demands a visit so once we were safely back on solid ground we immediately headed off to investigate what would prove to be the largest and best equipped playground any of us had ever seen. There was every combination of climbing apparatus a child could ever hope for. What made it even better was the large wading pool with a waterfall located in the same park.

Shortly after our children discovered that the world's largest wave pool was a short bus ride away, we went to visit the Sunway Lagoon water park for the day.

The wave pool was huge and there were slides, several smaller pools with climbing ropes and a 'lazy river' which flowed around the perimeter of one of the pools. It was great fun to jump in and be carried by the river, especially as it flowed under a series of waterfalls. To top the wave pool off it is spanned by the world's longest pedestrian suspension bridge.

The western edge of downtown Kuala Lumpur is bordered by a large green space called Lake Gardens. We spent several days wandering through the gardens and visiting the various attractions. Zachary is our bird-watcher and was really taken with the walk through the aviary. This large, covered enclosure is filled with many varieties of birds and is in the process of expanding to include even more species. Coming from Canada it was enthralling for us to see so many beautifully coloured birds. Not far from the aviary is the Butterfly Park. Here we saw some of the largest and most colourful butterflies that we have ever seen. In addition to the aviary and Butterfly Park, Lake Gardens also contains the National Planetarium which – while small in size – is extremely well put together and all three kids found it fascinating. Just outside the gardens, on the way to town, is the Police Museum. It contains a wealth of information, not only about the Malaysian police force but also about the country in general and the kids described the museum as 'really cool'. The boys particularly liked the vehicles outside the museum and loved the collection of firearms, while Genevieve enjoyed reading up on the history of Malaysia.

"...the 10 days we spent visiting Kuala Lumpur is remembered as one of the biggest vacations we have had as a family."

Other places we visited included the Petronas Science Centre which was an unexpectedly pleasant surprise. Located in the twin towers it provides a detailed description of the search for and use of energy in Malaysia and is filled with hands-on activities for the kids, including a virtual helicopter ride out to an oil rig. We also visited the National Zoo which has an outstanding collection of animals in large enclosures; the African animal exhibit and the reptile exhibit both caught the kids' attention.

Outside Kuala Lumpur we visited the Genting Highlands which are easily reached from the city. To reach the summit where the amusement park and casino are located, you ride up the mountain on what is billed as the busiest and fastest gondola ride in the world. The view from the top is spectacular and there are plenty of activities to keep you busy for a day.

Kuala Lumpur has all the ingredients to ensure a successful family holiday. We all look back on our stay in Kuala Lumpur with fond memories and hope to return in the future.

things to see & do

In Yangon, Shwedagon Paya is an early-morning wonder and children can take part in lighting incense amid the glittering surroundings. An afternoon rickshaw ride to an ice-cream or lassi shop can do wonders for young travellers.

Outside Yangon, sample the water culture of Inle Lake's floating gardens and island temples; or join the Buddhist pilgrims at Kyaiktiyo's balancing boulder stupa – perched on a mountain cliff.

Explore Mandalay by rickshaw and visit the stone carvers outside sprawling Mahamuni Paya. Then travel by ferry to ancient Bagan and pile the kids into a shaded horsecart to see the temples and in the evening catch a marionette show at a riverside restaurant.

festivals

Prepare to be doused with cold water during Thingyan, the three-day water festival in April. There's dancing and open-air theatre, too, but the main idea is to soak and be soaked.

cultural issues

Be cautious about discussing Burmese politics with locals, not so much for your safety but for theirs. You should try to simply explain the issues of local politics with your kids.

PHILIPPINES

Filipinos are crazy about kids and rather fond of their parents too. Your children won't be lacking in playmates. Most Filipinos speak excellent English, though accents may take some sorting out for littlies.

You can buy disposable nappies, infant formula and long-life milk in the main towns, but it's best to stock up before straying too far. Most hotels and resorts welcome families with children. Philippine food is not too spicy, and a variety of fresh fruits and vegetables is readily available.

manila

Manila's pollution quickly drives most families away, but in the short time you're likely to be there, check out the kid-friendly Museo Pambata with interactive science exhibits and lots of levers and buttons to keep children busy for hours.

The Chinese Cemetery is more like a miniature town of streets and houses with all the amenities including hot water and air-conditioning. Kids find it more fascinating than macabre.

around the philippines

Impressive to kids and adults alike are the stunning 2000-year-old rice terraces around Banaue, which are like stepping stones to the sky.

Nearer to Manila, and relatively undeveloped, the peaceful beaches of Puerto Galera and rowdier Sabang are great for snorkelling and sailing.

Bohol Island is a short ferry trip from Cebu City, and home to the famous Chocolate Hills, eerie hillocks which make for good hiking in the dry season from December to May. For kids, the best part of little Borocay Island is its dimensions; at 9km long and only 1km wide you can walk across in just 15 minutes. The thing to do here is enjoy the splendid beaches, like White Beach.

Palawan stretches down to the Malaysian state of Sabah and has the strongest ecotourism ethics in the Philippines. The caves and underground river of the St Paul Subterranean National Park are a must for kids. The mouth of the river can be reached by boat or via a two-hour walk along the monkey trail. In the town of Irawan visit the Crocodile Farming Institute – a breeding centre for endangered crocs. There are guided tours for families and it's all free.

books

For a mischievous illustrated folktale, pack a copy of Robert San Souci's *Pedro and the Monkey*.

SINGAPORE

Singapore is a prosperous city-state with a taste of great Asian cultures squeezed into a small, easy-to-get-around package. It is safe and clean beyond reason, and children will discover a surplus of attractions and backstreet delights.

Singapore has an extensive transport network and cheap taxis to boot. Accommodation ranges from guesthouses to colonial throwbacks like the celebrated Raffles. The variety and quality of food is legendary. Sample the best of Chinese, Malay, Indian and European cuisine from lively hawker food stalls.

Cheap food aside, Singapore can quickly bust a family budget. Still, there are nominal discounts for families and you can save a lot by taking advantage of free park and river activities.

practicalities

Infant supplies are widely available. Attitudes toward breastfeeding are positive, and many department stores feature a 'mothers' room'. In public, discretion is the norm.

things to see & do

wild things At the Zoological Gardens, youngsters can breakfast with an orang-utan or ride a pony in one of the world's best zoos. The hugely popular Night Safari allows you to view animals at their most active.

The Jurong Bird Park features a wondrous walk-through aviary with penguins, flamingos and birds of prey atop rainforest perches. Kids can wander around or treat them to a ride on the 1.7km Panorail – a luxurious monorail.

After six exhausting weeks visiting relatives and friends in Germany, the Philippines was our stopover on our way back to Australia. Fourteen days of sun, sand and turquoise waters sounded appealing, so we decided to find a little island to relax. Our choice was Malapascua Island as there was no malaria risk.

philippines LOOKING out for LINUS

Dore Stockhausen and her partner, Marcus Foley, travelled to the Philippines for two weeks with their two-and-a-half-year-old son, Linus.

I had some doubts on arrival in Manila as both Linus and Marcus had caught a nasty virus in Germany. They arrived in the Philippines with fever and nausea. On top of that Marcus had a very painful root-canal infection and had visited a dentist in Germany on several occasions. Would there be any reasonable hospital and dentists in the Philippines? Especially on an island barely 3km long?

I shouldn't have worried. After the first night in polluted Manila they both felt much better. We had pre-booked a hotel room for the first night in the capital, though unfortunately no record of our booking seemed to exist. It took at least an hour to find the heavily guarded ticketing office of Philippine Airlines, not the greatest of joys with a two-and-a-half-year-old, luggage and hot weather.

But we got our tickets and arrived in Cebu City the next day and found a reasonably clean hotel room. Going nappy shopping and acclimatising, Linus and Marcus didn't have the slightest temperature. The toothache disappeared miraculously. Linus learned the most important form of conversation on his first day there – smiling. No matter where we went, people smiled at him and said a few nice words. Although most Filipinos speak excellent English, Linus had trouble understanding them. Consequently he resorted to smiling. We were actually asked if he spoke any English.

In darkness, at 5.30 am the next day we continued our travelling. On arrival at the bus terminal we were immediately surrounded by 10 helpers, who asked our destination then stowed our three pieces of luggage somewhere and shuffled us onto one of the buses. For the four-hour trip we worried for nothing, our backpacks were on the bus. At one of the stops everyone left the bus. We followed. There was a little snack bar and yes, we were a bit thirsty. Bright red or green soft drinks, that was the question. What would Linus like? Linus? I felt as though the blood had drained from my body. He was just standing between us and now he was nowhere. The second day in the Philippines and our child had been kidnapped. Strange that all the locals kept on smiling at us. We had panic written all over our faces, till a nice Filipino led us around the corner. Who was sitting on the lap of the biggest, most tattooed Filipino, sharing peanuts – our small son, pale and happy. A picture made in heaven. Travelling on the bus worried me a little as Linus gets carsick. Fortunately he waited until we reached the bus terminal and all the passengers had left the bus before being sick.

A short trip by boat and we arrived at 'our' beautiful beach with 'our' fantastic hut. As we were travelling out of season we didn't have to pre-book. Three days out of 10, we had the whole resort to ourselves. Linus was spoiled rotten by the female employees. In the mornings his favourite breakfast of mangoes was served (until there weren't any left on the whole island) then he would be carried around and taken into the kitchen. Generally the food was very suitable for kids. Not too spicy and lots of variety. We didn't experience any stomach upsets during our trip.

In the evenings he would be taught such important skills as playing cards and gambling. On our strolls across the island we were shown many beautiful young girls for Linus to marry. But we decided to leave the decision up to him and perhaps wait a few years.

"Linus learned the most important form of conversation on his first day there – smiling. No matter where we went, people smiled at him and said a few nice words."

We enjoyed a wonderful holiday – boating, swimming, snorkelling and relaxing. The night before we were planning to return to Manila a typhoon hit. Its peak winds struck in the middle of the night and Linus didn't wake up once. Marcus and I couldn't possibly sleep. The coconut palms beside us were horizontal and the waves were breaking under our hut. The next morning the wind had calmed down. The beach was scattered with plastic, building materials, coral and a couple of dead dogs. The waves remained huge. We actually wanted to set off on our return trip but as no boat would brave the crossing we were stranded.

The next morning the waves were still huge but despite this a friendly local told us of a fisherman who was going to make the crossing to Cebu City sometime that day, so by lunchtime we had the trip organised. Our flight was leaving that night.

Up and down, up and down, I didn't feel too comfortable in the boat. Linus? At first I thought he had fallen asleep on me, but he was hiding his face in my lap and had decided not to move at all. The captain's big grin and the fact that he had two of his own children on board was reassuring. We survived the crossing and made it in time for our bus and plane. Unfortunately we had a lot of trouble with our airline and ended up spending three boring days in one of Manila's hotel rooms. But that's another story.

pure entertainment The theme-park island of Sentosa is Singapore's answer to a floating Disneyland. There are beaches, cable-car trips and multimedia displays where children learn about Chinese mythology.

activities

Catch a sampan (small boat) and cruise the Singapore River, then dine at one of the floating restaurants at family-oriented Clarke Quay.

parks & playgrounds

The fountain at Bugis Junction is a kid favourite as they duck and dive around the shooting water. Older kids may want to check out the bicycle and in-line skate rentals at East Coast Park and Pasir Ris.

A good place for kids to run around is the green and clean Singapore Botanic Gardens, a combination jungle, orchid garden, jogging and tai chi space – especially enjoyable in the morning.

Visit Bukit Timah Nature Reserve, a beautiful patch of rainforest with giant butterflies and flying lemurs. There are walking and mountain bike trails.

festivals

In December traders along Orchard Rd put on a dazzling light show and shopping malls provide plenty of free, family entertainment leading up to Christmas.

cultural issues

Fines for gum chewing and spitting in public are among the more famous expressions of control in this tightly run society. Even so, Singapore's diverse ethnic communities are lively, tolerant and inviting.

THAILAND

Thais love children, who will find ready playmates among Thai kids and a temporary nanny at practically every stop. Foreign kids under 12 usually pay half the fare or fee for most attractions.

It's a good idea in crowded Bangkok (and other large cities), to have your kids carry the address and phone number of their hotel, written out in Thai – just in case the family becomes separated.

All the usual health precautions apply in Thailand – such as basic hygiene and malaria prevention. Children should especially be warned to avoid playing with animals as rabies is relatively common and you should be aware that smaller children may not always report a bite.

Breastfeeding is common in Thailand, but modesty is expected, so carry a shawl for nursing. Nappies and infant formula are easily found in Bangkok and Chiang Mai.

bangkok

Simply getting around Bangkok can become a family adventure. For a thrill ride in Bangkok traffic, nothing beats a ride in a *tuk-tuk* (motorised three-wheeler), but limit the frequency due to Bangkok's heavy pollution. For more relaxing transport, look to the Chao Phraya River and the surrounding network of canals and river tributaries with many water-oriented homes, trading houses and temples. Floating markets are fascinating, though in Bangkok visitors often outnumber vendors. Try going to an early morning market to keep kids out of the heat and away from the hordes.

things to see & do

wild things Join the Thai families escaping the city chaos at Bangkok's fine and relaxing Suan Sat Dusit (Dusit Zoo), formerly a royal garden, that has a collection of over 300 mammals, 200 reptiles and 800 birds.

On the outskirts of Bangkok, Samphran Elephant Ground & Zoo features elephant 'roundups' and crocodile shows. Safari World is a 5km drive-through park with both African and Asian animals.

interesting & educational Widely known as the Snake Farm, Queen Saovabha Memorial Institute is a serious research facility where kids can watch as venomous snakes are milked daily to make snake-bite antivenins.

Despite the parental tendency to overdo it, children often enjoy visiting 'all those Wats' or temple-monasteries – like the Wat Phra Kaew (Grand Palace) complex. Thai monks tend to be very friendly and tolerant of kids who are free to run around. Take the kids on a river ferry to the Wat Arun (Temple of Dawn) where they can climb halfway up the steps of the 82m tower.

pure entertainment Siam Park, 10km from Bangkok, is a huge and well-managed recreational park with pools, water slides and a wave pool; Saturday is less crowded than Sunday.

The 8th floor of the World Trade Centre contains Bangkok's premier antidote to the tropics, the World Ice Skating Centre. Like most shopping centres in the city, it also has a small children's play centre, including video games.

parks & playgrounds

Lumphini Park is Bangkok's largest and most popular park, with a lake surrounded by wooded areas and walking paths and paddle boats for rent. During kite-flying season (February to April), Lumphini becomes a favoured flight zone, with colourful kites for sale.

around thailand

Chiang Mai is Thailand's second-largest city – a vibrant capital with lively night handicraft markets. A visit to the Young Elephant Training Centre on the road from Chiang Mai to Lampang makes a great day trip. Kids and parents alike can ride the elephants and even feed them fresh fruit in a relatively natural setting.

Thailand's mainland and island coastlines have some of the finest beaches and marine parks in Asia. The islands of Ko Samui, Ko Samet, Ko Pha-Ngan and

Phuket are especially popular, but there are many others to discover.

The well-developed system of national parks includes Khao Sok, where families can sleep in a tree house under limestone crags or explore jungle streams and waterfalls. Khao Yai is Thailand's oldest national park – home to wild elephants and 50km of hiking trails, many formed only by the movement of wildlife through the area.

books

Check your library for a copy of *Thai Tales: Folktales of Thailand* retold by Supaporn Vathanaprida or soothe your own little savage beasties with *Hush!: A Thai Lullaby* by Minfong Ho.

cultural issues

One of the delights of Thailand is the concept of *sanuk* or fun, and anything worth doing – even work – should have a bit of *sanuk*; otherwise it becomes drudgery.

Thai modesty calls for respect in dress and speech. The loud foreigner often gets served last.

VIETNAM

Vietnamese are extremely friendly to Western visitors in general and the presence of foreign children only increases personal contact in a society that pities the unmarried and childless.

The marvellous Vietnamese cuisine offers many variations on standard kid fare – from spring rolls and noodle soup *pho* to baguettes and ice cream. Accommodation around the country is variable, but decent guesthouses and affordable hotels are on the increase as tourism grows.

After decades of war, Vietnam's infrastructure is a work in progress. Domestic air travel is reliable, but other transport is less predictable. The train service is notoriously slow and uncomfortable. Public buses suffer from frequent breakdowns, zero legroom and chronic overcrowding. The salvation for foreigners with impatient kids are the faster and more reliable mini-buses.

Families with younger children must watch out for the frightful traffic and reckless driving, not to mention drive-by 'snatch thieves' or marketplace pickpockets.

Basic infant supplies like nappies and infant formula are available in larger towns. With food and water, the usual precautions apply. Milk is often unpasteurised.

ho chi minh city (saigon) & the south

things to see & do

wild things The city Zoo and Botanical Gardens with their shady, spacious grounds, small lakes and flower beds is a relaxing hit with families, with kiddy rides, a small train and a house of mirrors.

interesting & educational Kids can enjoy water puppet performances at the otherwise sobering War Remnants Museum – the country's most visited reminder of the conflict Vietnamese call the American War.

pure entertainment When the kids are feeling overdosed on pagodas and museums, head for the delightful Saigon Water Park, in a riverside suburb of Ho Chi Minh City. Families can spend an entire day splashing in a variety of pools, fountains and circular streams, or braving a range of water slides. Other newer water parks include Vietnam Water World and Sharks. Or check out Saigon Superbowl near the airport to while away an afternoon or a delayed flight.

activities

In Ho Chi Minh City, a *cyclo* (pedicab) ride around town – with frequent stops for the best ice cream in South-East Asia – can keep an otherwise easily bored child engaged for hours.

In the southernmost region of the country is the Mekong Delta's wetland patchwork of rice paddies, rivers and islands, which kids will love exploring by boat.

Along the central coast, visit the turquoise waters of Nha Trang, the nicest municipal beach in Vietnam, with excellent and easy snorkelling.

hanoi & the north

Hanoi is changing quickly, but most foreigners still find a slow-paced and charming city with lakes and shady boulevards for pleasant walks through colonial architecture.

things to see & do

pure entertainment Hanoi's world-renowned water puppets are a guaranteed hit with adults and younger children, and may even impress an adolescent. There are nightly performances on the shore of Hoan Kiem Lake. At the tranquil Temple of Literature you can inspect second hand puppets on sale.

One Russian tradition that has survived in Vietnam is the Central Circus, featuring talented gymnasts, jugglers and animal trainers. The circus performs nightly in a huge tent near Lenin Park, and also puts on a special children's show every Sunday morning.

activities

Nature-loving kids will like hiking in one of the national parks or nature reserves near Hanoi. Cuc Phuong National Park is the site of the Endangered Primate Rescue Centre, where kids can learn first hand about pressures on the environment and the plight of endangered monkeys.

Halong Bay is one of the natural marvels of Vietnam. Besides the magnificent vistas, youngsters can explore countless caves of all shapes and sizes. Reasonably priced family trips can be arranged easily in Hanoi and the family can sleep on a boat in the bay.

We went to Ho Chi Minh City (Saigon) for the weekend several years ago. That time, people in Ho Chi Minh City were remarkably welcoming of foreigners and foreign children. Now we wanted to go further afield. Overland travel from Phnom Penh brought us to Ho Chi Minh City, we were headed for Hanoi and Hué seemed a logical halfway point.

vietnam LITTLE EMPRESS

Damien Coghlan spent three weeks travelling in Vietnam with his partner, Barbara, and their daughter, Theodora, eight.

At the Saigon Water Park we spent a great day splashing in a wonderful variety of pools and fountains or taking gentle tyre rides in circular streams of slowly moving water. Younger parents (we're both on the wrong side of young) seemed unconcerned about the availability of chiropractors and braved the water slides that ranged from gentle to death-defying. The cafe had food and drinks enough to please the fussiest palate (we explored fussy), and the atmosphere was relaxed and friendly. We'd left our camera behind, but skilful photographers set up, then processed excellent photos of children far faster (and cheaper) than we could. Young wannabes can even pick up some modelling tips – ours did.

Ho Chi Minh City's combined Zoo and Botanical Garden was a hoot, not so much for the animals, but for the shady, spacious grounds, the weird concrete gates to the aquarium and the other children brought there by friendly parents. The parents initiated connections between our child and theirs. Say hello to the foreigner was the name of the game.

At the other end of a very long country, Hanoi provided some quite different experiences. Seeing Ho Chi Minh's body under muted lights and in stony silence, was quite awe-inspiring. Luckily, we'd had a preliminary chat about issues of decorum, because the guards and the oppressively sombre atmosphere were almost enough to precipitate an attack of nervous giggles. This was really serious stuff.

Hanoi's old quarter was like an overcrowded medieval European town with the heating and the volume turned right up. The energy, the intensity and the noise were overwhelming. For the first few hours, we were well and truly stunned – but lolling around a small hotel room soon lost its attraction. Solution? First we went for a walk around the lake and found Fanny's Ice Cream Parlor. That was lovely, helped a little and encouraged us to think about a swim. A few hotels allow outsiders to use their pools, and at the 'Cuban' hotel we had the place to ourselves until early afternoon.

In the dawn light of the next day, the area around the central lake was transformed: no motorbikes, no incessant horns, no *cyclo* bells, no shouting. Thousands of people, old and young, thronged the area around the lake, engaging in every kind of exercise imaginable – and quite a few we'd never have imagined.

There are always a few things to watch out for. Our little vegetarian has a proclivity for pet shops, so she was drawn to big bowls of small, live crabs at the markets. She had a little trouble dealing with the next bit, when handfuls of these cute little things were scooped into a pestle and, right in front of us, were efficiently crushed into paste. Ditto when a local dog vendor paraded his wares, dragging a carcass by the back legs from a container on the back of his bicycle. Travel broadens the mind – and the emotions.

Life wasn't all fur, shell and gristle. Hué gave us a mid-country rest-up in a gentle city that was easy to explore by bicycle. In the ancient citadel, grown-up kids can be dressed up as the emperor or empress, enthroned and photographed. Being emperor for even a couple of minutes was a powerful experience and our daughter wanted takeaway. In the building opposite hard bargaining provided a child-sized *ao dai* (traditional costume) – genuine, beautiful, and very light to pack. Worn to the cafe for dinner that night, the outfit generated enthusiastic comments. The restaurant waitress, not much older than our eight-year-old, asked to show her off, 'have ice cream with my friends' and then disappeared with her into the night on a bicycle. Irresponsible? It didn't feel like it, we'd been in Hué a few days by then. As promised, they came back 20 minutes later – just 15 minutes after we started worrying.

"In the dawn light of the next day, the area around the central lake was transformed: no motorbikes, no incessant horns, no *cyclo* bells, no shouting. Thousands of people, old and young, thronged the area around the lake, engaging in every kind of exercise imaginable – and quite a few we'd never have imagined."

While we were there, it was impossible not to realise that even though life in Vietnam is very hard for most people (including children), people still enjoy having kids around and are more than happy to accommodate them, wherever they're from. Travelling with children is always rewarding, but in Vietnam, it's often also really good fun.

festivals

Besides the difficulty in booking transport and accommodation, the Tet Festival – announcing the arrival of the lunar New Year – is a wonderful time to visit Vietnam. People take extra care to bring good luck for the coming year, and no-no's include sewing, sweeping, swearing and breaking things.

The Mid-Autumn Festival of Trung Thu is celebrated with moon cakes of sticky rice filled with lotus seeds, the yolks of duck eggs, raisins and other ingredients best understood by children, who carry colourful lanterns in the form of boats, dragons and toads in procession accompanied by the banging of drums and cymbals.

books

To get kids in the mood try *A Taste of Earth and Other Legends of Vietnam* by Thich Nhat Hanh or for pre-readers get a copy of Darell HY Lum's *The Golden Slipper* with bright illustrations to impress the littlest traveller.

cultural issues

Never point the bottoms of your feet toward other people or Buddhist statues. In general, shorts are considered inappropriate wear for all but children.

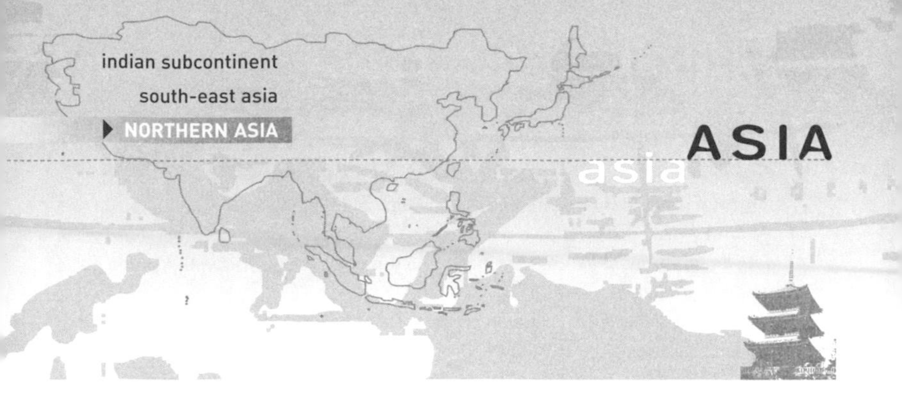

CENTRAL ASIA

Children can be a great icebreaker, but travelling in post–Soviet Central Asia is difficult even for healthy adults. Long journeys between oasis cities and the endless landscapes of the Silk Road are especially trying for children. Despite the difficulties, there are always a few helping hands.

practicalities

Hygiene is patchy and Central Asian food is an acquired taste. But fresh produce is available in season, and naan and rice dishes go down well with most kids.

Accommodations range from overpriced city hotels to friendly guesthouses and charming home-stays. Nappies are available at city department stores, but bring your own medicines. Generally there are few highchairs, car seats or any equipment designed specifically for kids, so be prepared to improvise or bring your own.

things to see & do

In addition to more demanding treks, there are kid-friendly day hikes from bases in Ala Archa Canyon near Bishkek in Kyrgyzstan. Families can arrange a horse trek around the Köl-Say lakes in Kazakhstan or a camel trek through the Karakum Desert in Turkmenistan.

Children like the colourful open-air bazaars reminiscent of the Silk Road caravans such as the popular markets in Bukhara, Uzbekistan. The legendary Kashgar market can be found across the border in Xinjiang, China.

festivals

Navrus (New Days) is Central Asia's main holiday and the best time to see traditional horse races and the wild-beyond-belief sport of *buzkashi* (polo with attitude), dating from the time of Jenghiz Khan.

CHINA

One of the greatest advantages of travelling with children is that you appear almost normal to the locals. People give up seats, help you through a crowd and generally make extra allowances. Nevertheless, the big cities can be hard work with children, so take time to seek out bustling markets, parks with boating lakes and playgrounds.

Travel in China tends to be uncomfortable and uncompromising – picture long distances by train, in hard-seat carriages where everyone smokes and spits. *Xiao laowai* ('little foreigner') and *yang wawa* ('foreign baby') are often prime targets for cheek-pinching and head-patting.

Foreigners are subject to inflated prices all across China and there are few discounts for children. Ridiculous as it may seem, you'll find it worthwhile getting any child an ISIC student card to wave at temple, garden and museum entrance counters.

Infant basics like nappies, formula and medicine are generally available, though the range and quality may be limited. Breastfeeding is not a problem, but in public it will draw inevitable stares from curious eyes.

Chinese food seems to go down well with most foreign children. Infant formula and sweetened cereal is available everywhere, but fresh milk is harder to find. For toddlers not accustomed to chopsticks, bring along plastic spoons.

beijing

things to see & do

wild things The Beijing Zoo got its start as a private garden for the Empress Dowager Cixi who imported 700 animals from Germany for her own amusement. The quality of the zoo hasn't improved much since Cixi's time and – with the exception of the pampered pandas – most animals live in tiny cages with little shade. Kids tend to like the Blue Zoo which features a smallish but well-executed underwater tunnel complete with baby sharks.

pure entertainment The immense Lakeview Water Park features an inner-tube course and a web of twisting and turning water slides. Ritan Park offers bumper cars, miniature golf and swings; the China World Trade Centre has an indoor ice rink; Five Colors Earth in Poly Plaza offers arts and crafts.

activities

Off limits for 500 years, the Forbidden City is China's best-preserved cluster of ancient buildings. Head to the Summer Palace, one of the most popular places to visit in the city, with several lakes and parklands.

Beijing is the jumping-off point for the Great Wall with several walking routes away from the crowds of tourists, including a 4km walk near Huanghua perfect for little legs.

shanghai

Circus acts in China are legendary and Shanghai is home to several troupes whose talents range from magic and mime to clowning and amazing bicycle stunts.

Parks like Ocean World and Jinjiang Amusement Park are popular, and the Botanical Gardens have a children's playground. All department stores and malls have entertainment complexes.

south-west china

Far from the throbbing hubs of Beijing and Shanghai are South-West China's colourful villages, peoples, weekend markets and exciting festivals with folk games, song and dance. After long bus and rail trips, the traveller-friendly centres of Dali and Lijiang in Yunnan Province may well be what the whole family needs: thinner crowds, child-friendly food (like banana porridge), swimming, boat trips, country walks and bike rides.

Though not as famous as the three-day boat ride along the Chang Jiang (Yangzi River) between Chongqing and Wuhan, the six-hour boat trip on the Li Jiang (Li River) between Guilin and Yangshuo is easy on kids and the river is said to resemble a Chinese silk scroll.

around china

China's immense scale is a challenge to family trip planning. Whether you head for the 2000-year-old Army of Terracotta Warriors around Xi'an, or the Yungang Shiku (Cloud Ridge Caves) around Inner Mongolia, consider flying to overcome the enormous distances and save some energy for your children and yourself.

festivals

During the Dragon Boat Festivals held in June, pyramid-shaped packets of glutinous rice wrapped in bamboo or banana leaves are handed out to children and adults alike. Across China, be prepared to stand at a distance if little ears prove sensitive to festival firecrackers.

tibet

This is a region of spiritual wonders, but children need to be prepared for the push and shove of crowds along with fascinating street performers and stalls hawking everything from prayer flags to yak skulls.

Most of Tibet lies on an immense high plateau so altitude sickness can be a major problem for adults and children alike. Tibetan food can take getting used to and sanitation is a problem in many areas. Bring essential medicines and other basics with you. Many hotels have family rooms which normally have three or four beds arranged in two connected rooms.

books & films

Part of the Tintin children's adventure series, *Tintin in Tibet* is a delightful read for small children and parents. Older kids will enjoy the colour and culture of *Kundun* (1997) which follows the life and exile of the 14th Dalai Lama.

The Silk Road – the legendary ancient trade route from China to Europe – was the home to merchants and beggars, kings and thieves, and was also one of the most amazing trips we had ever been on.

uzbekistan

NAPPIES on the SILK ROAD

Tanya Seaward travelled with her husband, Bern, and son Jeremy, 11 months, to Samarkand and Bukhara.

Our family had been living in Moscow for five years, and had decided to return to Canada. We had heard so much about the famed Silk Road, that it seemed a shame to leave the region without seeing it. Many of our friends had been to Samarkand and Bukhara and raved about their beauty and amazing architecture.

I researched the trip by doing a lot of reading in guidebooks and did a lot of asking around in Moscow about the specifics of travelling in Uzbekistan. I even found a couple who had taken their 18-month-old there the previous year. We also consulted a doctor at a travel clinic before the trip. She had excellent advice on vaccinations, food and water, and we felt more reassured after receiving professional advice.

Our itinerary was Tashkent–Samarkand–Bukhara–Khiva, and return to Tashkent by plane. We rented an air-conditioned (absolutely a must!) minivan, which was not terribly expensive, and turned out to be a very convenient way to travel with a baby/toddler. Before we booked the minivan, we told the tourist agency that we were bringing our baby car seat and would need seat belts. We had already learned from our experiences in Moscow that seat belts are not standard options on many Russian vehicles. When the minivan turned up, without seat belts, we were not overly surprised, but nevertheless had to quickly rig up a way to fasten the car seat in. A piece of rope purchased at the local market did the trick, although I wouldn't recommend this as a long-term solution and I'm sure that the car seat manufacturers wouldn't either.

The next transportation hurdle that we had to solve was whether to bring the stroller or the backpack. Our stroller was the sturdy sort, and was already used to bumping and pitching along potholed pavements in Russia. We also felt that it would be more comfortable than the backpack for Jeremy to nap in and would shade him better from the sun.

For accommodation, we stayed in guesthouses the entire trip. The owners were all friendly to Jeremy and accommodating for special requests, such as warming up his cereal in the mornings, arranging for laundry, etc. And all the guesthouses had spacious courtyards, which made for a relatively safe, clean place for Jeremy to stretch his legs when he got tired of the confines of the room. Also, the rooms in the guesthouses all had little fridges, which was handy for storing the fruit and huge, delicious tomatoes that we bought for him along the way.

The Uzbeki people are incredibly friendly towards children and this really added to our enjoyment of the trip. Everywhere we went, people were coming up to us, and smiling and making faces at Jeremy. Jeremy has blond hair and blue eyes, so this created quite a stir with the dark-eyed, dark-complexioned Uzbekis. And despite the language barrier, many local women would bring their babies over to us to 'compare notes' – what sex, what age, and why is he still in nappies. One young woman even brought her newborn out of the house to show us, wrapped up in three or four layers of clothing in the boiling heat! It was also clear that older children have responsibility for looking after younger siblings, as quite often children would approach us, and try different ways to make Jeremy laugh.

"Jeremy has blond hair and blue eyes, so this created quite a stir with the dark-eyed, dark-complexioned Uzbekis. And despite the language barrier, many local women would bring their babies over to us to 'compare notes'."

In Tashkent and Samarkand, we easily found fresh fruit and vegetables, and fresh, delicious naans in the markets. And Jeremy really enjoyed *plov*, the national dish of rice, carrots, raisins and meat. In Bukhara and Khiva, we ate at the guesthouses for breakfast and supper, so safe food was never a concern there. We generally ate lunch out during the day and the vast majority of places we ate I would not consider hygienic enough for children. A few weren't even hygienic enough for adults!

Oddly enough, Jeremy enjoyed carpet shopping in Bukhara. The market was located in an old stone building, that was blissfully cool even on the hottest days. Each vendor would lay out their carpets all over the floor and walls of the little cave-like rooms, and it made a cosy, clean place for Jeremy to crawl around in. And there was no shortage of smiling faces to entertain him while Mum and Dad looked around!

In Khiva, the historic centre was more like a museum than a living centre, as Samarkand and Bukhara are. They have many mini-museums set up in the buildings, with displays and life-size Uzbeki figures. A woman working at one of these displays was so excited to see Jeremy, that she took him and climbed into the display, and they posed there for pictures.

All in all, it was definitely worth the additional planning and time we took to take Jeremy with us. He wasn't able to say so, but I think he had a great time too.

cultural issues

Chinese culture took a beating during the Cultural Revolution, but not the traditional and all-important concept of 'face' and avoiding embarrassment in front of others.

You should remember that despite its holy appearance, Tibet is a Chinese police state and political discussions can invite trouble.

HONG KONG

Except for the dangers posed by traffic, most visitors should have few problems getting around Hong Kong with children. Taxis are cheap and efficient, and the MTR (Mass Transit Railroad) is safe, clean and fast. There is a wide range of Western and Chinese food. Even young sceptics are fascinated by the variety and presentation of dim sum – the uniquely Cantonese small portions of steamed delicacies served in swift succession.

Many hotels offer reduced rates for children and most public transport is half price for kids under 12. Infant formulas, nappies and medicines are widely available throughout Hong Kong. Breastfeeding in public in Hong Kong is not uncommon, but modesty is expected.

things to see & do

wild things The spacious Zoological and Botanical Gardens are one of the world's largest centres for captive breeding of endangered species.

pure entertainment To join Hong Kong kids at play, visit Ocean Park – a modern amusement and marine park with a dragon roller coaster, dolphin shows and a walk-through shark tank. Nearby is Water World with a full array of first-class pools, slides and diving platforms.

activities

There are numerous family-friendly trails on Hong Kong Island, the New Territories and the outlying islands. A favourite itinerary begins with a ride to the top of Victoria Peak aboard the Peak Tram, followed by a hike along the Hong Kong Trail, which passes through Aberdeen Country Park and usually takes longer than a single day. Most little visitors don't leave town without a ride on the Star Ferry, an essential mode of transport for commuters. You should try to take the trip on a clear night if possible for the best views.

festivals

Many of Hong Kong's best festivals take place on the water. At the Tin Hau Festival (April/May), decorated fishing junks sail around the harbour, followed by lion dances and Chinese opera. The Dragon Boat Festival (June) features rowing teams in dazzling boats going at it with intensity.

around hong kong

On Kowloon, the hands-on robotics exhibit at the Hong Kong Science Museum is a kid favourite and at rambling Kowloon Park kids can run around or take a swim. There's not a lot for kids on Macau, but the Hyatt Regency Hotel offers to occupy kids (aged nine to 14) at activity-packed five-day summer camps which include wind-surfing, tennis, rock climbing and theatre.

films

Kung-fu films with Jackie Chan – such as *Young Master* (1980) – blend comedy and martial arts in a good-natured manner, and give kids a glimpse of Hong Kong street life.

JAPAN

Contemporary Japan is a land of striking opposites and kids will be equally intrigued by the hi-tech glitter of crowded Tokyo and the sparsely populated mountain hamlets of another era.

Many Japanese restaurants allow kids to order simply by pointing to look-alike bowls of plastic noodles or gooey desserts in the window display. Children usually love *okonomiyaki* ('cook what you like') as they're armed with their own spatula and chopsticks to fry up their own choices. If this doesn't impress there are plenty of the usual fast food places.

Breastfeeding is accepted without question, though women are so discreet in public that you might not notice them. Make sure you give younger children a Japanese version of their address and phone number.

tokyo

information

Grab a copy of *Japan for Kids* by Diane Wiltshire Kanagawa and Jeane Huey Erickson for a look at kid highlights.

practicalities

Tokyo is one of the world's most expensive cities and can be a real challenge for families on a budget. The kids will enjoy the novelty of eating food from vending machines and you'll appreciate the prices. Try *bento* (boxed lunches) or self-catering to keep costs down. Public transport is usually excellent, but can be expensive. Wherever possible avoid taxis as they can be costly and time-consuming in traffic.

things to see & do

wild things Ueno Zoo features pandas, snow leopards and a great little petting area for the animal-obsessed. For a more peaceful experience try feeding the carp at Yasukuni-jinja or Rikugi-en, which is reputed to have the most beautiful carp in Tokyo. There are daily dolphin shows at Shinagawa

Aquarium and kids can go eye to eye with tuna and sharks at Tokyo Sealife Park.
interesting & educational Devoted especially to kids, the Tokyo Metropolitan Children's Museum has lots of play areas with a hands-on emphasis including pottery, origami and an impressive manga library. Kids love sailing in the ship-shaped Museum of Maritime Science that includes detailed model ships and a pool for piloting remote control submarines. If your kids are into hell on wheels check out the vehicles on display at the Transportation Museum that range from rickshaws to steam engines.
pure entertainment There's bound to be something to put a smile on every young face at the National Children's Castle which has swimming pools, puppet theatres, play areas and organised events. Tokyo Disneyland is always a sure-fire hit with littlies and has a similar layout to the California original. For the real danger ride freaks, there's the thrills of Koraku-en or Toshimaen Amusement Parks. Tokyo also has a huge variety of video game rooms around the city, but for cutting edge games treat the kids to a visit to the Sony building where they can test the latest games if they can wait in the longest queues.

activities

Check out a sumo bout at Ryogoku Kokugikan or a baseball game at the Tokyo Dome. For the more active kids there are traditional sports like aikido, judo, karate and kendo.

parks & playgrounds

Right next door to an amusement park is Koishikawa Koraku-en, a beautiful, 17th-century garden that shows off classic Japanese landscaping. For a bit of healthy exercise try a walk through the wild woods and swamps of the Nature Study Garden.

around japan

Nothing symbolises Japan more than the venerated Mt Fuji though the climb might be too much for tots. They'll prefer the Fuji Five Lakes even if it's just for the amusement parks. There's spectacular hiking and great skiing in Daisetsuzan National Park to escape the big city crowds. To give them a look at Japan's history visit the palaces and temples of Kyoto or Nagasaki's A-bomb Museum, a powerful memorial to the nuclear destruction of 1945.

books & films

You won't have to work to hard to get your kids interested in Japanese *anime* (animated films) with *Digimon: The Movie* (2000) and the Pokémon series making the genre popular worldwide. Older children may enjoy *Mononoke Hime* (1999), which is set in a traditional Japanese setting. For books, pre-teens will enjoy *Shipwrecked: The True Adventures of a Japanese Boy* by Rhoda Blumberg. Also have a look at illustrator Mark Crilly's Akiko series that starts with *The Menace of Alia Rellapor*.

cultural issues

Japanese are generally gracious and forgiving when it comes to slip-ups by foreigners, but your attempts to follow social conduct will be appreciated. Kids enjoy learning the varieties of bowing and you should bear in mind that being direct is not a virtue in Japan. In discussion silence seldom signifies agreement.

KOREA

Koreans tend to be hospitable but not overbearing and your children will often be invited to join in play. Korea is also one of the easiest Asian countries to navigate for travelling families. Transport is uniformly reliable and cheap. Hotels are plentiful, but traditional *yogwan* guesthouses are charming alternatives.

practicalities

Infant supplies are widely available in Seoul and most other cities. Breastfeeding in public will attract curious eyes only because a foreign child is involved.

seoul

Amid the mega-modern and appealingly ancient sites of Seoul, it's good to know that you are never far from a park, often in the popular palace areas, where children can run around.

things to see & do

Seoul's Lotte World is a rambling kid-tropolis with ice skating, swimming, shopping and more. Children's Grand Park offers kiddy rides, ponds and a small zoo. The tasteful Korean Folk Village features pottery and weaving workshops for older kids, a marketplace and Confucian school.

around korea

The Korean peninsula is easy to explore, and national parks like Puk'ansan and Songnisan feature family-friendly walking trails through spectacular landscapes.

Skim along the coast for a three-hour hydrofoil ride through Hallyo Haesang National Marine Park, stopping briefly at the islands or main towns along the way.

festivals

One of the most beautiful festivals to celebrate with Koreans is Buddha's Birthday, when worshippers illuminate their prayers by hanging paper lanterns and candles in temples.

books

Follow as average week of a young Korean girl in Patricia McMahon's *Chi-Hoon: A Korean Girl*, while younger readers will love the cheeky illustrations of *The Green Frogs: A Korean Folktale*, retold by Yumi Heo.

cultural issues

Koreans are naturally curious, and questions about your children and relatives (present and past) are commonplace.

TAIWAN

Children will be a constant source of attention, opening up plenty of opportunities to interact with Taiwanese families. There are also discounts for children at most public places and there are no special health considerations for children.

However, Taiwanese cities are heavy on traffic and crowds, and short on parks and public playgrounds. Most children attend afternoon cram schools and have little time to play.

Baby food is available everywhere. A foreigner breastfeeding her baby will attract some attention, but mostly from curious mothers.

things to see & do

interesting & educational If you're short of time forget about finding interactive displays at Taipei's excellent National Palace Museum and limit a visit with children to a morning or afternoon. Visit the amazing and carnival-like Huahsi Night Market, better known as Snake Alley, where skilled snake handlers play with live cobras as if they were affectionate house pets.

pure entertainment In Taipei, the Children's Recreation Center features kiddy rides and science displays. The underwater passage at Fin's Sealife Tapei gets good reviews from kids.

activities

At the Alishan mountain resort, take a day hike on the easy Alishan Loop past Two Sisters Ponds, a few temples and the Sacred Tree which is said to be 3000 years old. There are more good walking trails at Taroko National Park on the east coast.

books

New readers will get an introduction to modern Taiwanese culture with Priscilla Wu's *The Abacus Contest: Stories from Taiwan and China.*

cultural issues

What seems to be Taiwanese materialism is more about gaining 'face' or prestige through possessions. Flattery is one way of giving your host face and of course any flattery is expected to be modestly deflected.

canada

NORTH AMERICA

Travelling in the USA and Canada can be rewarding for kids and parents – whether they're sampling the wonders of the West or visiting the busy urban theme parks from coast to coast. Whether your family chooses to drive, fly, take a bus or train, just getting around will be part of the adventure. Travel in both the US and Canada is generally easy, safe and affordable. Sunday newspapers usually have extensive listings of local family-oriented activities, exhibits and festivals.

Accommodation varies from state to state, but family rates are commonly available. Motel chains often advertise that 'kids stay free', though there may be a small charge for an extra rollaway bed or baby crib. Camping grounds cater to families and facilities are often generous – playgrounds, swimming pools, games, etc. Some hostels can handle families, but B&Bs are generally for couples. Vacation homes and condos (apartments) are available in most states, usually found on the Web, or through local Convention & Visitors Bureaus. Laundry facilities are available in every town, and at many motels and camping grounds.

Most eateries in both countries have highchairs or booster seats. Unlike the US, however, few Canadian restaurants have children's menus. Of course, eating out all the time can get expensive in a hurry. Many motels offer kitchenettes where you can do a bit of cooking or at the very least take care of breakfast. If not a kitchenette, a small refrigerator may be available, so even if the family goes out to eat you can bring home the leftovers. Almost any restaurant in every price range is happy to do this.

Breastfeeding in public should not be a problem though discretion is recommended. Because of rare instances making the news where mothers have been asked to leave a public place for breastfeeding, many states have legislation pending that protects the right of a mother to nurse her baby in public. Such action is also pending in the US Congress for government buildings and tourist spots. In Canada, successful campaigns have been carried out nationwide to support breastfeeding-friendly restaurants, stores and other environments, and to encourage women to breastfeed 'anywhere, any time'. In some settings there are nursing rooms or special areas available where women can comfortably nurse their children.

Driving is still the easiest way to get around, especially in the west. Good public transport is available, but often limited due to the tendency of Americans to rely on the automobile. Rental car agencies rent by the day or week, and weekend rentals (usually Thursday to Monday) offer some of the best deals. It's required by law in most states to have car seats for all children under four years of age, or less than 40 pounds (approx 18kg) in weight.

Amtrak has an extensive rail and bus system throughout the US and most trains have a two-deck viewing car which helps kids pass the time. Canada's VIA Rail operates a transcontinental train which rolls across some spectacular landscapes between Vancouver and Montreal. Both systems offer good-value passes for families.

Supermarkets are the most common source of supplies for infants and toddlers: nappies, baby food, bottles, fresh milk, formula and over-the-counter medicines such as children's aspirin or cold remedies. Pharmacies, in addition to medicines, will also have nappies, sunscreen, etc. Baby carriages (prams), strollers and backpacks are found at children's shops, department stores or large discount chain stores like Wal-Mart or K-Mart. International visitors may be met with blank stares when asking for nappies, which are known throughout North America as diapers.

ALASKA

Camping is relatively cheap and the best of Alaska – like hiking and wildlife watching – is free. Children aged two to 11 receive a 50% discount on the Alaska Marine Hwy ferries and infants travel free. The Alaska Railroad and bus companies extend decent discounts to kids – as do museums, national and state parks.

anchorage

things to see & do

wild things Put the family in a glass-domed car of the Alaska Railroad and head north to the wilderness and Denali State National Park, where it's easy to spot moose, caribou, wolves and brown bears.

interesting & educational The Alaska Native Heritage Center is devoted to the history and arts of Native Alaskans. A half-mile (1km) trail passes a smokehouse and carving shed. Inside exhibits include splitting and drying salmon, or sewing animal skin boats.

The Alaska State Museum is a showcase of Alaskan heritage, but the most impressive sight for kids is the full-size eagle's nest that sits on top of a tree surrounded by a circular staircase.

Twenty-five miles (40km) east of Anchorage at the Valdez Museum, kids can view oil-spill exhibits and a model of the controversial Alaska pipeline.

south-east alaska

things to see & do

A cruise through the Inside Passage waterway is a trip to remember for a lifetime. You can board an Alaska Marine Hwy ferry in Bellingham, Washington, and then cruise the 14 ports from Ketchikan to Haines. Along the way you can jump ship for a day or two to watch whales, hike, go kayaking or check out a frontier town. If you want to take under-fives on a wilderness trip, consider a rental cabin in Tongass National Forest. Most cabins are reached via a float plane, an exciting beginning for any child.

Near the scenic capital Juneau, kids can watch brown bears snatch leaping salmon out of the air at Admiralty Island. For true hiking beginners, Juneau Parks & Recreation rangers conduct family hikes.

CALIFORNIA

Getting around California with kids is easy, but the distances are great. Public transport is limited, though Greyhound offers weekly Ameripass tickets, and children receive a 50% discount.

san francisco & northern california

information

In the San Francisco Bay Area, look for the free *Parents' Press* monthly paper, for family resources.

things to see & do

wild things At Pier 39 near Fisherman's Wharf in San Francisco, kids love watching the sea lions that gather daily to soak up the sun – or fog. Across the bay, the very walkable Oakland Zoo is especially good for young children with an outdoor eating area, animals to feed and pet, pony rides and a sky ride chairlift.

State and national parks dot the coastal and mountain areas. Point Reyes National Seashore and Point Lobos State Reserve are great for spotting exotic shore birds and watching sea lions up close. For family camping, try Calaveras Big Trees State Park in the Sierra Nevada mountains where children can spot woodpeckers and walk through a tree-tunnel in a magnificent giant sequoia grove.

interesting & educational The art and science Exploratorium in San Francisco is enormously popular, especially the pitch black Tactile Dome that kids can crawl, climb and slide through. The Zeum is a cool combo of art and technology, where kids from eight to 18 can create and see their own video productions in the Performing Arts Lab.

Berkeley's Habitot Museum has construction and well-supervised art activities for very young children. Down the coast at the Monterey Bay Aquarium, kids can press their noses against a two-storey tank filled with jellyfish, sharks and other graceful creatures of the deep. The old prison at Alcatraz is a popular ferry trip for families, but you can't leave the kids there.

pure entertainment At the northern end of Oakland's Lake Merritt, Children's Fairyland is a low-key delight dating from the 1950s (and an early inspiration for Disneyland) featuring fairy-tale displays, puppet shows and rides.

Around San Jose, Raging Waters theme park offers adrenaline-rush rides, while Paramount's Great America offers similar thrills while re-creating action scenes from blockbuster movies like *Top Gun* and the Star Trek adventures. The Boardwalk in Santa Cruz is an old-fashioned and affordable amusement park with rides for both small children and older kids.

parks & playgrounds

San Francisco's Golden Gate Park and smaller Dolores Park have good playgrounds with climbing structures and merry-go-rounds. The Marina Green on the bay is perfect for kite flying and playing catch. Berkeley Marina's one-of-a-kind Adventure Playground is a kid-designed rambling fort with hammers, saws and paints to continue the work.

los angeles & southern california

things to see & do

wild things The excellent San Diego Zoo features more than 3000 animals, representing over 800 species, in a beautifully landscaped setting. At the animal nursery, children can glimpse the zoo's newest arrivals. The Los Angeles Zoo overlooks the city from Griffith Park. Highlights include a walk-through aviary and Adventure Island children's zoo.

interesting & educational The Dinosaur Hall at the Natural History Museum of LA County is a crowd pleaser, along with the giant farm at the museum's Insect Zoo. For a lively introduction to Hispanic culture, take the kids to downtown LA's bustling Olivera Street, a one-block open-air Mexican market since the 1930s.

pure entertainment Southern California's amusement parks are legendary and Disneyland is the still the fairest of them all. In Fantasyland's Toon Town, young kids can still pose with Mickey Mouse.

Nearby Knott's Berry Farm is a delightful Old West amusement park with gold-panning demonstrations and staged gun fights. Universal Studios Hollywood offers a great glimpse into the world of make-believe and special effects, plus they have cool and scary thrill-rides like *Back to the Future* and *Jurassic Park*.

Legoland, between LA and San Diego, is geared to small children, but parents often seem to have trouble keeping their hands off the little plastic bricks. There are bicycles to ride around, and boat tours of the bigger exhibits.

activities

For dinosaur lovers, there's the La Brea Tarpits, whose bubbling black pools were a trap for animal life since the last ice age. Families can watch the ongoing excavations, plus there are low-cost sleepovers requiring only a sleeping bag and a torch (flashlight).

parks & playgrounds
Nestled in the Hollywood Hills, Griffith Park is the nation's largest city park, with a 1926 carousel, pony rides and picnicking. The Santa Monica Pier features carnival-style rides overlooking the Pacific Ocean.

festivals
Around the end of January, Chinese New Year kicks off with parades, food and fireworks – especially in San Francisco and Los Angeles. Cinco de Mayo on 5 May celebrates Mexican culture and history with festive parades in San Diego, Los Angeles, San Francisco and other sizeable Hispanic communities.

FLORIDA

Florida is very kid-friendly – it's hard not to be with all those beaches. But Florida also has forests, lakes and parks galore, where there's camping, hiking, biking, canoeing and an incredible diversity of wildlife.

miami
information
Friday's *Miami Herald* newspaper has a pullout section called *Weekend*. The excellent *Places to Go with Children in Miami & South Florida* by Cheryl Juárez and Deborah Johnson is great for keeping the little darlings calm and entertained.

things to see & do
wild things Miami's Metrozoo is first class, a natural habitat where animals have plenty of space to move around. Take the Zoofari Monorail for a great orientation tour. The excellent Miami Seaquarium goes overboard to preserve, protect and explain aquatic life.
interesting & educational Miami's Historical Museum of Southern Florida is excellent for kids with exhibits ranging from prehistoric Florida to a beautifully restored Miami trolley circa 1920. The Miami Museum of Science & Space Transit Planetarium is a total treat for kids, with over 100 hands-on exhibits.

activities
For swimming or lounging about, Miami's classy Venetian Pool is hard to duplicate. It's a fantastic spring-fed pool with caves and waterfalls that kids will love exploring.

parks & playgrounds
South Pointe Park in Miami Beach is a wonderful place to spend a sunny afternoon with a good playground, fishing pier, short boardwalk and very nice beach. Trendy Ocean Drive is fun for people-watching on a family walk, or you can rent bikes and cruise the boardwalk on wheels.

When my dad asked me if I'd like to go California with him, alone, I didn't take him seriously. I have three sisters and a brother, who I knew would all be insanely jealous. My dad is a foreign correspondent and we have travelled all over Europe, war-torn or not, but America had always seemed a no-go holiday area. Too expensive is what my mum always says, but I know she's just scared of the flight.

california ONLY in AMERICA

Twelve-year-old Ben Judah accompanied his father, Tim, on a two-week business trip to California.

Despite that, a few weeks later, I was waiting in a half-empty departure lounge, anxiously playing my Game Boy and hoping my plane wasn't going to splat into the middle of the Atlantic. The flight was great and at last I had a chance to see the movie *South Park: Bigger, Longer & Uncut* (for age 15 and over!). During the 11-hour flight I talked with my dad so much that I got a sore throat which didn't go away until the following morning.

My first surprise after we had negotiated our way out of Los Angeles International Airport was to come face to face with a huge department store called the Erotic Megastore. Next door was a huge Dunkeroo Donuts, complete with six-foot-high spinning doughnut. These were my first impressions of an entirely new continent. We checked into the Standard Hotel, on Sunset Boulevard, and as soon as we got to the room I passed out from jet lag.

We woke up at four in the morning LA time, because of the time change. Dad had an incredible craving for a doughnut, but the Dunkeroo Donuts in central LA was closed. So we went to examine Beverley Hills. At six in the morning, it was full of Hispanic servants cleaning convertibles. By 10 we had been to Santa Monica and had an ice cream on a completely deserted beach.

That evening we visited the Mann's Chinese Theater where most of the early movies were premiered. On the pavement outside is the walk of fame, which is set with more than 2000 polished marble stars, bearing the names of stars I'd never heard of. The thought of the glory of having my name on this pavement suddenly faded as my dad said that anybody who works in Hollywood can have his name on it for a mere US$7500! I decided to give Hollywood – as a career – a miss.

I was very pleased to have spent an entire day with my dad and realised how much I'd learnt about him as a real person – not just someone who nags me to get out of bed and tidy up. I didn't even give a thought to the rest of my family.

The next day we hired a car and set off for the San Fernando Valley about 50 miles (80km) away – an eight-lane motorway the whole way! We were visiting my distant cousin who lived in what my dad said was a large suburb. When we arrived in the San Fernando Valley I realised this wasn't a large suburb – this was suburb city! Living here must drive you mad, I thought. My cousin showed off his car, house, pool, shed, three-year-old daughter and even his microwave. The visit wasn't a waste of time as it turned out his wife worked for Universal Studios Hollywood theme park to which she gave us free tickets.

Universal Studios Hollywood had some really original rides. The Jurassic Park ride has to be the best, having to avoid the dinosaurs as you plummet down a water chute. It was great to go a theme park that wasn't all about Mickey Mouse. I loved Disneyland though. Well, everyone does, don't they? The rides are far more exciting than Disneyland Paris and I didn't think it was as commercial – if that's possible!

Dad was determined to go to Death Valley because my aunt had been there. Nobody told me it was a four-and-a-half hour drive. We shot past a couple of Las Vegas clones and then Trona – a real industrial hell, where there was so much pollution I had to shut the window to stop coughing. We passed the entrance to Edwards Air Force Base – landing site for the space shuttle – and all along the route were signs to military sites with a different number for each one. It was like the 'X-Files'. I wondered where they kept the aliens. At 11 at night we arrived at a small ranch hotel. There were more stars than I had ever seen before and cows mooing in the distance.

"We passed the entrance to Edwards Air Force Base – landing site for the space shuttle – and all along the route were signs to military sites with a different number for each one. It was like the 'X-Files'. I wondered where they kept the aliens."

The next morning my dad had to work. I was sent off on a three-hour horse ride round Death Valley. My first thought was that horse riding was very sissy, but since there was nobody from school in a thousand-mile radius I decided to risk it. The trek went up a cliff, through sand dunes and down a ravine but I couldn't really enjoy the amazing scenery because I was wrestling with my horse, which refused point blank to move and at one moment nearly threw me off a cliff!

I was exhausted after my horse ride and slept most of the long drive back to LA International Airport. I could have settled down quite happily in California, but even though it was great travelling with Dad, I realised that I really missed my family back home.

around florida

In Orlando, the newest venture at Walt Disney World is the realistic Animal Kingdom, where visitors go on safaris, riverboat rides and trails to see wild animals up close. The Magic Kingdom is still home to Cinderella's Castle, but newer attractions include Alien Encounter and Space Mountain – a wild roller-coaster ride through space that is usually more terrifying for parents than kids. A variation on the Disney World theme is the Orlando Science Center, which has an overnight program for families.

On the East Coast the Kennedy Space Center is among the most popular attractions, where kids can feel the powerful sensation of the Apollo 8 lift-off in a reassembled control room. At Titusville, the US Space Camp has cool overnight programs for kids.

Busch Gardens in Tampa is an African-themed thrill park with upside-down roller coasters. Take the kids on the Skyride which passes over the park's Serengeti Plain's 80-acre (32 hectare) habitat populated by giraffes, zebras, hippos, lions and camels.

There are terrific zoos in Florida, but no kid should leave the state without seeing a bit of Florida wildlife for real. Everglades National Park is the crown jewel, but several state parks are well worth a family outing. The name alone should attract kids to Corkscrew Swamp Sanctuary on the Gulf Coast north of Naples, and at Myakka River State Park near Sarasota, the big draw is the 70-person airboat ride through a dense wetland preserve with alligators and exotic birds.

THE GREAT LAKES

The Great Lakes region (Michigan, Illinois, Ohio, Indiana, Wisconsin and Minnesota) of the country's Midwest includes boxy urban centres and rolling rural plains, but the 'Windy City' of Chicago is still the gritty city that holds it together.

chicago

information

Check out the 'Friday Guide' of the *Chicago Tribune*, and 'Weekend' in the *Chicago Sun-Times* for family-friendly places to go with kids.

things to see & do

wild things At the Shedd Aquarium, the multi-level Oceanarium is a spectacular space where huge mammal pools seem to blend into the lake outside the floor-to-ceiling windows. The compact Lincoln Park Zoo is a Chicago favourite, and it's free.

interesting & educational The Field Museum of Natural History has a bit of everything from everywhere, including Egyptian mummies, Native American artefacts, dinosaurs and more dinosaurs – especially one named Sue, the best preserved skeleton of a Tyrannosaurus Rex yet unearthed. To see the sky at the Adler Planetarium and Astronomy Museum, you head underground. Interactive exhibits allow kids to glory in simulated cosmic events such as a meteor smashing into the earth.

activities

Although the most famous view of the elegant Chicago skyline is from the Sears Tower Skydeck, a similar experience awaits families at the John Hancock Centre, which benefits from having much shorter lines, along with a zippy 40-second ride to the 94th floor.

parks & playgrounds

At the popular Navy Pier, kids can take their chances dodging (or not) scores of water jets which squirt at unpredictable intervals or ride a 150-foot (45m) Ferris wheel. In the summer the large public pool at Holstein Park is refreshing and even rents swim suits. So that excuse is out.

around the great lakes

Indiana Dunes National Lakeshore has decent beaches and wetland hiking trails, and it's only about an hour by train from Chicago. In Ohio, Cleveland's lively Rock & Roll Hall of Fame & Museum pays homage to the roots of rock with some dazzling interactive exhibits ranging from Motown to hip-hop.

HAWAII

The spirit of aloha is alive and well, especially when it comes to children. Hawaiians love kids and there are outdoor activities from surfing to horseback riding, along with cool sightseeing attractions for *keikis* (children) of all ages. Hawaii has a wide range of accommodation, from breezy seaside camping to luxury digs with daily programs for children.

information

Check out the Friday 'TGIF' ('Thank God It's Friday') insert of the *Honolulu Advertiser*, and the free *Honolulu Weekly* for updates of family activities around Oahu. Even the numerous free tourist magazines distributed on the islands are worth a look for maps and discount coupons to everything from fish sandwiches to sunset cruises.

honolulu

things to see & do

wild things In Kapiolani Park young children enjoy the patting area of the small Honolulu Zoo. The nearby Waikiki Aquarium has a touch tank geared specifically for children. At Hanauma Bay Park kids can glimpse schools of parrotfish and other colourful reef inhabitants glistening in the turquoise waters beneath a rugged volcanic ring.

interesting & educational The fine Bishop Museum has a bit of everything, from ancient Hawaiian temple images and shark-toothed war clubs to barter items brought to the islands by Yankee traders of the 19th-century. Twice daily, families can enjoy demonstrations of Hawaiian quilting and lei making, or take in a Hawaiian music and hula performance.

The Hawaii Maritime Center on Honolulu Harbor's Pier 7, is home to the double-hulled sailing canoe *Hokulea* which was built to retrace the routes of early Polynesian seafarers. Older kids used to everything electric are often fascinated to learn about the age-old methods of navigation and survival at sea.

activities

The safest beaches for families of small children are generally on the leeward (south-facing) side of the islands. Besides famous Waikiki and Diamond Head, try little Sans Souci Beach with outdoor showers and a lifeguard station. Older kids can take surfing lessons and boogie boarding is easy for youngsters to learn in the gentle swells of Waikiki.

From November to March, take the kids and a camera to the island's north shore to watch big-wave surfers go for it at Sunset and Waimea beaches, where the north swells of winter can produce 20- to 30-foot (6–9m) waves on any given day.

parks & playgrounds

Beach parks are hard to miss in Hawaii, but the combination of grass and sand at Ala Moana Park near Waikiki is popular with families and the calm ocean lagoon is perfect for wading and easy swimming.

around hawaii

On the Big Island, Hawaii Volcanoes National Park is a true wonder and still growing – lava continues to creep slowly to the sea from the active Puu Oo vent. The Park's Crater Rim Road is a pristine path through lava flows past, present and future. Kids especially like walking through the Thurston Lava Tube with a flashlight. At the Kilauea Visitor Center, children sit spellbound at the Nature Center's popular short film of the volcano's fiery history and there is a junior ranger day program for children five to 12.

Snorkelling south of Kailua-Kona is spectacular, safe and accessible for kids. Kahaluu Beach teems with colourful fish and is especially good for beginners. Whales can often be spotted from the shore, especially along the west coast of Maui. To get even closer, take one of the whale-watching cruises or hop on the 24-passenger Maui-Lanai ferry.

In the old whaling town of Lahaina, the Old Lahaina Luau is one of the few such attractions available to tourists that is not a total family rip-off. The seaside setting is idyllic, the food is plentiful and the entertainment includes traditional hula dancing.

Teenagers old can join the group of cyclists who gather at the top of 10,000-foot (3000m) Haleakala for the thrill of coasting 38 miles (61km) down the winding mountain road. Bikes are modified with special safety brakes and each group is followed by an escort van.

A drive to Waimea Canyon Lookout will confirm why Kauai is called the Garden Isle.

NEVADA & THE SOUTH-WEST

Living deserts and snowy peaks, high mesas and meditative plateaus fill the vast south-west sky over Nevada, Utah, Arizona and New Mexico. Kids will know neon-lit Las Vegas, but there are cactus-filled deserts, limestone caves and ski trails – along with the magnificent Grand Canyon and the USA's oldest capital, Santa Fe, a centre for south-west Native American culture.

las vegas

Traditionally, downtown Las Vegas and The Strip existed for gamblers, and most casinos preferred that you left the little ones at home. Lately, the city has made a big effort to lure families to the city, and rugrats are nearly as common as ratpack gamblers. Kids are welcome, except perhaps in serious gaming areas.

information

Despite the many 'Tourist Information' signs posted around town, the city's only true tourist office is the Las Vegas Convention & Visitors Authority just inside the Las Vegas Convention Center.

practicalities

Even Las Vegas has real neighbourhoods with supermarkets and well-stocked pharmacies that provide all the necessities for infants and toddlers – from diapers and baby food to simple medications.

Childcare is available on The Strip, and the cost is reasonable; the operators assume they'll get your money in other ways. Three hotels in town have childcare centres: the Gold Coast, the MGM Grand and the Orleans. All others encourage parents to contact childcare agencies such as Around the Clock Childcare and Precious Commodities.

things to see & do

interesting & educational The Las Vegas Natural History Museum sports full-size dinosaur models and a diorama of Nevada's flora and fauna. The nearby Lied Discovery Children's Museum houses a giant bubble-making device and other hands-on exhibits for kids aged three to 12.

pure entertainment Few people cruising The Strip overlook the Circus Circus hotel-casino-cum-theme park. Animals, acrobats and magicians perform from

11 am to midnight daily for free. Adventuredome is a rambling amusement park enclosure within Circus Circus, with everything from kiddy aeroplanes and free clown shows to the Extreme Zone for the young and brave.

The 26-acre Wet 'n' Wild water is the coolest place on The Strip from early May through to September, featuring more than a dozen slides, chutes, floats and a simulated white-water rafting adventure.

activities

The Scandia Family Fun Center is a family amusement centre a few blocks west of The Strip, featuring three 18-hole miniature golf courses, bumper boats, batting cages, midget Indy cars and more than 200 video arcade games.

around the south-west

Las Vegas is a good base for exploring the Grand Canyon in Arizona and Death Valley in California. And just 20 miles west of The Strip, the contrast between the glitzy brightness of Vegas and the natural splendour of Red Rock Canyon couldn't be greater.

An hour's drive away, Lake Mead has 500 miles (800km) of beautiful shoreline with good swimming and boating spots. At graceful Hoover Dam, older kids like the 30-minute power plant tour.

Utah's Zion and Bryce Canyon national parks offer great hikes through otherworldly rock formations. The Museum of Indian Arts & Culture in Santa Fe is a great introduction to the rich native history of the region.

NEW ENGLAND

The six states of New England – Massachusetts, Rhode Island, Connecticut, Vermont, New Hampshire and Maine – have preserved much of their 'Early America' character. Most of the area is ideal for exploring with children. There's something for everyone from graceful farms and villages to rugged and dramatic coastlines, granite mountain ranges and thousands of glacial lakes and ponds.

boston

information

Kidding around Boston by Helen Byers and *Kids Explore Boston* by Susan D Moffat are both useful books for parents.

things to see & do

wild things Whale sightings are practically guaranteed at Stellwagen Bank, a fertile feeding ground 25 miles (40km) out to sea. The enormous humpback whales are awesome, breaching and frolicking, and in the spring and fall, huge pods of dolphins make their way to and from their summer holidays in the Arctic. Regular tours are easily organised.

interesting & educational An area of restored old brick buildings known as the Museum Wharf is the waterfront home to the Boston Tea Party Museum, where children enjoy the re-enactment of dumping bales of tea into the harbour. Nearby the Museum of Science is serious hands-on fun, especially the lightning-bolt generator. Next door, the most popular exhibit at the Computer Museum is the enormous, functional Walk-Through Computer.

The iconic giant white milk bottle on Fort Point Channel is the only sign necessary for this delightful Children's Museum. Children of all ages can be entertained for an entire day with interactive exhibits, bubble displays, dress-up areas and a two-storey climbing gym.

pure entertainment The Salem Willows Amusement Park, 20 miles (32km) north-east of Boston, features safe beaches, children's rides and games, and short harbour cruises.

activities

The New England Aquarium is teeming with sea creatures of all sizes, shapes and colours. A giant, cylindrical saltwater tank swirls with over 600 creatures, including turtles, sharks and eels. Kids will love Boston Harbor with its ferries to nearby Georges Island and the old sailing schooner, the *Liberty Clipper*.

books

Robert McCloskey's *Make Way for Ducklings* is a delightful story set in Boston, and a great read for small children. Check out the statues in Boston Public Garden that immortalise these lovable characters.

around new england

Salem offers a glimpse of the Salem Witch Trials of 1692, a dark chapter in American history which often appeals to children's gruesome curiosity. Down the coast, explore the sandy dunes of Cape Cod or visit a re-created 19th-century working coastal town in Connecticut's Mystic Seaport Museum.

North of Boston, take the kids for a ride on an antique steam train to the top of New Hampshire's Mt Washington; sample the great maple syrup in Vermont; then explore the rugged granite-and-pine coast of Maine.

NEW YORK

When most people think of New York, it's the city of skyscrapers that comes to mind. But there is no end of things for children to do across the state.

new york city

New York City has it all for kids, from the Statue of Liberty and the Empire State Building to neighbourhood parks and subway musicians. Several museums are dedicated to children, and travelling circuses never miss New York.

Our daughter, Ava, was going to camp for a week so we decided it was a good opportunity to do something worthwhile with our son, Trevor. At 14, he was pretty hard to impress and didn't seem overly enthusiastic about the plan Colleen and I had hatched. Or at least it appeared that way. At his age true feelings and outward manifestations are not always in sync.

new hampshire on TREVOR'S TRAIL

Mark Lightbody and his wife, Colleen, went hiking for a week in New Hampshire with their 14-year-old son, Trevor.

We wanted to do something alone with him that we couldn't do with his younger sister, something suited to his age and a challenge. We decided on hiking peaks in the White Mountains of New Hampshire. It was an area Colleen and I knew something about from a visit many, pre-child years ago.

After sketching a plan, we showed Trevor the details, looked at maps and listed our mutual equipment and supply needs. We had him select his own clothes and personal supplies, and then divided up the gear. With the packs all loaded Trevor's was heaviest. All he said was 'No sweat'. Colleen and I realised we'd hit a new phase and it held promise. Forget sherpas.

The park warden recommended arriving before 9 am so we got up at 4 am (Trev loved that!) and drove from Montreal. We breezed through customs and made the camping ground in time to grab one of the few remaining sites.

With chores shared and completed, we tuned up the legs and lungs on a short trail. Later around a quick campfire we joked about tomorrow's adventure. Being alone with one child totally changes the family dynamic and we all enjoyed each other's company and a chance to talk. The absence of the usual bickering and teasing all parents of siblings know, wasn't missed.

With morning came the disheartening patter of rain on taut nylon. I beelined to the lodge for the latest weather service bulletin only to read rain and relentless heavy cloud for the next million days with a chance of something slightly better for the next day only. We all thought briefly (but silently) of quitting but headed for the trail head in the drizzle.

Totally alone, we soon discovered this was no manicured path. Aside from the steepness, the muddy trail was endlessly twisted, strewn with rocks of every size and crisscrossed with roots and stumps. Impressively, Trevor dug in. We climbed for hours, stopping regularly to peel off more clothes. We couldn't tell if the clinging wetness was sweat or rain. By mid-afternoon we arrived at the camping area. Stumbling across the slippery rocks to the wooden tent platforms dispersed amongst the trees was like entering a magical world. Trevor picked up on it right away saying, 'It's like the land of the gnomes.' Dripping tree branches hung down, a smiling, straggly-haired munchkin-hiker ambled by and two women swaying in hammocks said, with strong French accents, 'You made it, there are empty platforms further along. Pick one you like.'

As we pitched camp, a lanky, humorous Webmaster from Boston strolled up and started chatting, informing us that his stove had died, what that had done to his dinner and what his plans were. Trevor was amazed at the friendliness and camaraderie.

The next morning I stuck my head out of the tent and couldn't see a thing. At first I thought 'My God, the fog's thick,' but then realised that my head was in the clouds. The idea was to hike to the summit and walk along the ridge to some of the other peaks at about 5000 feet (1500 metres). After several hours ending in almost blindly crawling over massive boulders, we reached the tree line and open ridges.

"With the packs all loaded Trevor's was heaviest. All he said was 'No sweat'. Colleen and I realised we'd hit a new phase and it held promise. Forget sherpas."

Visibility was nil and the wind so strong it literally nearly blew us over. We found an outcrop to hunch behind out of the wind where we could have lunch. We just got the daypack open when the entire world seemed to brighten. We looked up and a patch of sky opened as though it were a window. The scene took our breath away. There were forests, valleys and mountains as far as the eye could see. In an instant, the window slammed and the clouds folded in on themselves again. Suddenly, the same thing happened again behind us. Loud involuntary oohs and ahhs erupted from our mouths. The same process occurred over and over – our euphoria and jubilation increasing each time. Within 10 minutes the entire sky had cleared, the clouds had lifted as though by drawstring and we could see perhaps 50 miles (80km) in each direction. We whooped and patted each other on the back, and heard others along the ridge also shrieking with delight. All of us were sharing something we knew was special and well earned. Within minutes various adults joined us tucking into their food bags. Teenagers in North America generally do not get much respect and are not often spoken to, rarely as equals. Here with the incredible scene around us and a collective sense of exhilaration Trevor was greeted, asked questions and treated like a peer.

Days later Trevor led the entire way down. My knees hurt, Colleen's back ached. We stopped for a snack once and that was the last we saw of him until the parking lot. Sprawled out on the grass, he looked tired but happy, healthy and pleased with himself. That look alone was worth the trip for me.

information

For helpful ideas on activities for children pick up the free *Big Apple Parents' Paper* which is available at kids' shops around the city.

things to see & do

wild things Begin a tour of the huge Bronx Zoo on the Skyfari aerial tramway. Back on the ground, kids can glimpse the nocturnal world of bats, sample a skunk scent or crawl up a rope spiderweb.

At the smaller Central Park Wildlife Center, toddlers can pat llamas or delight in the antics of seals and penguins.

interesting & educational The American Museum of Natural History is popular for its dinosaur hall's 'please touch' displays which allow kids to handle the bones of extinct dinosaurs. The century-old Brooklyn Children's Museum features a world playground that celebrates different cultures and a greenhouse designed to teach kids about environmental preservation. Each June, the museum holds an international balloon festival. The manageable scale of New York Aquarium makes it a perfect place for young children. At the touch pool, kids can handle starfish and other small forms of sea life.

pure entertainment The Big Apple Circus visits Lincoln Center each winter, and the Ringling Bros and Barnum & Bailey Circus takes over Madison Square Garden every May and June with lions and tigers, jugglers and clowns.

parks & playgrounds

In sprawling Central Park, horse-drawn carriages and in-line skaters happily share New York's most famous open space. Other kid-friendly city parks with sand, slides and swings include Manhattan's Riverside Park, midtown's Hecksher Playground and Brooklyn's Prospect Park.

festivals

Hardly a week goes by without a parade, street fair or celebration of some sort in New York. The St Patrick's Day parade in March, and Macy's Thanksgiving Day parade are two of the bigger show stoppers. The annual Christmas Tree Lighting attracts thousands of visitors, and semi-officially kicks off the city's holiday season.

around new york state

Rochester's outstanding Strong Museum is a hands-on history centre for children and home to a whimsical environment made up of Sesame Street characters, whaling ships, cooking shows and time labs.

The small and family-managed Six Nations Indian Museum near Saranac Lake offers a delightful introduction to Native American culture.

The National Baseball Hall of Fame and Museum is what brings most visitors to Cooperstown. The museum houses all the important baseball artefacts: famous players' bats, gloves and uniforms and balls hit by Babe Ruth, Willie Mays and other stars of the national pastime.

For serious amusement-park type fun, take the kids to Lake George Action Park, an 1890s-style theme park with rides and shows; or nearby to New York's largest amusement park, Great Escape Fun Park, with raft rides, roller coasters and live shows.

Honeymooners and daredevils have made Niagara Falls famous, but no-one enjoys a big waterfall more than a kid. Niagara Falls' biggest tourist attraction has been the half-hour boat ride on the *Maid of the Mist*, where a ticket gets you an up-close feel for the fury of the water hurtling over the cliffs above. Families can buy a discount pass which covers entry to several attractions around the falls.

Lake Placid Village high in the Adirondack Mountains is the picturesque site of both the 1932 and 1980 Winter Olympics. It has a great deal to offer year-round, from family skiing and ice skating to summer biking and hiking.

LOUISIANA

new orleans

Nothing ever goes too fast or grows too worrisome in New Orleans, a city where the unofficial motto is *laissez les bons temps rouler* (let the good times roll). And it's exciting to let children discover the confluence of cultures that makes New Orleans so unique. African, French, Italian, Spanish and Caribbean influences flavour both the food and the music.

information

For specially scheduled children's activities around New Orleans, check out the brief 'kid stuff' listing that appears in the *Times-Picayune* 'Living' section each Monday and in tourist magazines like *Where*.

practicalities

Accent on Children's Arrangements is a service that takes the kids off your hands and engages them in organised activities.

things to see & do

wild things Among the country's very best zoos, Audubon Zoological Gardens is a must for kids and parents. Its Louisiana Swamp exhibit displays a Cajun cultural setting with alligators, bobcats, red foxes, black bears, snapping turtles, huge butterflies and giant anaconda snakes. At the Aquarium of the Americas, kids can go eye-to-eye with spotted moray eels from Caribbean coral reefs, and other slippery creatures of the Amazon basin, the Mississippi River and the Delta wetlands.

pure entertainment Storyland is a low-key and low-cost children's amusement area known for its Last Carousel – a restored gem with carved wooden animals and Wurlitzer organ.

activities

The Audubon Zoo Cruise offers a unique way to see the zoo and the Aquarium of the Americas, which the kids will love. Combined discount tickets for the riverboat cruise, zoo and aquarium are available. Walking and casual bicycling can be had in City Park and around the lakefront; and in a loop around Audubon Park and the riverside Levee Park.

festivals

New Orleans lights up with Mardi Gras madness – beginning in early January with Carnival and reaching a costumed climax at midnight in late February or early March. But parents should be forewarned that the French Quarter, jammed with merrymakers, can easily overwhelm and frighten small children.

around louisiana

It's easy enough for families to explore Louisiana's small towns, bayous and back roads by car. In south-west Louisiana's Cajun Country, Cajun and zydeco music is played at many restaurants and Cajun festivals are common on weekends. Along the banks of the Mississippi between New Orleans and Baton Rouge, a dozen old plantations are open to the public as historic sites, usually with costumed guides.

PACIFIC NORTHWEST

seattle

things to see & do

wild things Seattle's Woodland Park Zoo was one of the first zoos in the country to free animals from their restrictive cages in favour of ecosystem enclosures, including an Asian elephant forest and an African savannah.

interesting & educational The Pacific Science Center is a hip museum with hands-on exhibits of holograms and a robot that challenges kids to a game of tick-tack-toe (nought and crosses). At the Burke Museum, the North Coast Indian totem poles – showing various animals and humans stacked on each other – are a dramatic introduction to the spiritual world of Native Americans.

Seattle's ode to the future is the Space Needle, built for the 1962 World's Fair and overlooking the whole of Seattle. The view is impressive, but kids seem just as happy with the 41-second ride to the top of the 520-foot (156m) architectural icon.

parks & playgrounds

During those brief summer interludes when Seattle gets hot, locals make the pilgrimage to Lake Washington to sprawl out on the small, sandy-grassy beaches. There are bike paths and play structures for small children, too.

around pacific northwest

The two Pacific Northwest states, Washington and Oregon, have some of the most diverse and dramatic landscapes in the country, from the majesty of the Columbia River Gorge to the volcanic blast zone of Mt St Helens. For a wholesome break, Portland, Oregon has something many American cities envy – a friendly reputation and a thriving downtown centre, plus fountains and whimsical statues of animals.

ROCKY MOUNTAINS

Birthplace of the fabled Wild West, kids may also find that the real Wild West is quite different than the stuff of Hollywood movies. Old mining and frontier towns like Leadville (Colorado) and Helena (Montana) have historical sights which show that – for Native Americans – a lot was lost when the West was 'won'.

The biggest problem you're likely to encounter is skirting the summer crowds at tourist meccas like Yellowstone and Rocky Mountain National Parks.

colorado

things to see & do

interesting & educational The Denver Museum of Natural History features several hands-on geological and dinosaur exhibits, as well as affordable half-day parent-kid workshops which focus on crafts, health and wildlife topics.

activities

Among national parks, Mesa Verde in south-west Colorado is unique for its focus on a native culture over 1000 years old. Nimble kids can climb a stone stairway and four ladders to discover a labyrinth of family shelters at Cliff Palace.

wyoming

activities

Kids will love exploring Yellowstone National Park, established in 1872 to preserve the area's unique geological features – spectacular geothermal hot springs, fossil forests and alpine lakes, along with abundant wildlife including grizzly bears. The Yellowstone Association offers affordable and ranger-led overnight horseback tours for families with kids at least eight years old.

Summer visitors swarm Rocky Mountain National Park to take in the stunning peaks and catch sight of elk, bighorn sheep, moose and beaver.

montana & idaho

things to see & do

interesting & educational In Bozeman, the Museum of the Rockies is the most entertaining museum in Montana – from its procession of dinosaur dioramas to the planetarium's 'Tour of the Night Sky' which is told from a Native American perspective.

activities

The Glacier National Park is the state's most revered attraction and still sacred to the Native American Blackfoot nation who called the region the 'backbone of the world'. The 50-mile (80km) long Going-to-the-Sun Rd crosses the Continental Divide at Logan Pass and affords magnificent views of glacial activity and often mountain goats and bighorn sheep.

Idaho's Sun Valley is heaven on earth for skiing families with trails for all abilities, discount children's lift tickets and lessons for beginners. Craters of the Moon National Monument is a surreal experience for any kid, with short trails to the edge of craters and into cool tunnels and lava caves.

TEXAS

Here's your kids chance to play cowboy for real. It's fun to show children the Texas of your imagination – wide-open spaces, working cowboys, cool geology and unusual animals. In child-friendly Texas, hotel discounts and travel packages for families are common.

things to see & do

wild things South-west of the Dallas-Fort Worth metropolis, the Fossil Rim Wildlife Center at Glen Rose is dedicated to endangered wildlife, including the African white rhino and the Mexican red wolf. The classy Fort Worth Zoo features unique animals such as koalas and Komodo dragons.

interesting & educational At NASA's Space Center Houston, kids (and former kids) can strap themselves into the Lunar Jumper, then literally jump for joy in the low-gravity simulator which approximates body weight according to the moon's gravity.

Picturesque San Antonio is home to the Alamo – a former Spanish fort and mission – popular for its beauty and famous for the most pivotal battle in Texas history.

pure entertainment Sea World San Antonio does behind the scenes tours for aquatic youngsters and Six Flags theme park in Arlington is always a hit with the roller coaster set. At Fort Worth's Cowtown Coliseum, junior cowboys and girls can rejoice at the sight of grown men getting thrown by wild bulls in impressive rodeo displays.

activities

For kids who want to jump in the saddle, horse riding is popular across the state, from remote Big Bend National Park on the Rio Grande to dude ranches in Central Texas.

Austin has a reputation as a music town, but from March to November kids might prefer the tradition of watching a million bats taking off from under the Congress Ave Bridge at sunset in search of yummy insects.

WASHINGTON, DC

With all its historical, cultural and recreational attractions, the Capital Region is a popular destination for families with children. In Washington, DC, many of these attractions are free, offering budget travellers unsurpassed opportunities for kid-friendly entertainment and enrichment.

things to see & do

wild things The National Zoological Park is one of DC's crown jewels, following the natural contours of its woodland-canyon setting. Visit early on summer weekends to beat the crowds and the heat.

interesting & educational The cavernous halls at the National Air & Space Museum trace the history of aviation and space exploration through interactive displays including the Wright Brothers' *Flyer*, Charles Lindbergh's *Spirit of St Louis* and the *Apollo 11* command module.

The National Museum of Natural History sports a giant IMAX theatre and hands-on science exhibits where children can examine shells, bones, geodes, costumes and more.

pure entertainment The regal Arts & Industries Building's Discovery Theater hosts performances and puppet shows for kids and across the street, an antique carousel offers rides.

activities

Kids love the delightful National Sculpture Garden which is studded with oversized and whimsical sculptures like Roy Lichtenstein's *House* and Louise Bourgeois' leggy *Spider*.

parks & playgrounds

Outdoor enthusiasts head north-west to Rock Creek Park, with extensive trails for cycling, hiking and horseback riding.

around washington, dc

Virginia is just across the Potomac from DC, and full of colonial sites, Civil War displays, and the excellent Richmond Children's Museum.

NORTH AMERICA

Like the US almost all attractions in Canada offer child rates, and at many major attractions family passes (meaning two adults and two children) are an even better deal. Some hotels may no even charge at all for younger children. Best of all, families will find a rich cultural patchwork of people from European, Asian and Native American roots.

MONTREAL

things to see & do

wild things The Insectarium in the Jardin Botanique (Botanical Gardens), a huge collection of bugs from all around the world, which will definitely fascinate children – and if you're lucky, you might even get to taste a chocolate-covered grasshopper.

interesting & educational Montreal Planetarium is popular with families for the multimedia shows about the power of the sun and the earth's magnetic fields. There are several interactive exhibits and nightly star shows alternate between French and English. The YMCA on Rue Stanley offers educational and affordable day programs for youngsters ranging from 18 months to 12 years of age.

pure entertainment It's easy (if expensive) to keep kids entertained in the summer at the La Ronde amusement park with its classic wooden roller coaster and tamer kiddy rides.

activities

In the summer, Montrealers like to stroll around the Vieux-Port (Old Port), and it's great for family picnics by the river, bike rides or just watching a slice of Montreal life. And in May and June, you might catch the marvellous Cirque du Soleil's original circus theatre.

At the city's Olympic Park (built for the 1976 Olympics), a cable car ride provides great views of the city. Family activities range from swimming at one of the six public pools, to exploring the Biodome's rainforest global ecosystem, complete with monkeys and alligators.

parks & playgrounds

The splendid Parc du Mont Royal overlooks the entire city, and Parc La Fontaine is popular with young kids who can enjoy either the puppet theatre or the wading pool.

TORONTO

Canada's largest city makes for children, as the city is famous for the downtown area's cleanliness and vibrancy. The subways and streetcars are very safe, though strollers may be awkward to lift onto some forms of public transport.

things to see & do

wild things At the rambling Toronto Zoo, little kids can take a break on the small train that circles the grounds. A constant favourite with kids is the Black-Light Zone where they can spy on nocturnal animals.

interesting & educational Long a model for kids' science museums, the Ontario Science Centre has hundreds of hands-on exhibits, from a hair-raising electric generator to a computer-generated time-travel exhibit. At the Children's Own Museum there are play areas and interactive exhibits for children under eight, including garden and construction sites, a wall of musical instruments and an art workshop.

pure entertainment In summer it's easy to keep kids entertained at Paramount Canada's Wonderland with several roller coasters and a huge kiddy area with wandering Hanna-Barbera cartoon characters. From May to September, Ontario Place is a family-friendly scene with strolling musicians, mimes and a Children's Village with a Lego play centre.

activities

Harbourfront organises kids' programs ranging from summer concerts to free winter ice skating.

parks & playgrounds

The city's biggest park is High Park, a popular escape for a little picnicking, cycling, in-line skating or strolling through the flower gardens at sunset. At the west end of Ward's Island is a cool children's play fort.

festivals

At the International Children's Festival in May, Harbourfront stages come alive with international puppetry, theatre, dance and musical performances especially for kids.

Canada isn't an exotic destination when it's your northern neighbour which speaks the same language. Still, I'd heard rave reviews about travelling with children in Canada – spotless cities, picture-postcard countryside and fewer people than the state of California. Over the border we went.

canada THE GREAT NEXT DOORS

Stephanie Levin-Gervasi and husband, Luis, took their daughter, Camille, eight, on holidays to Canada.

Our plan was to fly into Vancouver, British Columbia, and take the train to Whistler. Since it was my husband's and daughter's first trip to Canada, we spent a few days moseying around Vancouver.

It's so easy to get around Vancouver with kids that it makes you want to pull up your roots and move there. We shuttled around the city on buses and boats, criss-crossing numerous bridges and bays. It's hard to do justice to Vancouver in a few days. Don't try to do it all in a weekend, it's too exhausting. It's best to combine outside activities with a good mix of kid-friendly museums.

We chose two museums – the first was Science World with its golf-ball shaped silver dome looming over the city. It's a busy place, full of hands-on extravaganzas. We liked the robot-backscratcher best and the spinning spiral, which shrunk our faces or turned them into a jelly mould when spun. At the HR MacMillan Planetarium and Space Centre, in Vanier Park, Camille jettisoned to Mars inside a space simulator and climbed a space tree.

After two days in Vancouver, we boarded a 7 am train to Whistler, a two-and-a-half-hour ride. Since the exchange rate in Canada is favourable to the American dollar, we checked into the Chateau Whistler – a regal hotel at the base of Blackcomb Mountain.

Whistler might be the king of the mountains in the winter, but it's full of families and oodles of outdoor activities in the summer. Our first family adventure was a canoe trip on the River of Golden Dreams. Since we have not canoed a great deal, we rented a guide who paddled next to us in another canoe. Good thing!

We were classified as 'tranquil paddlers' – novices who wouldn't be running into any white water on this narrow stretch of the river. Harnessed into life jackets, just in case, I sat front, Camille sat centre and Luis weighed down the rear. We were a balanced threesome as long as no-one stood up. Nevertheless, we ran into a snag. Luis and I couldn't coordinate our oars and things became rather testy as we bounced downstream. The front of the canoe crashed into brambles and spiky branches along the bank, careening from one side to the other. At first we laughed, but after a dozen bank bounces, I was barking at my husband.

The kind guide kept encouraging, 'Hey you're doing great.' Camille knew better; she could sense disaster and a kid's natural instinct is not to sit and wait for disaster to strike. She began moving about the canoe. We didn't tip, but we had enough water on the bottom to wash dishes for a week. We arrived at the end of the River of Golden Dreams with badly bruised tempers, but physically unscathed.

We cooled off in the pool at the hotel. Camille headed to the opposite end and hung out with a convention of kids. If we'd allowed her, Camille would have spent the entire time in the pool. But Whistler is an ever-changing canvas of colour and wildlife with numerous trails to explore. Camille reluctantly left the pool for land.

From a kid's perspective, the best spot in the village is the kid's centre at the base of Blackcomb Mountain. During the winter it's a ski school, but in the summer it transforms into a square of activity – a climbing wall, pony rides, and bungy trampolines. We plunked down $10 on tickets and Camille spent all of them on the bungy trampoline. After the second day of jumping, everyone knew the kid from California with the long curls.

"It's so easy to get around Vancouver with kids that it makes you want to pull up your roots and move there."

When we weren't in the pool we walked around the village, had lunch or wandered around the shops. One afternoon, we took the gondola up to the Round House for lunch and saw a baby bear cub sitting in a patch of wildflowers.

On our last day, we spent the better part of the morning in the pool before I insisted on one more mountain activity. We rented mountain bikes in the village and the shop assistant pointed out the easiest route, a loop, and assured us we wouldn't get lost. Camille had trouble shifting the gears, but once we got that worked out we sped through verdant forest, secret paths and other cycling families. And we got lost.

What's great about travelling in Canada with kids is the seamless sense of perfection, the idea that you're in good hands. So, we were surprised when a fire alarm went off at the hotel at 3 am and we discovered there was also no power. Wrapped in robes, we opened the door and joined the line of heads bobbing out the doors. When we all stampeded the lobby, hotel employees shaking flashlights waved us back up. 'There's no fire, it's just a generator blackout in the village.' Of course, no-one could go to sleep after all the excitement, so we did the next best thing – pulled out a deck of cards and played Go Fish. Who said Canada couldn't be exotic with kids?

VANCOUVER

Vancouver brags about being kid-friendly with many sights and activities geared towards the littlies.

information

From a tourist information centre, pick up the free brochure, *Kids' Guide to Vancouver*, which lists more than 100 places to take youngsters.

things to see & do

interesting & educational HR MacMillan Planetarium and Pacific Space Centre, part of the Vancouver Museum Complex, offers entertaining star shows projected onto a dome 20m across.

pure entertainment At much-beloved Stanley Park, small kids like the low-key children's farmyard and miniature railway. Playland at Hastings Park features over 35 rides and attractions. SplashDown Park has 13 slides and 10 acres (4 hectares) of mostly wet activities.

activities

The Vancouver Aquarium displays over 8000 creatures from the sea, the most popular being the dolphins, the orcas (killer whales) and beluga whales. Kids eight and older can sign up for the Sleepover with the Whales.

parks & playgrounds

The heated Kitsilano Outdoor Pool at Kitsilano Beach Park is the only one in the city to use salt water. Lighthouse Park in West Vancouver is a great dense forest with old-growth Douglas fir trees, a 1914 lighthouse, rock formations and tidal pools which kids love to explore.

festivals

The Vancouver International Children's Festival is held annually in Vanier Park, during the last week in May. The festival is a world of fun and entertainment for children of all ages and attracts about 200 Canadian and international acts, including musicians, actors, mimes, clowns, puppeteers, jugglers and storytellers.

SOUTH & CENTRAL AMERICA

While the Caribbean is a popular family destination, only a few foreigners visit South and Central America with children. Latin Americans share a widespread affection for children and they are likely to be a social asset. Children with fair hair and light skin are especially likely to receive attention, so parents may need to protect them from unwanted affection.

Children generally enjoy discounts on local transport or in hotels and theatres. Age limits for particular discounts vary from place to place, but are rarely rigidly enforced. In hotels the general rule is to bargain. Children should never have to pay as much as an adult, but whether they stay for half price or free is open to discussion. Most hotels also offer free accommodation or greatly reduced rates for children staying in their parents' rooms. A child is usually defined as being 12 years old or younger, but some places classify under-16s as children. If you are staying in one spot for a while it's a good idea to prearrange necessities such as babysitters, cots and baby food.

It's perfectly acceptable to order a meal and split it between two children or an adult and a child. For light, cheap meals shop at the supermarkets and self-cater. Always be careful with water and ice, and boil milk as it is often unpasteurised.

Children pay full fare on buses if they occupy a seat, but often ride for free if they sit on a parent's knee. Children under 12 pay half fare on most domestic airline flights and get a seat, while under-twos pay 10% of the fare without a seat.

Nappies are widely available, but creams, lotions, baby foods and familiar medicines may not be so easy to find outside larger cities and tourist towns. Consider the health risks for particular countries and take extra care to avoid sunburn and heat exposure. Poorly maintained public bathrooms may concern some parents, so carry your own toilet paper. While a woman may take a young boy into the women's toilet, it's socially unacceptable for a man to take a girl into the men's room.

You may find that safety standards are different to those of your own country. Children's car seats are not always available in car rental agencies, so bring one if you're driving. Seat belts are often nonexistent in rear seats. Swimming pools are rarely fenced which doesn't make for a relaxing time with a toddler, but with a little caution and common sense you can still have a safe holiday.

Although breastfeeding in public in Latin America is considered normal for low-income mothers, middle- and high-income mothers often prefer to use the bottle. Even so, there is no problem if you discreetly breastfeed in public. It's an image thing – the bottle is a sign of social status. Breastfeeding an older baby will sometimes attract attention.

ARGENTINA

Argentina, especially Buenos Aires, is extremely child-friendly in terms of safety, health, people's attitudes and family-oriented activities.

Babies and children are welcomed everywhere and people are always friendly towards them. While breastfeeding in public is uncommon, people won't be offended by it. In the more indigenous areas, women breastfeed their babies in the markets.

In parts of northern Argentina cholera is a problem, so play it safe by not eating uncooked vegetables or unpeeled fruit and use bottled water to brush teeth. No sane person would recommend driving in Buenos Aires; the city has an extensive, if rundown, public transport system.

Restaurants, while often smoky environments, provide a wide selection of food suitable for children. Waiters are accustomed to providing extra plates and cutlery for children, though some places may add a small additional charge. Regional foods – such as *empanadas* (turnovers stuffed with meat or cheese) – tend to be spicier than in the central or southern parts of the country, but pasta and grilled meat is available everywhere. Budget hotels will often allow you to use their kitchen. For sweet-toothed kids, Argentina's high-quality ice cream is a real treat.

Once children are old enough to cross the street safely and find their way back home, parents don't hesitate to send unaccompanied pre-adolescents on errands and visits to friends or neighbours. While most visiting parents won't feel this comfortable, they can usually count on children's safety in public places. Children under the age of 14 travelling without both parents theoretically need a parents' consent form.

buenos aires

information

Ambito Financiero, the capital's financial daily, publishes an excellent Friday cultural section with listings of children's activities, including films, music and theatre shows. Many of these activities take place during winter holidays (early to mid-July) and can be very crowded.

practicalities

People are generally very helpful on public transport, often giving up a seat for a parent and child or offering to put children on their laps. Sometimes this happens so spontaneously that you find someone pulling a child out of your arms. People frequently touch each other so your child will be patted on the head and caressed regularly.

things to see & do

interesting & educational Older kids enjoy the guided tour of the Teatro Colón with its scale models of theatre sets or the Museo Histórico Nacional and the Museu de Arte Moderno. Go for a stroll in La Boca, down by the port, to see the colourful houses built by Italian immigrants. Teenagers will appreciate seeing a soccer match. There are lots of cinemas with foreign children's films and cartoons are usually Spanish dubbed for a free Spanish lesson.

parks & playgrounds

Buenos Aires' numerous plazas and public parks are popular gathering spots for families; the most attractive are the wide open spaces of Palermo. Palermo has the city's Jardín Botánico Carlos Thays, Jardín Zoológico and Planetario. Plaza Alemania is where skateboarders go to show off their moves; younger children also bicycle and Rollerblade in the area.

festivals

Horse-loving kids won't want to miss Palermo's annual horse breeders' fair in late March and there is an agricultural fair in July.

around argentina

Unless you are travelling by plane, remember that distances are long and trips seem never-ending for younger children. There are organised tours to Esteros del Iberá – a wetlands wilderness which is a great spot to see wildlife. Península Valdés has unique scenery and also has abundant wildlife. In summer, older children will appreciate a trip to the awesome Moreno Glacier in the Parque Nacional Los Glaciares way down south. Up north, the Iguazú Falls are one of the continent's most breathtaking sites.

BOLIVIA

Few foreigners visit Bolivia with children, but those who do are rewarded with great kindness by Bolivians. Children with fair hair are especially likely to receive local attention.

la paz

practicalities

La Paz – one of the world's most scenic cities – is nearly 4km above sea level so bring warm clothing for littlies and be aware that altitude sickness can be a problem (see the Health chapter for more information).

things to see & do

interesting & educational The children's museum features science-oriented displays and hands-on experiments. The planetarium is great for an hour of astral entertainment. At the Academía de Música there is musical instruction (in Spanish) on traditional Andean instruments.

activities

La Paz has bustling markets and pleasant botanical gardens. Children will probably enjoy the ubiquitous Bolivian video arcades as well as outdoor activities, such as horse riding, river trips and light hiking.

around bolivia

Day tours from La Paz give your family a great chance to explore Bolivia. For a taste of archaeology there's Tiahuanaco Ruins – a partially restored ruin that includes a pyramid to scale and museum to browse. Teenagers love the downhill mountain biking at Zongo Valley or skiing at Chacaltaya – the world's highest ski fields.

festivals

Peñas – traditional folk music programs – are held at least weekly in most larger cities and towns. Kids will like the riotous carnival La Diablada (the 'Dance of the Devils' in Oruro during Holy week) for its colourful parades and dancing.

BRAZIL

brasil

Brazil has loads of beaches and in major cities. Kids can be occupied forever in their museums and attractions. Brazilians are very family-oriented and children are generally treated like little princes and princesses. Malaria and yellow fever are health risks in some states (see the Health chapter for more information).

Many hotels let children stay for free, although the age limit varies. Babysitters are readily available. Most restaurants have highchairs and meals large enough to be shared. Self-serve *a kilo* (pay by weight) restaurants are common and convenient. There is also lots of great Brazilian children's music available, which makes for lots of fun dancing even if kids can't understand the Portuguese lyrics.

rio de janeiro

information

For kids' activities try the entertainment pages of the weekend issues of the *Jornal do Brasil* and *O Globo* Portuguese-language newspapers.

practicalities

City traffic is chaotic; there is a good metro and bus system but avoid rush hour with younger children.

things to see & do

wild things Children will enjoy the Jardim Zoológico at Quinta da Boa Vista with its native animals and endangered species. Also in the park is the Museu Nacional, which is bound to appeal to gruesome kids with its sabre-toothed tiger skeletons, huge meteorite and gory displays of tropical diseases.

interesting & educational Older kids will like the Plánetario in Gávea, showing the southern sky to the accompaniment of classical music; there are also activities for younger children on weekends.

pure entertainment Mini-Rio in Barra Shopping Mall has a small amusement area with dodgem cars and boat or plane rides for the tiny tots. Tivoli Parque in Lagoa is a popular amusement park for both adults and children. Thrill-seeking kids will love Terra Encantada – a large amusement park in Barra da Tijuca including Cabum, a 100km per hour free-fall which is not for the faint hearted. Water Planet and Wet and Wild at Grota Funda have water play for all ages. Rio has lots of cinemas though foreign movies are usually not dubbed, so make sure your kids have some basic language skills.

activities

As well as the cable car ride to Pão de Açúcar (Sugar Loaf), kids will love the cog train up the mountain to Corcovado (Hunchback) and the huge statue of Cristo Redentor (Christ the Redeemer). Cruise in paddle-boats on Lagoa Rodrigo de Freitas in Parque Tom Jobim or hire bikes to take to the path around the lake. Praia do Grumari is the most isolated and unspoiled beach close to the city and is quiet during the week but packed on weekends.

parks & playgrounds

Kids will like exploring the Parque Nacional da Tijuca – a tropical jungle with waterfalls, excellent trails, restaurants, picnic areas, iguanas and monkeys. The lovely Jardim Botânico is quiet on weekdays and overflowing with families and music on weekends. Parque Lage nearby is tranquil with no sports allowed and a favourite with families of small children.

around brazil

Older children will enjoy the awesome waterfalls of Foz do Iguaçu. Or there's the spectacular train ride from Curitiba to Paranaguá through mountains covered in Atlantic rainforest. Show your kids Brazilian history at the gold rush towns of Minas Gerais. Athletic kids will love hiking in Brazil's vibrant national parks or exploring the Pantanal – a sanctuary for some of South America's most exotic wildlife.

festivals

Carnaval in Rio (February or March) is probably too full-on for children, although it can be fun in small country towns. The folkloric Festas Juninas (June parties) are more child-friendly with children dressing up as country bumpkins and square dancing.

Planning began long before the trip. We succeeded in timing our pregnancy so that the baby would be a suitable age to travel for the *Brazil* guidebook update assignment – young enough to still be breastfeeding and light enough to be easily carried around. The Amazon seemed a bit too adventurous this time (malaria and yellow fever) so we figured the south-east region would be more manageable for research as a family.

brazil REWRITING the BOOK

Lonely Planet authors Robyn Jones and Leonardo Pinheiro travelled to Brazil with Alex, four, and Nicholas, 6–9 months.

This would be far from a normal family holiday – as any LP author will tell you the image people have of travel writing is far from the reality. So, how to travel as a family and get our work done at the same time? The logistics were daunting. We had to cover around 10,000km, visit more than 50 towns, cities and national parks, confirm a few million facts, and move hotels almost every day. We imagined the possible scenarios and drew up a list of all the assorted paraphernalia and time-saving tricks we would need for our scheme to have any chance of working. We ended up hiring an air-con car for most of the trip – a kind of mobile hotel – with a spacious boot, of course.

We were prepared for a bit of a rough time, but then there is always the odd nightmare day at home with children anyway. Even though we faced a lengthy air trip – a total of 45 hours including airport stopovers – we decided against an extended stopover so we could take as little hand luggage as possible and avoid seeing all our gear until Rio. Alex loved the buttons on the plane, asking for drinks and calling the attendants – all of which tested their patience. He also loved running up and down the aisles.

While on the road we often couldn't afford to stop just to entertain the kids, so we involved Alex in our work as much as we could and endeavoured to expose him to the fun and colourful side of Brazilian culture. He helped us checking the hotel rooms. He became quite discerning and even appreciated the architecture of the Niemeyer hotel we stayed in (the long passages and modernist open plan were fantastic for running in). We bought local toys, handicrafts, books and music so he could learn some Portuguese. We encouraged him to order his own meals, talk to the locals and play with kids along the way. By the end of three months he was quite fluent and preferred speaking Portuguese to English. He also learnt about some of the negative aspects of Brazil when we saw hungry and homeless children on the streets.

We had been worried that the kids might get unsettled and cranky with so much moving but it didn't seem to stress them at all. Home was wherever their parents were. Of course any concept of a strict routine went out the window. Our kids would sleep well in the car, though, if we did most of our driving in the afternoon. They even slept through our tantrums when we repeatedly got lost in the traffic chaos and bedlam of Sâo Paulo (driving here is not something we recommend). The *praças* (town squares) of the country towns were great for expending our toddler's energy. Alex would zoom around following the curvaceous designs in the pavement. We would have liked more late afternoon dips at the beach. He also loved the parks in the mineral spa towns where he had his own canteen and ran around tasting the waters from the 12 different springs.

While the baby was happy as long as he was near the breast, bribery was a handy tool for the toddler. Alex collected loose change in his pockets and became obsessed with lollies. If we had to wait too long for meals he would be tearing around the restaurant like a wild thing, the baby would be writhing or squealing, other guests would be scowling, and we would be bickering and in no mood to appreciate the meal. We usually opted for quick buffet style/pay by weight. Alex learnt to eat Brazilian style: black beans and rice; sushi (Sâo Paulo has a large community of Japanese descendants); chilled coconuts from roadside stalls; and from the wandering beach vendors, cured cheese on a stick and coconut couscous with condensed milk. He was close to heaven when pigging out in a mango plantation with the juice dripping down his face.

"We had been worried that the kids might get unsettled and cranky with so much moving but it didn't seem to stress them at all. Home was wherever their parents were."

So would we recommend a trip to Brazil with kids? Definitely, especially if you are actually on holiday. Just give the big crowded cities short shrift and head for rural Minas Gerais and coastal Rio and Sâo Paulo. We loved going off the beaten track to the mountains, exploring the fascinating colonial towns, talking about the panthers in the Atlantic jungle, feeding the wild wolves at the monastery in Minas Gerais and relaxing in car-less Ilha Grande, the farm where Alex milked a cow, rode a horse, fed the chickens and exclaimed 'It's great fun here'. We managed to combine life on the road, being with the kids full time, getting our work done and – one of the best bits – escaping three months of tedious everyday chores like cooking, dishes and cleaning. In that sense it was almost a holiday.

CHILE

You'll find Chile extremely child-friendly in terms of people's attitudes and family-oriented activities.

santiago

information

There are many activities for children; check out the listings in the Spanish-language newspapers like *El Mercurio* or the English-language *News Review* for ideas on how to keep kids entertained.

practicalities

Santiago streets are congested so it's often quicker to get around by metro rather than bus, though it can be difficult to get a seat. Often someone will give up a seat for parent and child or offer to put the child on their lap. Bottled water is a good idea for delicate young stomachs. Most restaurants offer a wide variety of dishes suitable for children and Chilean cuisine is generally bland despite the occasional spicy sauce. Portions are usually large enough that smaller children won't need separate meals.

things to see & do

interesting & educational The Museo Infantil is terrific for young children and has different playrooms focussing on construction, ecology and optics. The Museo de Ciencia y Tecnología with its planetarium and multimedia exhibits will fascinate older kids. For kids who like to be scared the Museo Nacional de Historia Natural has a creepy mummified body of a 12-year-old child sacrificed at least 500 years ago.

parks & playgrounds

Santiago – like most other Chilean cities – has large public parks with playgrounds. West of downtown, the cool, woody Parque Quinta Normal attracts walkers and picnicking families with impromptu soccer games, rental rowboats and several museums. The large Parque Metropolitano has an aerial tramway to the summit of Cerro San Cristóbal. On the way up the tramway stops at the zoo.

around chile

Chile's tremendous Andes are bound to impress the kids. Older children will appreciate the spectacular mountains and glaciers of the southern national parks and there are organised tours and four-day sailing trips around the fjords. Car ferries cross to Isla Grande de Chiloé, heartland of Chilean folklore, where you can explore extra-friendly small towns.

Distant Easter Island with its giant stylised statues will capture children's imagination. Adventurous families can visit the remote Isla Robinson Crusoe, where the real-life model for Daniel Defoe's fictional character was marooned. The archipelago is a national park and a World Biosphere Reserve.

ECUADOR

Foreigners travelling with children are still a curiosity and will be met with extra, generally friendly, attention and interest. Kids will love the stunning Andean scenery and the unusual and fun ways to travel. You'll probably prefer they don't join in the locals and ride on the train roof from the dizzy highlands to the coast!

quito

Ecuador's capital is a great place to give children a look at colonial history just by strolling the streets on a quiet Sunday afternoon when traffic is quiet.

things to see & do

wild things If you miss them in the wild the best spot to acquaint the kids with Ecuador's flora and fauna is at the natural history museum, Museo de Ciencias Naturales. Live animals including boa constrictors and poisonous snakes can be seen at the Vivarium.

interesting & educational The Museo de la Ciudad has exhibits depicting daily life in Quito through the centuries with interactive computer displays. Older kids might like the Fundación Sinchi Sacha which exhibits artwork and utensils of the Amazonian people.

parks & playgrounds Quito has little green space and playgrounds are few and unsafe. The Parque El Ejido has impromptu games of soccer and volleyball, as well as the strange giant marble game common in Ecuador.

festivals

Quito's annual *festa* (early December) gives kids a chance to mix with local people and have fun. New Year's Eve celebrations will thrill kids with the burning of elaborate life-sized puppets at midnight. Kids will love Carnaval (the weekend preceding Ash Wednesday) which is celebrated by intense water fights.

around ecuador

From Quito you can rent a car or take bus trips to the more relaxing smaller towns to chill out restless kids. Interesting day trips will have kids exploring the colourful Indian crafts market in Otavalo and Saquisili.

While the Galápagos Islands are very expensive to visit compared to the rest of Ecuador, their wildlife is truly phenomenal and a visit is worth considering if you have animal-crazy older children. Kids will be thrilled by rainforest trips or staying in jungle lodges. Also on offer are guided wildlife-watching opportunities.

Yellow fever vaccinations and anti-malarials may be required on many tours.

Shortly after Alexa's second birthday we took our first big trip abroad. I chose Ecuador partly because I knew someone there but primarily because I thought it would be easy to travel around – a small country with a central capital to use as a home base. It also offered the diversity of beach, rainforest, cloud forest, mountains and urban areas. I took a lot of luggage including games, nappies and bottles which I kept in the capital, Quito. Alexa was always glad to return 'home' after our jaunts to other parts of the country. In retrospect we spent too much time in the city, there isn't much for kids to do there. The playgrounds were few and dangerous with the only thing resembling a safe play area at the fast food chains which we resorted to at times. We were both more relaxed in smaller towns with little traffic and more green space.

ecuador WET & WILD

Susan Roedl and her daughter, Alexa, two, spent eight weeks in Ecuador.

We travelled mostly by bus and our only long trip was a 12-hour journey to Guayaquil, which we broke up with a night's stay along the way. It is not recommended to travel overnight anyway because of robbers. The buses were comfortable but we did have to occasionally walk to get to some of the places we stayed. I rented a car for a week to go to Otavalo because the bus schedule was inconvenient and I wanted to stop at some places along the way. I was a little apprehensive about driving in Quito. In the end it was so easy that I had a hard time giving the car back.

We had the most fun when we found water to play in or other kids to play with. And there were so many water spots and so many other kids in Ecuador that we stayed happy. Banõs is a touristy but charming town built around natural springs. The bus ride there is fantastic because you see the snow-covered mountains much of the time. We got a hotel with a pool where we could use our water toys (a wide variety were on sale in town) and we met and played with an Ecuadoran family.

Although Ecuador isn't known for its beaches, in keeping with our water theme we tried out two of them: Manta and Atacames. Both were crowded but Atacames had a carnival atmosphere that was really fun for kids as well as adults. The beach was lined with restaurants, bars, and vendors selling all types of goods and services. I had my hair braided as Alexa played in the sand. The activity goes on far into the night which kept Alexa entertained while I got to have a drink and socialise. Cars are banned so the only mode of transportation is bicycle taxi.

One of the only places we stayed that I didn't learn of through my guidebook was Aldea Salamanca – a small eco-friendly place run by an Ecuadoran man and his Canadian wife. The couple had a son the same age as Alexa and they had fun playing together. The owner took us for a day-long outing through the woods and to a waterfall and made the trip fun for us all by showing and telling us things about the plants and insects we saw.

One of our best trips was to El Reventador, a small town, really just a very large bus stop on the edge of the rainforest. We went there because I like bird-watching and I had read of a resort nearby that boasted some of the best birds in Ecuador. I had been forewarned that the resort was closed but went anyway hoping that the caretaker would let us stay. He agreed but told me I would have to buy my own food and candles in the nearby town. In the town we met a bored little girl who offered to show us around. At two years old my daughter was a magnet for older girls; they thought she was a toy and she found the big girls just as fascinating. On our tour we met some people, chickens, pigs and ended with a climb up the big hill to get a 'really good view of town'. At the top of the hill we encountered llamas, cows and steers behind a fence. It was so beautiful to watch the sunset that we stayed up there until it was almost dark. All of a sudden the cows and steers were let out from behind their fence and were coming toward us. I started to run to the road but it was covered with the steers, a couple of whom were charging. I panicked but our young guide led us to a giant pipe that we jumped up onto, safely away from the animals. We walked down to safety on the pipe.

"At two years old, my daughter was a magnet for older girls; they thought she was a toy and she found the big girls just as fascinating."

When we got to the resort it was more than I had hoped for. In our cabin we were completely alone in the woods. The following morning we got up early and walked to San Rafael waterfall where we ate lunch. On the way back we played in a stream and I had to carry my Alexa as she was so tired. Head on my shoulder, almost asleep, she pointed and whispered 'red'. I looked into the forest and saw the bird. It was the cock of the rock that all bird-watchers come to Ecuador to find. We sat and watched it until it flew away.

PERU

Peru's a great place for kids fascinated by archaeology. Travellers with children are still rare in Peru, though they are usually met with friendly curiosity. Health risks include yellow fever and malaria in the Amazon region and altitude sickness in the Andes, so keep an eye on the kids in those areas. See the Health chapter for more information on malaria. You'll have to stick to bottled or well-boiled water. Public toilets are rare and, where available, often dirty. Hiring a car with a driver is often not much more expensive than renting a vehicle.

lima

things to see & do

Lima is an interesting, if nerve-racking, place to visit with a dismal climate and polluted beaches. To introduce the kids to Peruvian fauna try the Museo de Historia Natural or the zoo. There are half-day sailboat rides to offshore islands to see sea lions and seabirds and many companies offer guided natural history tours to national parks and jungle lodges.

Older kids will like the Museo de la Nación's excellent models of Peru's major ruins. The Museo de Oro del Perú with its thousands of gold pieces ranging from earplugs to ponchos is sure to dazzle the kids. Don't miss the Museo Rafael Larco Herrera with a great collection of mummies and a weird cactus garden that will fascinate the kids for hours.

Kids can explore the minor pre-Inca ruins around Lima and the catacombs at the San Francisco monastery, the site of an estimated 70,000 burials. The changing of the guard at the Plaza de Armas will also appeal to military-minded littlies.

around peru

Kids will enjoy exploring the famous Inca ruins in the Cuzco area, especially breathtaking Machu Picchu. You could try to get older kids to walk the popular Inca Trail, but with three days of difficult hiking you might find younger attention spans wandering and tantrums becoming more frequent. A better option is to take the train or splurge on a helicopter and take a few short walks around the ruins.

In Chan Chan (the huge adobe capital) the pyramids will appeal to kids and they'll like the huge herds of domesticated alpaca and llama and colourful wild fiestas on Lake Titicaca. Kids also love a light-aircraft flight over the Nazca lines – the huge, mysterious drawings on the desert floor depicting animals and geometric shapes.

festivals

Check out Cuzco's colourful Inti Raymi (Festival of the Sun) if you're visiting in late June for a real taste of traditional culture.

VENEZUELA

Venezuelans adore children and due to a high population growth they are omnipresent. Few foreigners travel with children in Venezuela, but those who do easily find plenty of local companions.

Basic supplies are usually no problem in Caracas or in other cities. Bottled water is readily available and you can buy disposable nappies and baby food in supermarkets and pharmacies. Health is a bit more of an issue, given numerous potential hazards (see the Health chapter for further information or consult your doctor for more information).

Free rides on buses and the Caracas metro mean that your child doesn't occupy a separate seat.

caracas

things to see & do

The capital holds little appeal for many children and is considered more dangerous than the rest of the country. You can check out the native birds, reptiles and mammals at Parque Zoológico do Curicuao, easily accessible by metro. The Museo de los Niños (children's museum) is an excellent hands-on museum; avoid the busy weekend period. The largest city park, Parque del Este, is a good place for the kids to visit the snake house, aviary, cactus garden or see a weekend show at the planetarium.

around venezuela

Organised tour operators in the capital will tailor trips to suit children including trekking in the *tepuis* (flat-topped mountains), flying over the world's highest waterfall, Angel Falls, or visiting the marvellous Parque Nacional Mochima. If you head to smaller towns children can experience more of the traditional way of life.

festivals

The dancing devils – colourful horned demons, monsters and fantastic animals – are bound to scare at Diablos Dazantes on Corpus Christi.

SOUTH & CENTRAL AMERICA

COSTA RICA

Costa Rica is the one of the safest countries to visit in Latin America and one of the friendliest. It also has tasty food and an agreeable climate. Don't be surprised if you're met with curiosity by Costa Ricans as few international visitors bring their children with them to Central America's most ecologically minded nation.

san josé

practicalities

The transportation system is inexpensive and extensive, radiating from San José, making it a convenient base for ventures. Although driving a rental car around the capital is difficult, leisurely drives through the countryside can be fun. Roads vary from barely passable to very good. Hiring a taxi for a day can be cheaper than a tour and allow you to enjoy the ride as much as the kids.

information

The *Tico Times* has a what's on page for children.

things to see & do

wild things Kids will like the Serpentario – a small but weird collection of live snakes and lizards and the Spirogyra Jardín de Mariposas that houses Costa Rica's most dazzling butterflies.

interesting & educational Older kids will have fun at the Museo de los Niños (Children's Museum), a big place with hands-on displays, part of the old jail. The gruesome exhibits that include criminals' severed limbs at the Museo de Criminología may interest older children.

pure entertainment There is the Children's Theatre group which makes a performance a fun Spanish lesson. Also consider taking a family dance class. Movies are often screened in English with Spanish subtitles. A few kilometres west of town is the Acua Mania water park – great for the whole family.

parks & playgrounds

The littlies will enjoy the playground in the Parque Morazán. Teenagers check each other out and meet at the Plaza de la Cultura where there are several fast-food joints and ice-cream bars.

around costa rica

There's lots do around the capital in the Central Valley region including horse riding, river rafting or kayaking and visiting volcanoes, national parks or wilderness lodges. West of San José there is a butterfly farm in La Guácima and nearby, in Alajuela, Zoo Ave has lots of birds and some monkeys and reptiles. Over-fives can go on the aerial tram through the rainforest canopy near the Parque Nacional Braulio Carrillo. The topiary garden in Zarcero with its bushes in animal and human forms will appeal to small children.

festivals

In July there is the Fiesta of the Virgin of the Sea in Puntarenas and Playa del Coco, with a colourful boat regatta as well as many land-based festivities.

GUATEMALA

Children are highly regarded in Guatemala and can often break down barriers and open the doors to local hospitality. Guatemala, however, is so culturally dense with such an emphasis on history and archaeology that children can become easily bored. Water parks, recreation centres (called *turicentros*) with pools and games, playgrounds and hands-on activities such as weaving can all break up duller activities.

Buses are the cheapest way to get around. While kids might think it's fun for short trips, they may not have the patience to ride cheek by jowl with the masses and their produce (vegetable *and* animal) on longer trips. Rental cars are expensive and navigating very narrow roads alongside hell-bent drivers is no treat.

Bring extra warm clothes for kids. Hotels of all price ranges can be damp and musty; choose upstairs rooms, preferably non-carpeted. Bottled water (with an unbroken seal) is the way to go and you'll need to be strict about food (avoid salads and ice cream sold on the streets).

guatemala city

Guatemala City – the largest urban agglomeration in Central America – is a sprawling smoggy place though the city's Zona 2 has a couple of interesting spots.

things to see & do

The large Parque Minerva is a tranquil place where the kids can run among the eucalyptus trees. There are carnival rides and games for children near the Mapa En

Relieve, an odd but fun map of Guatemala including mountains that are exaggerated for dramatic effect. The Autosafari Chapín makes for a great day-trip south of the capital. This drive-through safari park with animal conservation projects is a great place to show kids some native species including deer, peccaries and macaws.

antigua guatemala

Antigua is a better base for families – it's one of the more kid-friendly Guatemalan cities with playgrounds, Spanish classes for children and food for the finicky. Nestled between three dramatic volcanoes, it's one of the oldest and most beautiful cities in the Americas.

things to see & do

On sunny days kids can frolic with the butterflies at the lush Mariposario Antigua farm. Casa K'ojom is a cultural museum dedicated to Mayan music and ceremonies that kids will enjoy with an excellent audiovisual show. Another favourite with kids is the convent of La Merced, left in ruins by earthquakes in the 18th century. It has a huge 27m-diameter fountain – one of the largest and certainly the most impressive in Central America.

Older children might enjoy bike riding or horse-riding tours into the countryside. There are also cultural tours of the town, and to nearby villages and farms. Teenagers will love the challenge of treks to the summit of Volcán Pacaya. The Antigua market is chaotic, colourful and busy, but an interesting insight into local culture for kids. On most weekend nights you can hear mariachi or marimba bands playing in the Parque Central – the town's gathering spot.

festivals

The most exciting time to visit Antigua (and also the busiest) is during Semana Santa (Holy Week) when hundreds of people dressed in deep purple robes parade along streets that have been covered in elaborate carpets of sawdust and flower petals. The busy crowds and the clouds of incense won't be much fun for those with younger children though.

HONDURAS

There are few children-specific activities in Honduras, but clever parents will include kids in their plans. Larger hotels usually have swimming pools to keep kids cool. There are a couple of ecotourism ranches near Omoa and Copán Ruinas which offer activities. You should be safety conscious, especially in La Ceiba where robbery is becoming more common, and if you intend to go hiking in wild places read up on the health risks first, especially potentially dangerous animals and insects.

Buses are an easy and cheap way to get around, ranging from the odd air-conditioned bus with videos and soft drinks to the more common used school buses from the USA.

tegucigalpa

things to see & do

Tegucigalpa – the busy, noisy capital – has a zoo with some local wildlife and an area where iguanas are bred to be released into the wild again. There are organised tours to Parque Nacional La Tigra and fascinating old Spanish mining towns.

around honduras

The safest beach for swimming is probably West Bay on Roatán in the Bay Islands, off the north coast. When swimming you should be aware that many beaches have rip tides, annoying sandflies and mosquitoes, along with the chance of catching dengue fever and malaria. Horse riding at the spectacular Maya ruins at Copán is great fun for older children, while children of all ages can enjoy organised jungle tours through Honduras' lush parks such as Parque Nacional Pico Bonito.

MEXICO

Most children are excited and stimulated by the colours, sights and sounds of Mexico. Apart from the obvious attractions of beaches and swimming pools you can find other special attractions, such as zoos and aquariums. Plus there are the stories of the Aztecs and the Olmecs to delight littlies.

Children are welcome at all kinds of hotels and in virtually every cafe and restaurant. It's usually not hard to find an inexpensive babysitter; just ask at your hotel. Children pay full fare on Mexican long-distance buses unless they're small enough to sit on your lap.

mexico city

information

Tiempo Libre (in Spanish), the city's weekly what's on magazine, includes lots of entertainment for children.

practicalities

Mexico City has a good, cheap metro and bus system. However it can get extremely crowded. Some trains have cars reserved for women and children, but avoid the metro except late in the morning, the evening and on Sundays. At peak times the platforms can become dangerously packed with passengers and younger children may be intimidated by the large crowds.

Crossing from Belize into the Petén region in the north-east corner of Guatemala, we had a relaxed and friendly border crossing. The friendliness of the Guatemalan people struck us immediately – from the cheerful border guards (who were intrigued by our bikes and spent a long time telling us where we should visit in Guatemala) to people running out to the road to wave at us as we drove by. Throughout Central America, André was treated royally. The people here have a great respect for family and children are very special.

guatemala LIVING with LOCALS

Cathy Sather, her husband, Doug, and son, André, 12, travelled through Central America, spending three months in Guatemala.

We stopped at El Remate, a small village spread along the edge of Lago de Petén Itza. On our first morning, we arose at 5 am so we could be at the ancient Mayan city of Tikal for sunrise. We hurried in the fresh morning air to try to get to Temple II so we could climb it and watch the sun rise over Temple I. Here we sat – high on top of this temple, listening to the sounds of the jungle and imagining the civilisation that once existed here. André was fascinated by the ruins themselves, the jungle life, the stories about the people who had lived here and especially by the grandeur of these structures and the fact that they were built by human labour. Another great thing about these temples is that they provide a great opportunity for kids to be active. André raced up all of the temples and explored every nook and cranny that was there to explore. As the day wore on and I grew a bit tired he was often my inspiration to climb one more temple.

The other extremely special part of our time in this village was the opportunity we had to live with a family. It was especially fun for André because there were lots of kids for him to play with. The family we lived with had six children and their relatives next door had another four children. We stayed in a *palapa* (thatch-roofed building) that had an open-air window that overlooked the lake with a western view of the sunsets. There was a system for running water which we soon found out really didn't work; the lake really provided all of the water. Everyone had little stands built out in the lake where they washed their clothes and bathed themselves – a daily ritual we would soon partake in.

The village had just got electric power for the first time the month before we arrived. There was a neighbour who had a fridge and often the kids were sent on their bikes to get something from their fridge. Soon André was invited to go along on these trips. He really became part of the family even more easily than Doug or I. He went with the kids when they did many of their errands for the family. These included the daily trip to the *molino* where the corn was ground into meal for the tortillas; a visit to an elderly family member; a day with the kids at school where they were celebrating carnival; many trips to the store; and many to the neighbour with the fridge. The kids also played hours' worth of soccer and threw stones in the lake. We learned so much Spanish living with this family, but more importantly we were allowed into their lives and developed a wonderful relationship with these people who we will never forget. André absolutely loved his experience here and we all found it quite difficult to move on.

From here we travelled south for two days through an area that had been known for its guerilla activity. The only hair-raising experience we had was on a windy dirt road which narrowed to one lane every time a vehicle was coming in the other direction. At the end of the first day we arrived at Finca Ixobel, a beautiful oasis for travellers owned by an American woman who has lived there for years. The *finca* (farm) had cabins and camping, a wonderful organic garden and the most delicious and social meals you can imagine. Doug and André went on a day-long horseback trip and the next day they went on an all-day hike up into a cave. They saw stalactites and stalagmites, sometimes swimming through deep water holding their flashlight above the water. The cave hike ended on a ledge with a huge pool below. They had the choice of climbing down or jumping into the pool. Needless to say, both André and Doug chose the latter. André also re-climbed and plunged into the pool as many times as he could. He came back just bursting to tell me about every detail of their day!

"André raced up all of the temples and explored every nook and cranny that was there to explore. As the day wore on and I grew a bit tired he was often my inspiration to climb one more temple."

We went on to spend another few months in the more densely populated areas of Guatemala and wondered how we would ever return to our 'normal' lives. We'd had time to enjoy music, reading and drawing. The trip gave André a great chance to read – he became a voracious reader, reading everything he could get his hands on. We had experienced the wonders of vibrant jungle life and ocean life. We all became fairly fluent in Spanish and had lots of fun soaking up the wonderful culture and atmosphere. But mostly, we'd had lots of great time with each other!

things to see & do

interesting & educational Kids won't want to miss the Papalote Museo del Niño, a marvellous hands-on children's museum. The Museo Nacional de Antropologia is fascinating exploration of Mexican culture, however it is very large with more than most adults, let alone children, can absorb in one visit. Close by, indigenous Totanac people perform their spectacular *voladores* – suspended by their ankles from a 20m pole.

pure entertainment For free entertainment, you can't beat the musicians, comedians and mimes who turn Coyoacán's central plazas into a big open-air party most evenings and all day on weekends. At Plaza Garibaldi in the evenings you can treat the kids by wandering around and listening to the mariachi bands decked out in their fancy costumes. Foreign movies for children are usually dubbed into English.

parks & playgrounds

The Bosque de Chaptultepec is a large inner-city woodland expanse with lakes, a zoo, several excellent museums and La Feira – a large amusement park with some hair-raising rides. To chill out try the Parque Ecológico de Xochimilco which has lakes, an incipient botanical garden and a truly surprising number and variety of water birds.

festivals

Mexico has lots of fiestas but on Día del Niño there is a special Kids' Day Carnival in late February or early March with parades, music, food, drink, dancing, fireworks and fun. On 12 December children are taken to the Basílica de Guadalupe dressed in brilliant indigenous costumes.

around mexico

Some of the best things to see and do in Mexico are within a day's travel of the capital. Archaeological sites can be fun if the kids are into climbing pyramids and exploring tunnels. The ancient city of Teotihuacán – the site of two enormous, spectacular pyramids – is an easy day trip. The region also has volcanoes, ruins and national parks. One of the best places for kids to see wildlife is Africam Safari east of Mexico City.

If you intend to travel to more isolated towns and villages renting a car or taking an organised tour is often easier and more convenient than the bus for families. Kids will be amazed at the cliff divers in Acapulco and love the handicrafts (masks, marionettes, musical instruments) found in most towns.

SOUTH & CENTRAL AMERICA

THE BAHAMAS

The Bahamas pursues the family traveller aggressively and the larger hotels compete by providing facilities for children. Most offer free accommodation or greatly reduced rates for children staying in their parents' room, and will provide a babysitter, cots and baby food if you make an advance request. Several all-inclusive resorts cater specifically to families, offering a full range of activities and amenities for their young guests. Rental villas and apartments are also a good option for families. Most come fully staffed, allowing you to leave the children with the housekeeper (you'll need to check that this is in accordance with rental terms).

nassau

practicalities

Exploring the island of New Providence with kids is easy – it's only 21 miles (34km) long and seven miles (11km) wide. There are organised tours and minibuses as well as car rental.

things to see & do

Paradise Island, just offshore from Nassau, has great beaches or cruise to Blue Lagoon Island where the movie *Flipper* was filmed. Kids can swim with trained dolphins in a protected lagoon. Toddlers can stand in the shallow lagoon where the dolphins will also let you touch them.

The endangered Bahama parrot is bred in captivity at Ardastra Gardens and Zoo and West Indian flamingos are trained to strut their stuff on voice command.

At Crystal Cay Marine Park – a spaceship-shaped structure hovering above the ocean – the kids can see sharks and turtles, and handle starfish and other seabed critters. You can also cruise to the coral reefs of the offshore marine park aboard a submarine.

Kids adore Fort Charlotte, an old-style castle featuring guides decked out in period costume. They can explore the moat, dungeon, underground tunnels and a re-created torture chamber including fierce torturers and their victims.

parks & playgrounds

Let the children loose in the Botanical Garden with its lush Fantasia section with hundreds of species of tropical plants plus lily ponds, grottoes and a waterfall fountain.

books

For encouragement, you might like to check out Nan Jeffrey's *Bahamas – Out Island Odyssey*, her tale of travelling through the islands with two teenage sons and an infant.

BERMUDA

Although Bermudians are family-oriented, Bermuda can pose some challenges to travellers with children. There are no car rentals and while large resorts and hotels don't place restrictions on children, many other hotels and guesthouses tend to be formal and gear activities solely toward adults; a few don't accept children at all. Cots or highchairs can be rented from the Bermuda Red Cross if your hotel can't provide them.

things to see & do

As well as beaches and swimming pools, Hamilton has kids' snorkelling tours, mini-golf, a wonderful aquarium and zoo, limestone caverns, and plenty of cool forts to explore. At Fort Hamilton the kids can scurry about in the dungeon-like magazine and in the fort's narrow moat which has been turned into luxuriant gardens.

The Bermuda Underwater Exploration Institute in Pembroke Parish has interactive displays featuring state-of-the-art sound and video technology. The Crystal Caves tour in Bailey's Bay is a fun little excursion through impressive subterranean caves. Kids will like the story of how it was discovered in 1907 by two boys looking for their lost cricket ball.

CUBA

Cuba is a pretty safe place to bring children; the traffic on the roads is limited and security is good, and most Cubans are extremely courteous towards guests.

Most tour companies will offer reduced prices for children under the age of 12, provided they share their parents' accommodation. Only a token amount is charged for children under the age of two. Families can often get a room for the normal price of a double if children are young. Some resorts offer special daycare programs for young guests and almost any hotel reception will be able to arrange a babysitter for a nominal amount. Electrical safety in rooms may be poor – inspect the appliances for exposed wiring.

If you're not on a tour, it may be tough to find food children will eat. Omelettes, fried potatoes and bananas are a safe bet for young stomachs.

havana

practicalities

Playgrounds are only open at certain times. Getting around in vintage cars, horse-drawn carriages and *bicitaxis* (three-wheel tricycles) can be fun, although city buses can involve long waits and are usually extremely crowded.

things to see & do

The Parque Lenin has so much for kids to do – beautiful old trees, a large zoo and an aquarium with freshwater fish and crocodiles, a children's railway line, an amusement park and rowboats for hire on the artificial lake. Join the Cuban families who flock to the amusement park at Expo Cuba, bypassing the rather dry propaganda displays.

The Museo del Aire has aircraft of all descriptions and kids can check out Che Guevara's personal plane or the space suit used by Cuba's first cosmonaut.

Havana has several theatres and cinemas such as Cinecito behind Hotel Inglaterra which frequently shows kids' films. On weekends there are puppet shows and other performances for children in the main theatres.

around cuba

Besides an organised tour, renting a car is the easiest – if not the cheapest – way to see Cuba. Take kids snorkelling or bird-watching on Península Guanahacabibes. For a taste of Spanish history, there's Santiago de Cuba – a treasure trove of cultural events, castles and museums – or check out the preserved cobbled streets and courtyards of Trinidad.

DOMINICAN REPUBLIC

As in most of the Caribbean, children are highly regarded in the Dominican Republic, making for easy and comfortable family travel. Buses and taxis can take you almost anywhere. Rental cars are expensive and driving is risky. Malaria and dengue fever are both endemic. See the Health chapter for more information on immunisation.

santo domingo

Santo Domingo is a colourful, historic city with the oldest church, the first paved road in the New World and the oldest surviving European fortress. The Museo de las Casas Reales is filled with treasures recovered from Spanish galleons that sunk in the nearby waters.

The Parque Zoológical Nacional has a variety of animals and a lovely flamingo-filled pond and the aquarium has an underwater walkway where sharks pass overhead.

Let off some steam at the Jardín Botánico Nacional, the Parque Colón or the Plaza de la Hispanidad – a large, open area closed off to traffic. The latter are both good places for parents to have a well-earned beer while the little darlings play nearby.

festivals

Music and dancing at the Merengue Festival (July/August) is a little less wild than the city's other carnivals and is perfect for funky kids.

around dominican republic

If you're tired of trying to keep the kids entertained yourself, the Costa del Coco is synonymous with an all-inclusive resort where there are lots of activities, gorgeous palm-lined beaches and an amusement park featuring dancing horses, dolphins and sea lions. There are organised tours for whale watching, encountering crocodiles and visiting iguanas.

JAMAICA

With family travel common in the Caribbean, Jamaica actively encourages you to bring the kids along – offering babysitters if you arrange them in advance. All-inclusive resorts – such as Poinciana (Negril), FDR Resort (Runaway Bay), Superclubs Boscobel Beach (near Ocho Rios) and Sandals Beaches (Negril and Whitehouse) – all let parents take it easy while kids are kept busy with a range of activities. When staying at hotels other than family resorts, it's a good idea to pre-arrange essentials like cots, baby food or highchairs.

For independent travel rent a villa or an apartment; many are fully staffed which can include a babysitter or housekeeper who is happy to help out with child minding. Despite the appalling driving habits of locals, Jamaica is great for scenic family drives.

montego bay

things to see & do

The Montego Bay Marine Park organises guided tours by canoe or kayak through mangroves for kids to spot herons, egrets, pelicans and waterfowl, while below juvenile barracudas, tarpon, snapper, crabs and lobsters play. Kids will love the semi-submersible trip that operates from Margueritaville that lets them see marine life through a bubble dome beneath the boat.

PUERTO RICO

Puerto Rico has probably the best roads in the Caribbean and while it's probably best to avoid driving in busy San Juan, renting a car and exploring the island can be lots of fun. It's relatively easy to travel with no fixed accommodation or book only a day in advance. Puerto Rican law requires that children younger than four be restrained in an approved child's seat.

If you'd prefer the predictability of a resort, all four of Puerto Rico's mega-resorts offer full-day, camp-style programs for children three to 15; these are the Hyatt Dorado and Hyatt Regency (both in Dorado); El Conquistador (near Fajardo) and Wyndham Palmas del Mar (near Humacao).

Staying out late in the streets and eating out in restaurants with young children, especially babies, is quite common. It is now legal to breastfeed in public, though previously it was considered indecent exposure. Most people will look away if they see breastfeeding or pretend not to have noticed. Attitudes are changing and some people will even come up and congratulate a breastfeeding woman.

san juan

things to see & do

The Museo del Niño is similar to many of the interactive museums in the USA, including a journey through the human heart. The Luis A Ferre Parque de Ciencias is a good value theme park – with a planetarium and interesting museums devoted to physics, electrical energy, transport and aerospace technology.

On Sundays, La Casita forms the backdrop for free performances of traditional music, dance and a puppet theatre. The Parque de las Palomas (Pigeon Park) is a shady cobblestone courtyard where kids can feed the pigeons. Get the kids to re-enact the days of the Spanish Conquistadors at the Fuerte san Felipe del Morro, an impressive six-level fort dating back to 1539. On weekends the fields around the fort are alive with picnickers and kite flyers.

around puerto rico

Puerto Rico's wonderful beaches are usually packed on weekends and deserted during the week. For beach-loving kids it is worth paying a few dollars to use a resort's beach and facilities. Good family beaches include: Balneario Condado in San Juan; pretty Playa Luquillo on the east coast; and on the north coast, Playa de Cerro Gordo, Crash Boat Beach and a cove near the Faro de los Morrillos.

El Yunque on the east coast is a beautiful forest for walking. The visitor centre here has interactive exhibits, a film in English and a walkway through the forest canopy. There is winter whale watching from the west coast – you can charter a boat from Rincón. To see animals you missed in the wild, take the kids to Zoológico Zoorico in Mayagüez. The archaeological sites at Tibes give kids a glimpse of ancient civilisations, including ceremonial plazas, *bateyes* (ball courts) and more than 180 preserved skeletons.

AFRICA & THE MIDDLE EAST

While many parents think that travel in Africa is out of the question with children, thousands of pint-sized travellers visit the continent each year without incident. Children are highly valued in many African societies, and travelling with them can mean special treatment and an open door into local society.

Health is the main worry for most parents travelling here. Malaria is endemic in many areas and you must ensure that children are well protected (see the Health chapter for more information). Other health hazards are listed under the relevant countries, but most are easily preventable with simple measures like wearing shoes or avoiding standing water.

You may also want to spend more on your accommodation to ensure that bathroom and sleeping facilities are better suited to your children's needs. For kids desperate to cool off in the heat, top-end hotels in many countries will allow littlies to use their pools for a fee.

With planning and flexibility, the benefits of exposing children to the amazing wildlife, landscape and history of the continent far outweigh the inconveniences.

EGYPT

Egyptians love children and welcome them almost everywhere. Children under 12 are admitted free of charge to most antiquities sites, museums and many hotels. Although all but the most basic hotels are perfectly suitable for children – depending on your fussiness about cleanliness and hygiene – only four- and five-star places have child-specific services, such as babysitting. Although breast-feeding is widely practised in public, it is usually done discreetly.

practicalities

Child safety awareness in Egypt is minimal, so if you're hiring a vehicle, check that there are seat belts in the back. You will need to bring your own car seat for younger children. When renting feluccas or other boats, don't expect life jackets; if you really need them, bring your own. Likewise with helmets for horse riding.

One concern with children is the high incidence of diarrhoea and stomach problems that plague travellers in Egypt so come prepared for any problems (see the Health chapter). Another potential health worry is hepatitis, which is endemic in Egypt. It is worth getting your children vaccinated against hepatitis A and B before leaving on your trip.

On the positive side, nappies, formula and wipes are readily available in pharmacies in major towns and tourist centres. High-SPF sunscreen, crucial when touring, is not always available outside Cairo and tends to be very expensive, so bring your own. Baby-changing facilities are nonexistent but people are tolerant about changing in public.

things to see & do

wild things Egypt's Red Sea coast is famous for its underwater flora and fauna, and although diving is not recommended for under-16s, there are plenty of snorkelling opportunities. Some of the larger resorts also have glass-bottomed boats that allow you to see the fish and coral.

interesting & educational In a country awash with five thousand years' worth of monuments, there's no shortage of culture and history on offer. You can make things more interesting to kids by finding gruesome reliefs in temples and tombs (a big hit with the over-fives) or searching in museums for the pets and toys that pharaohs took with them to the afterlife. A visit to Dr Ragab's Pharaonic Village – a theme park near Giza in which actors re-enact daily life in ancient Egypt – is another way of keeping history alive for young archaeologists. Fagnoon Art School about 15km south of Giza gets kids painting, making pottery and doing simple carpentry.

pure entertainment There are a number of great amusement parks around Cairo. Crazy Water has water slides, a wave pool and a playground. Sindbad Park, Merryland and Dreampark have the usual roller coasters and rides. Bowling and ice skating have also arrived at Cairo's many malls; the World Trade Centre and Arcadia malls are the most central.

activities

Horse and camel riding are an exciting adventure from stables near the Giza pyramids.

books

Locally-produced kids' history books, such as Salima Ikram's *The Pharaohs*, are excellent for kids and reasonably priced for budget-conscious parents. Hoopoe books is a local children's publisher with a fascinating list of titles related to Pharaonic and Islamic Egypt.

cultural issues

Egypt is a conservative society and while Egyptians are tolerant of foreign visitors, they do not appreciate nudity among young children in public. Make sure you have bathing suits, even for babies.

ERITREA & DJIBOUTI

Children receive a warm welcome in both Eritrea and Djibouti, although the lack of child-specific facilities means that travelling here with kids can be a challenge. Top-end hotels usually don't charge for under-twos and will have a supplement for under-12s.

practicalities

The very basic facilities in Eritrea and Djibouti mean that baby supplies are not easy to get. Although nappies, baby food and bottled water are available at upmarket supermarkets in Asmara and Djibouti Town, they cannot be found elsewhere. Bring high-SPF sunscreen with you from home. If you're renting a vehicle, bring car seats with you. Malaria is endemic in Djibouti, and in the western lowlands of Eritrea. Mild altitude sickness can also afflict new arrivals in the Eritrean highlands, so watch out for symptoms and take it easy on your first few days. See the Health chapter for more information.

activities

Away from hotel swimming pools (available for a daily fee) there are a number of activities on offer. In Eritrea, the islands of the Dahlak Archipelago offer beautiful sandy beaches and fabulous snorkelling, although they're not cheap to visit. Young children may also enjoy the bustling Monday livestock market in Keren. In Djibouti, hiking can be done at La Forêt du Day National Park.

books

Trouble, by Jane Kurtz, is the story of a young Eritrean boy who's always getting into trouble. *Fire on the Mountain and Other Stories from Ethiopia and Eritrea*, by Harold Courlander et al, is a collection of Ethiopian and Eritrean folktales.

ETHIOPIA

Ethiopians are very welcoming to travellers with children, although specific children's facilities are thin on the ground outside Addis Ababa.

practicalities

Disposable nappies, baby food and formula are available at the expat supermarkets in Addis Ababa but are not always in stock and can be very expensive. Addis Ababa has good medical facilities, including a special 24-hour children's clinic and medicines are available. However, outside the capital facilities are basic at best. You should bring your own high-SPF sunscreen as well as antibiotic eardrops, eye baths and wet wipes. Take care with food too; diarrhoea and vomiting are common so drink only bottled or boiled and purified water. Malaria is prevalent at lower altitudes. Bilharzia infects all lakes and rivers except Lake Langano, so keep swimming confined to pools.

things to see & do

wild things Almost all children will be amazed at the sight of 200,000 flamingos – they congregate on Lake Abiato in season. Mule treks through the Bale or Simien Mountains National Parks are an excellent way to see baboons, ibex and other wildlife.

interesting & educational The small National Museum in Addis Ababa has the fossils of the 3.5-million-year-old Lucy, possibly our earliest ancestor. The city's Ethnological Museum, with its examples of local crafts and exhibits on regions and people, make it an ideal place for kids to learn about Ethiopia's rich ethnic diversity. If the conflict with Eritrea allows, the city of Aksum, with its ruined palaces, underground tombs and field of huge, ancient carved stele (some as much as 25m tall), is a great place for children to explore.

activities

Older children may enjoy wandering around the impressive castles at Gondar though younger kids may find it too strenuous.

books

When the World Began: Stories Collected from Ethiopia, by Elizabeth Laird, is a collection of Ethiopian oral folktales for nine- to 12-year-olds. *Ethiopia, the Roof of Africa*, by Jane Kurtz, is another good read. Younger children will enjoy *Pulling the Lion's Tail* also by Jane Kurtz – an illustrated retelling of a folk story about a child who wins her stepmother's love by taming a lion.

GAMBIA & SENEGAL

Both Gambia and Senegal have a fairly well-developed tourist industry and large top-end hotels and resorts cater for families with children. In cheaper places there are no discounts for children and on public transport a seat is paid for, no matter how old the occupant. But while there are few facilities for children outside the most touristed areas, children are highly valued in West Africa and having them with you can make travel a more enriching experience.

practicalities

You can find baby food, disposable nappies and medicines – at a price – in the large cities but elsewhere you'll have to bring whatever you need with you. Car seats and life jackets for children should also be brought from home.

Egypt has long been considered the cradle of civilisation, abounding in tales and artefacts belonging to pharaohs of ages past. But Egypt is also the land of bargaining with people who may find you unintelligible, crossing streets meant for two lanes of traffic that have five lanes of traffic and waking up at 5 am to purchase a ticket for Tutankhamun's tomb.

egypt TEMPLED OUT

Debra Leung, 15, travelled to Egypt with her family for a three-week holiday.

Our family, including myself and a rebellious 10-year-old, and a friend's family, with two boisterous boys aged five and eight, packed our bags and set off for the land of the pyramids. Prior to our trip to Egypt we did as much research as we could to make the following three weeks as painless as possible and I strongly urge you to do the same. This will not only ensure that you are well prepared for the coming weeks but you will gain much more from the guided tours if you have some sort of background. We approached this as a joint family activity which also provided the family with hours of fun learning – including that embalming consists of pulling various bodily organs out of extremely small orifices which the children in our family found hilarious.

The plane trip to Egypt was long and taxing to say the least, especially for the young children, so an adequate number of pre-organised 'plane games' proved to be an excellent distraction. Once we arrived in Cairo we faced the daunting task of trying to relocate four grumpy children and four even more exhausted adults. This was definitely not the right state of mind to be facing the horrors of peak hour traffic in Egypt. The one piece of information that we managed to glean within the first day of our visit was that it is *always* peak hour in Egypt. And traffic rules are virtually nonexistent. A street meant for two lanes of oncoming traffic can comfortably fit five lanes of honking and abusive Egyptians. The closest thing to a pedestrian crossing is the small gap in the traffic caused by frantic tourists, such as ourselves, sprinting across.

The pyramids at Giza were a must-see and really epitomised why Egypt is referred to as the land of mystery. You can actually walk into the chambers inside the pyramids however I wouldn't advise it for families with extremely young children. The descents and ascents can be extremely steep and cramped and small children can get easily frightened. The Egyptian Museum in Cairo with its large collection of ancient artefacts including the mummy of Ramses II is great but could take an entire day and younger children will tend to lose interest.

Bargaining is a way of life in Egypt as we soon discovered and we used 'never accept the first offer' as a general rule of thumb. Most of the street vendors could understand English which was a great help for a bunch of confused tourists from Australia and many of them often enjoy a good haggle. I was once told by a friend that 'No matter how long and hard you shop for an item you will find it for less just after you've bought it' and this was no exception. After providing countless hours of amusement for the Egyptian locals with our very poor bargaining skills, we were annoyed to when we often found items for half the price in the shop just next door. Getting the younger children involved with the bargaining process was great fun for the whole family and at times could also prove an effective bargaining tool.

A cruise down the river Nile was an ideal way to view the Egyptian countryside. All cruises stop daily at various temples including the Temples of Karnak and Luxor Temple, to name some of the better known ones.

My advice for anyone contemplating a temple cruise is that it is most definitely a good idea to space out your visits to temples and more importantly be selective in what you visit, because it is extremely easy for younger children to get 'templed out'. Generally younger children enjoyed the visits to tombs as much as anybody, there seemed to be something reminiscent of Indiana Jones as we tramped down the narrow passageways admiring treasures of the golden age. But after the first five temples the children pointed out that several of them appeared to be almost identical and refused to even walk, resulting in piggy backs and adults with sore backs.

We soon found that it was possible to make history and temples entertaining by pre-reading legends and then explaining them to the kids. At the temples, we'd show them the associated hieroglyphics and images carved into the temple walls to keep them interested.

> "Once we arrived in Cairo we faced the daunting task of trying to relocate four grumpy children and four even more exhausted adults This was definitely not the right state of mind to be facing the horrors of peak hour traffic in Egypt."

Some of the more enjoyable activities involved several opportunities during the course of the two-week cruise for the whole family to get involved in traditional Egyptian activities. There were numerous dress-up parties and various activities, such as belly dancing, that provided a good chance for the whole family to really live the Egyptian experience.

And soon enough it was time for our travelling crew to return to Australia and the luxury of pedestrian crossings. Perhaps we were a little worse for wear, but rewarded with the knowledge that not only did we learn about the history of one of the world's oldest and most treasured civilisations but we had the unique opportunity to live it.

things to see & do

There are a number of wildlife reserves in both countries although almost all have to be visited by vehicle. Although the area is touristy, most children will be thrilled by a look at the crocs in the Kachikaly Crocodile Pool in Bakau, Gambia.

activities

Apart from the many beaches on offer, a pirogue (boat) trip through mangrove swamps in coastal areas or drive through a wildlife reserve will keep older children amused. The Casmance region of Senegal can also be toured by bicycle (however, check the security situation first). Older children will be sobered by a visit to La Maison des Esclaves and the IFAN Historical Museum on the Île de Gorée near Dakar, which was one of Africa's busiest slave centres in the 18th and 19th centuries.

books

Nine- to 12-year-olds might like *Senegambia: The Land of the Lion* by Philip Koslow, a history of West African communities from the 12th to 20th centuries.

KENYA

Kenyans are helpful and friendly towards children and parents. Your main worry travelling here is likely to be going between towns, where bad roads and poor public transport mean that journeys can be long. Children under two are not usually charged to stay in their parents' room, and two- to 12-year-olds are usually charged at 50% of the adult rate. You'll need to stay in a mid-range hotel if you want reasonable toilet and bathroom facilities. Note that some exclusive lodges impose an age limit of eight or over so as not to disturb the tranquil ambience; check in advance if you are planning to stay in lodges.

practicalities

Although baby food, formula and disposable nappies are available in large supermarkets, they are expensive, so bring as much with you as you can. Child-friendly insect repellent is not available, so make sure you pack some if you are taking children to malarial areas. Keep in mind also that running barefoot carries some risk: in areas of habitation children could get hookworm infestation, while on lakeshores bilharzia can be contracted. Scorpions, snakes and thorns are risks in other areas, so it's best to keep shoes on.

Car hire and safari companies rarely have child seats, so you'll need to bring your own; check in advance that there are seat belts available. If you're using public transport, keep in mind also that *matutus* (minibuses) and buses do not count young children as passengers so they end up sitting on adult knees – not a comfortable option on long journeys.

things to see & do

It goes without saying that wild things are high on most people's agendas in Kenya. Safaris can be made more enjoyable for kids if hotels and lodges have pools to keep them amused when not looking at wildlife. Around Nairobi, the Langata Giraffe Centre, the David Sheldrick Wildlife Trust and Snake Park at the National Museum all reinforce what children have seen out in the wild. Away from animals, the Railway Museum is a popular outing.

parks & playgrounds

Kaleidoscope is an outdoor adventure playground and restaurant on Miotoni Rd, on the way to Karen.

MALAWI

malawi

With its small domestic tourist industry used to catering to families, Malawi is an easy place to travel with children. Although most of its family-oriented hotels are clustered around the shores of Lake Malawi, there's plenty on offer. Family rooms and chalets are generally only slightly more expensive than a double room and arranging an extra bed or two for children in a double room is usually not a problem. Malawi's small size means that travelling between tourist sites is relatively brief and easy.

practicalities

Nappies and other baby supplies can be found in the capital and some main centres but not in remote areas. Medical facilities in main towns are good but expensive, so make sure your insurance has adequate cover. There is bilharzia in Lake Malawi, although people may try to tell you otherwise. Beaches away from human habitation and free of the waterweed that harbours the bilharzia snails are the least risky places to swim but are not totally safe. You should check local reports before swimming anywhere.

things to see & do

Malawi has a number of wildlife reserves, many of which can be visited on horseback or on foot, as well as in jeeps. Nyika Safari Company organises all activities in the popular Nyika National Park and is a good place to start when checking out child-friendly safari options.

activities

Horse treks are a good way of keeping kids entertained. Kayaking is offered at Cape Maclear and if your children are old enough, paddling through its offshore islands is a good way to spend a few days. You can also hike on foot through most of the national parks. That perennial option, swimming, is on offer at all the resorts.

Madagascar is the first country I've visited where the airline office didn't even have a phone. Post offices in major towns may have one, but they rarely work. The massive erosion of the landscape is mirrored in the decay of basic services. Mail, transport and all communications, if available at all, are erratic and unreliable at best. A bit like our eight-month-old baby! But leaving civilisation for chaos was still a highlight of our big trip.

madagascar STAYING SANE in MADLAND

Jane Bennett spent three weeks in Madagascar with her eight-month-old baby, Sacha, and partner, David.

Three-quarters of our way through an around-the-world ticket by the time we hit Africa, we figured we had travelling with a baby pretty well sussed – getting the right hand luggage contents for flights, groovy little packets of wipes, strategically packed cloths and toys, timing the breastfeeds, inventiveness with entertaining and food. Making it easy on ourselves, we had arranged to stay with family and friends most of the way and everything was swimming along nicely. A few days back we had been in suburban Pretoria, where two things stand out in my memory. Firstly, I will never forget sitting in a homey family living room watching the surreal barrage of news reports that was obviously a very brief summary of the daily violence, death and mayhem outside the security gates. The second is that Pretoria was where Sacha started to crawl.

We had entered a new dimension. Our baby could now wander off her floor mattress, fall off beds and potentially disappear in crowds. She wasn't just travelling with us any more, we were following her! We'd always scoffed at people carting huge mountains of kid-related baggage and had tried to keep it simple (definitely no stroller, OK!). We had the ergonomic baby backpack that she'd travel and sleep in for hours, and the clip-on feeding chair for restaurants, but it wasn't till we hit Madagascar that we learned that a port-a-cot (offered in sympathy) was also an indispensable part of the caravan. Besides, it had a mosquito net.

We had arrived in Madland, as our friends affectionately called it, the week after dissidents had burned down the old Rova (Queen's Palace). They had warned us not to walk outside after dark and not to carry money on the streets in the capital, Antananarivo (Tana). It is a destination so capricious and unpredictable, yet welcoming and playful that finally, in a perverse sort of way, it made travelling with a baby seem to make sense. It is a land full of frustration for the timebound, where we discovered how late French restaurants open (too late for hungry infants) and where we actually welcomed the scungy flea-ridden dogs that hung around our restaurant table. Not only did they clean up all the spilt food, but they kept Sacha entertained at a safe distance while we had a relatively peaceful meal.

Sacha enjoyed a diet of rice (thankfully), as well as the rice cereal flakes and jars of organic baby food we'd stocked up on in the US, though they didn't last long. She was still breastfeeding three or four feeds a day which made travelling easier – providing a constant diet, making her easier to settle and helping her ears on flights. We also took the village approch and fed her pre-chewed portions of our own meals for diversity.

People without phones and television have time for children. When our three-hour trip in an air-con 4WD with our friends and their baby turned into a 13-hour epic in a rickety taxi-*brousse* (bush taxi) with flat tyres and torrential rain and all, the travelling became an adventure. We exhausted our repertoire of songs lulling cranky babes to sleep (with two musicians, it was a huge repertoire, too!). The hours spent waiting for a replacement vehicle in dingy roadside huts with bemused locals became unexpected entertainment for all. We tasted village food and watched the pace of village life with a sense that this experience was a gift in comparison to fleeting glimpses through a frosty window. And we savoured the experience – now denied to us in the West – of cradling a sleeping baby on our laps during a long drive, taking it in turns when we cramped.

"We had entered a new dimension. Our baby could now wander off her floor mattress, fall off beds and potentially disappear in crowds. She wasn't just travelling with us any more, we were following her!"

We realised that babies don't necessarily get excited about dawn walks in the forest to see the giant panda-like lemur, indri. But Sacha slept quietly in the backpack and we'll tell her about it when she gets older. Come to think of it, she was asleep when we saw the gray whales off San Diego too. So for whose benefit were we doing this nerve-racking trip as new parents? With only passport stamps and photos to remember her first round-the-world trip, I'd have to confess it was a rite of passage for us. Somehow the home birth wasn't enough of a challenge. We also needed to grapple with the demands of travelling as a family to one of the world's most difficult areas to prove we could still do such crazy things – that there is life after becoming a parent!

Of course there were the inevitable frustrations of not getting the right food at the right time, or Sacha's moods and sleeps not coinciding with our plans. We learned to be prepared to alter plans at a moment's notice, but that you also meet different people and are treated differently with a baby in tow, especially a fair, blonde baby. Sacha's company certainly meant we probably had a slower trip with fewer destinations than without her, but we also savoured the time we had to see the chameleons and smell the ylang ylang.

MALDIVES

Sun, sand and sea are usually a hit with kids, and resorts are where most people head. They offer a safe environment with virtually no traffic and few hazards. Most resorts are very child-friendly and offer children's facilities, including babysitting services. Children sharing their parents' room are generally charged a supplement which is usually less than the cost of an adult.

practicalities

If you stay in a resort you should check in advance that there are baby supplies available. Even if they are, nappies, medicines and milk or formula will be a lot more expensive than at home, so bring what you can with you. Ensure also that you've got adequate sun protection; in addition to high-SPF sunscreen and hats, Lycra swimshirts are a good idea. Swim shoes are also useful for running in the water and are available at some resorts, but it's best to bring them with you.

activities

Swimming and running on the beach is most kids' idea of heaven, so you shouldn't have much problem amusing them. Most resorts have table tennis, tennis, volleyball or badminton. Older children might get bored after a few days so allow extra money for canoeing or fishing trips. Some resorts offer windsurfing or sailing courses and, while the minimum age for diving is 16, there are 'bubble blower' courses for younger children.

books

Older children might like to check out Roseline Ngcheong-Lun's *The Maldives*, in the Cultures of the World series, before travelling.

MAURITIUS, RÉUNION & SEYCHELLES

With their numerous resorts and fabulous beaches, Mauritius, Réunion and the Seychelles are all enjoyable destinations with children. Most resort hotels have babysitting services and organise children's activities. They may also have playgrounds and play areas. Most tour operators and many hotels offer 50% discounts on the adult rate for children between two and 12 and don't charge at all for under-twos.

practicalities

Although disposable nappies and baby supplies are available, the choice is limited, especially outside Réunion. Bring as much as you can with you. Given the heat and strength of the sun, be vigilant for signs of heatstroke and make sure you have plenty of high-SPF sunscreen with you. If you're worried about marine safety, best to bring a child's life jacket too. Avoid street food if you venture away from the beach and make sure you stick to bottled water.

things to see & do

In the Seychelles, kids love checking out the odd collection at the Natural History Museum in Victoria which includes the bones of the extinct Seychelles crocodile, giant robber crabs and the wreckage of a ship which sunk off the islands in 1570.

activities

The magic combination of beach, sun and water usually works wonders on children. Most resorts have windsurfing and sailing on offer to keep older kids happy and there are usually games such as table tennis and badminton. Kids will also enjoy sailing to Curieuse Island, where they can see one of the world's largest colonies of giant land tortoises and the second largest forest of coco-de-mer palms.

MOROCCO

As in other North African countries, children are welcomed in Morocco and often serve as icebreakers with locals, particularly women. Most hotels give discounts to children under 12 and under-twos usually stay for free.

practicalities

Disposable nappies and other baby supplies are widely available in large Moroccan towns, although they tend to be expensive. Bottled water and UHT or powdered milk are also easy to find. Although Moroccan food is delicious, you should steer clear of salads (if you have a child that eats them), and peel and wash all fruits and vegies. Because roads can be dangerous, and buses and share taxis are less than ideal with kids, try to plan your journey around Morocco's excellent rail system.

things to see & do

Kids will like exploring the maze of narrow, winding alleys in the Fès el-Bali medina (you'll have to keep up with them as it's easy to get lost!). They'll also enjoy the Djemaa el-Fna, the huge, atmospheric square in the heart of the Marrakesh medina which fills with musicians, snake charmers, acrobats and other performers in the evening.

books

For young readers, *The Storytellers* by Ted Lewinis is the evocative tale of a boy and his grandfather who work as storytellers in the medina of Fès. For older children, *Tales From Morocco* is Denys Johnson-Davies' translation of six Moroccan folktales.

Storm and I were travelling and were based in Paris for a few months during the European winter. I was trying to decide whether to go to Spain or Morocco for a break from the cold. I was hesitant to travel alone with Storm in Morocco and thought Spain might be a little tamer. I pulled out a map and some photos from travel brochures and asked Storm where he wanted to go. He replied 'Morocco' with no hesitation, so the decision was made. We got a great deal on a ticket and flew from Paris to Marrakesh.

morocco NORTH AFRICAN STORM

Maree Conroy and her five-year-old son, Storm, travelled for a month in Morocco.

In Marrakesh we stayed right near the Place Djemaa el-Fna, a big square in the old part of town. There was always something to entertain Storm at the square. The snake charmers and magicians were a big hit. There were rows and rows of juice stalls and the food stalls at night were a great place to eat. It was good for Storm because there was lots of great food on display and he could pick what he wanted. We had never had any problems with street food. One day Storm and I got some 'work experience' with one of the juice stallholders. We spent hours helping to squeeze juice for the customers and consuming a lot of juice ourselves. At the end of the day the stallholders cooked up a delicious seafood feast for us, washed down with the famous Moroccan mint tea.

Our next stop was Essaouira on the Atlantic coast. The architecture is magnificent and we stayed in a beautiful hotel with whitewashed walls and big blue doors. We could eat breakfast on the roof and look out to sea at the fishing boats, and at night view the stars. The rides along the beach on large one-humped dromedaries kept Storm amused, even though the next day we were very sore.

It was in Essaouira that we discovered *hammams* (public steam baths). These were one of the highlights of our trip, as the hotels that said they had hot water only seemed to deliver lukewarm water. Children are welcome with their parents, although females of any age would not go to the men's *hammam*. At the women's *hammam* it was the first time we had seen women interacting and there was lots of conversation and laughter. There seemed to be a hierarchal order of who got their hot water first, but we couldn't quite work it out. I bought Storm a little bucket that we used for all our visits to the *hammam* and he loved the ritual of collecting the water for washing. Storm got a massage and the woman was very gentle with him. He loved it.

Another highlight of our trip was Merzouga, where we stayed at the foot of the Erg Chebbi, Morocco's famous sand dunes in the Sahara. We ran off to explore the dunes as soon as we arrived, but it wasn't long before we soon returned for fear of getting lost. The next day we went with a guide and learnt the art of walking up the dunes the easiest way – follow the line of the dune; don't walk up the middle of the dune. At the top of the biggest dune we buried ourselves in the warm sand with only our heads peaking out. The view from the top of the dune was breathtaking. Storm had lots of fun rolling down the dunes and then climbing back up. It was exhausting to watch.

The villagers at the foot of the dunes were Berbers, North Africa's indigenous people, and the local children loved having a new child to play with. We were invited to lunch in their homes and got to experience village life. Every afternoon Storm would ride with the local children on a donkey to get their water supply from the well. This was a great experience for Storm, as he learnt that water doesn't always come out of a tap.

Storm got a lot of attention in Merzouga, as he had with him a prized possession – a soccer ball. The children from the village would ask him to play soccer and once there were more than 30 children involved in a game. It took him a long time to get the ball back that day!

"One day Storm and I got some "work experience" with one of the juice stallholders. We spent hours helping to squeeze juice for the customers and consumed a lot of juice ourselves. At the end of the day the stallholders cooked up a delicious seafood feast for us, washed down with the famous Moroccan mint tea."

We had one scary moment when Storm developed an abscess on his gums. He was in a lot of pain and after giving him paracetamol, he was still troubled by it. I was reluctant to visit a dentist so I went in search of some penicillin to clear the infection. The hotel manager took us to the community health centre on the back of his motorbike where Storm was attended to in a very professional and friendly manner. The doctor gave us penicillin and we were surprised to find out that this great service, including the medicine, was totally free of charge. The abscess cleared up in a couple of days, much to our mutual delight.

Storm and I loved our month in Morocco. It turned out to be a fantastic destination to travel with my son and we experienced friendly warm people who were helpful wherever we went. We did get a lot of attention as we were unaccompanied by a man, but people seemed to respect the fact that I was a mother and accept my imaginative story that my husband was working in France.

SOUTH AFRICA

South Africa has a strong domestic tourist industry aimed at families, particularly on the coast. Even away from the seaside hotels, you'll find lodges and camping grounds have facilities for children, ranging from play leaders and babysitting services to playgrounds. Family rooms and chalets are usually available in more upmarket hotels for only a little more than the price of a double room. In many cheaper hotels children pay as adults.

practicalities

With its relatively well-developed infrastructure, travel in South Africa is much easier than in surrounding countries. Baby equipment and disposable nappies are readily available in population centres. However, baby-changing facilities are not easy to come by and short-term daycare is not on offer. Health risks are minimal but there is bilharzia, so avoid letting children play barefoot in stagnant water and mud. There is also malaria in the eastern half of the country; preventatives are available over the counter in many South African pharmacies. Another thing to keep in mind is that when hiking, water from streams and even from huts and villages along the trail must be purified.

things to see & do

wild things With a number of national parks and a thriving trekking and safari industry, you're spoiled for choice when it comes to wildlife. The South African National Parks Board has useful information about the country's many national parks and reserves. With such a long coastline, there is also a lot of marine life to see and even urban coastal areas have enough to impress children. At Bertie's Landing on Cape Town's Waterfront you can usually spot seals. Cape Town also has an aquarium at the Victoria and Albert Waterfront, where there is an amazing kelp forest tank.

For those not put off by scary creatures, the Natal Sharks Board in Umhlanga Rocks, outside Durban, is a research centre dedicated to studying sharks. Cape Town's South African Museum has exhibits on marine life, mammals, dinosaurs and reptiles. Kids will love the machine that shows how whales sound when they're 'talking'.

interesting & educational South Africa's larger cities have museums devoted to wildlife and local history. In Johannesburg, Museum Africa has a large collection of rock art. In Durban, older children may be interested in the KwaMuhle Museum, with a display of the 'Durban System' by which whites subjugated blacks.

activities

Hiking and mountain biking are popular activities in South Africa's National Parks. For the less energetic take a ride in the cable car up Table Mountain in Cape Town.

books

Indaba My Children by Vusamazulu Credo Mutwa is an interesting book of folk tales, history, legends, customs and beliefs. For older children, *Waiting for the Rain: A Novel of South Africa* by Sheila Gordon is a story about a black boy and a white boy whose friendship is torn apart by apartheid.

TANZANIA

Tanzania's wildlife and natural beauty is always appreciated by kids as well as adults, and Tanazanians are very helpful and friendly towards travellers with children. To get decent bathroom facilities you'll need to stay in mid- or top-range accommodation. Some hotels and safari outfits have discounts of 50% for under-12s who share a room with their parents, but you should check when booking.

practicalities

Nappies and other baby supplies are available in major towns but not elsewhere. Decent medical facilities are also scarce outside large population centres. Pharmacies in major towns stock a wide range of medicines that can be bought without a prescription. Keep in mind that malaria is endemic in Tanzania. If you're going on safari or renting a car, bring your own car seat as they're rarely available.

things to see & do

A wildlife safari is why many people come to Tanzania and 38% of the country is allocated to national parks or marine and wildlife reserves. Older kids will love the spectacular Mt Kilimanjaro, but be careful trekking at this altitude (see the Health chapter for more information). For animal-loving kids, head straight for Selous Game Reserve – Africa's largest game reserve, which promises hippos, elephants and some of the last black rhino. For more information about child-friendly safari outfits, you can start at the Tanzania National Parks office or the Tanzania Tourist Board.

The Tanzanian coast has a number of upmarket beach resorts for a bit of luxury. Children might also enjoy watching traditional music on weekends at the Village Museum in Dar es Salaam. Boat rides, including dolphin spotting trips, can be done off Zanzibar. Older children will also enjoy clambering around the crenellations and towers of the fort in Zanzibar town.

books

The Clever Tortoise: A Traditional African Tale, by Francesca Martin, is an illustrated book that young children might enjoy. *My Rows and Piles of Coins*, by Tololwa M. Mollel, is the poignant story of a young boy working to save enough for a bicycle. *Is It Far to Zanzibar?: Poems about Tanzania* is a collection of humorous rhymes for children.

Before our nine-hour flight to Harare we were worried sick that we had made the wrong decision to take our 15-month-old son Zach. Never before had we ventured overseas with our little darling. He drank a bottle during take off and within 30 minutes was asleep, allowing Yvette and I to actually enjoy a drink and the in-flight movie.

zimbabwe

CUTTING TEETH in HARARE & BULAWAYO

Crispin Walker travelled to Zimbabwe with his son, Zach, 15 months, and fiancée, Yvette, as part of a two-month trip in southern Africa.

We were met off the plane by friends who were putting us up for the Harare leg of our adventure. Harare's heat wasn't too bad, but we dedicated our first day to acclimatising and ensuring that Zach – who had a nasty case of teething – was comfortable and settled.

Relaxing by a spacious pool, sipping wonderfully cool beers while our hosts cooked us a fantastic meal was ideal, as we could stagger off to bed whenever required. We kept Zach covered in SPF-30 sunscreen and after the first dousing he was fine with having it applied throughout the trip.

Despite warnings we felt completely safe in downtown Harare and spent a few great days wandering around the city-centre markets, shops and galleries. We were enthusiastically welcomed at eating and entertainment establishments and Zach loved the sculpture park behind the National Gallery of Zimbabwe. We were however quiet regularly cajoled – as the only white faces in the crowd – into public donations to talented buskers! Zach particularly enjoyed day trips out of Harare, in a hire car, to see elephants and lions at Ewanrigg National Park and Bally Vaughan Game Farm.

Our first big test of Zimbabwe as a kiddy-friendly destination was travelling to Bulawayo. Our friends reluctantly dropped us off at Harare Central, after arguing that we should fly around the country. Even they were amazed at the shiny new train which was doing one of its first dozen overnight trips to Bulawayo. Train travel was probably the unexpected highlight of the trip. We had booked a two-bed sleeper cabin, with Zach sharing Yvette's bunk. The wagon's gentle rocking had the nipper asleep quickly and we all enjoyed our first glimpse of dawn over Zimbabwe's beautiful countryside in the morning.

Bulawayo was undramatic but the impressive Museum of Natural History with excellent animals displays kept Zach amused. We stayed five nights at a grotty but cheap hostel, where Zach played with the owners' kids and dog, and felt right at home. They advised on good restaurants and guides for a day tour of the magnificent Matobo National Park. Our guide, Edmond, was excellent with Zach, insisting on carrying him so I could take photos. Edmond even allowed himself a chuckle when, as he was explaining that Prime Minister Mugabe had threatened to move founding father Cecil Rhodes' grave, we all turned around to see our offspring performing a song and dance on the great man's grave!

After such a positive initial experience with the trains we eagerly anticipated our onward journey to Victoria Falls. Rather than a brand new train this time we had a charming steam classic. Again Zach slept well even with plenty of rowdy young backpackers on board who we partied with. The town of Victoria Falls was inescapably touristy but the Falls themselves proved unmissable. We were all spellbound and Zach enjoyed the fine water mist and trekking through jungle around the top of the falls.

"He bought the apples and kissed the owner's two-year-old daughter, making both sets of parents laugh and smile."

One big mistake we made was underestimating the distance to walk to the Zambian border for a simple souvenir passport stamp. When we arrived back in Victoria Falls exhausted, tempers flared. But a cooling dip, cold drink, and baboons playing on the rooftop of a fancy lodge restored our humour. A violent African thunderstorm had us all gasping in amazement.

As our trip was based around city stops with side trips we opted to take Zach's lightweight collapsible stroller. It was a great move as it gave my back an occasional break and allowed Zach to indulge in his early afternoon sleep while we strolled around cooled museums and galleries.

One unexpected bonus of the stroller was that it turned out to be an icebreaker with local kids, who were usually ferried around on mum's back. Most stared and some even asked for a go! As for food, given the favourable exchange rate, we could afford to eat out most nights. However Zach was also happy snacking on the local maize dish *sadza* and stew, or noodles and veggies purchased from mini-markets.

We had a few unpleasant experiences with 'Rhodies' whose negative outlooks – harping about the 'good old days' of British influence – and nasty attitude to their staff, usually in restaurants and shops, left an unpleasant taste in the mouth. Also a barber's haircut I got in Bulawayo was an unmitigated disaster, after the barber attempted to shave me with the clippers (ouch) and it became clear the place was a front for hot car stereos! One of our endearing memories was, however, giving Zach money to buy fruit from the Bulawayo market. He bought the apples and kissed the owner's two-year-old daughter, making both sets of parents laugh and smile.

We loved Zimbabwe immensely and the trip was an unqualified success. By pacing ourselves sensibly and allowing Zach to dictate how long we lingered – especially around wildlife – we ensured we all had an excellent time. Zach even managed to forget, temporarily, about his sore teeth!

TUNISIA

The Tunisian state spares no effort in promoting itself as a family destination and many resort hotels offer special family rates or discounts for children. Children under five also travel free on buses and trains, while children under 15 pay half fare. Keep in mind that they pay full fare on *louages* (minibuses).

practicalities

Disposable nappies, UHT milk, formula and other baby supplies are easily obtainable at supermarkets and pharmacies in Tunisia and coastal tourist centres. Pharmaceutical drugs are widely available, often without prescription.

things to see & do

Camel treks are a good bet with kids and are usually arranged in the Douz region, south of Tunis. Older children may also be interested in Matmata, where the underground cave houses were used as the set for *Star Wars*. Clambering about the stairways and underground passages of the huge Roman colosseum in El Jem can keep kids happy for hours. Archaeology can be made fun at Dougga, one of the world's best preserved Roman towns. Kids will love joking about the communal Roman toilets, searching for Roman coins or patting the ubiquitous donkeys.

books

Editions Alif does an excellent series of pop-up books about Tunisian life; the only English title is *A Walk through an Arab City: the Tunis Medina*. Look out also for a series of books about Tunisian crafts aimed at seven- to 10-year-olds by author/illustrator May Angeli.

ZIMBABWE

Until recently Zimbabwe represented a fantastic African family destination with political stability and some fantastic wilderness to explore. At the time of writing unrest in rural areas has meant that safety is not guaranteed outside larger cities. While travellers should consider the current political situation before visiting Zimbabwe, there's still a lot see.

Some safari companies and lodges may have an adults-only policy, so check kids are welcome before booking.

things to see & do

wild things Seeing Africa's animals will be high on the list for most little travellers, but many can be easily seen without a safari by going to Mukuvisi

Woodlands just outside Harare, which has zebra, giraffe and hand-raised elephants. There are plenty of day safaris around Victoria Falls that entertain littlies. More adventurous families can organise an excursion to Matobo Park to see healthy populations of black and white rhino.

interesting & educational In Harare the National Gallery of Zimbabwe offers your kids a fantastic education in African art, though be warned this is definitely a hands-off exhibition.

activities

Fearless kids will love a hike along the Zambezi River with the best walks starting at the Livingstone Statue or taking in the majestic Victoria Falls.

parks & playgrounds

Harare Gardens is the capital's largest park with plenty of room for kids to run around or admire the scale model of the Zimbabwe-Zambia bridge. To really work off some energy there's Greenwood Park which includes a fun park with a miniature railway and cable car.

books & films

Younger children will enjoy the detailed illustrations of *Gugu's House* by Catherine Stock, which gives a good visual introduction to the country and culture.

AFRICA & THE MIDDLE EAST

africa & the middle east

With their emphasis on the family, Middle Eastern societies prize children – which means that anyone travelling with them has a ready-made icebreaker with locals. Don't be surprised if waiters whisk your little ones off to the kitchen for special treats, if you are given special treatment in queues or if kisses are planted on your toddler's cheek by total strangers (especially if the toddler is blonde). While this can be a bit overwhelming at first, it is a great way to meet people and enhances any visit to this historically rich area. It also makes up for the lack of child-specific facilities in some countries. But as long as you don't expect highchairs in every cafe and take a few commonsense precautions with food, there is little in the region to stop your children from enjoying their visit as much as you.

GULF STATES

With their strong emphasis on large families, the Gulf States are easy places to travel with young children. Under-12s are usually given discounts on admissions to museums, beach clubs and amusement parks. American-style fast food restaurants mean that there are few problems with fussy eaters. The Gulf is a very conservative place and you should not breastfeed in public.

practicalities

Disposable nappies and other baby supplies are widely available at supermarkets and pharmacies. Medicines are in good supply too. There are few health risks in the Gulf, with the exception of the searing heat in summer. Although most Gulf countries have begun enacting seatbelt laws, don't assume that car rental agencies will have car seats for babies and toddlers; always check before leaving home.

things to see & do

wild things Most of the Gulf States have aquariums but Muscat's is by far the best. All of the underwater creatures are native to Oman and have good descriptions in English.

interesting & educational Kids will also enjoy wandering through the reconstructed buildings and dhows (traditional fishing boats) beside Bahrain National Museum. They can see real dhows being built in Sur, Oman – a dozen or more of the traditional boats are usually under construction at any time. Older children will also be interested in taking trips on dhows. Nearby are great beaches and impressive forts to make the 150km trip from Muscat worthwhile.

pure entertainment Any child who's read *The Arabian Nights* – or watched the Disney versions – will be interested in visiting Sohar. This was Sinbad the Sailor's home port and now has a large whitewashed fort that will fire young imaginations.

All of the Gulf States have amusement parks; don't miss Aladdin's Kingdom in Qatar, which has one of the biggest roller coasters in the region. Camel or jeep safaris are always popular with kids and are easy to arrange.

books

Summer 1990: A Young Adult Novel by Firyal Al-shalabi tells the tale of a spoiled 13-year-old on holiday in Disneyland when the Gulf War breaks out.

cultural issues

You should ensure that young children and babies have bathing suits when at the beach or pool; nudity – even in tiny children – is not appreciated. Likewise, older girls should dress more conservatively than they would at home, avoiding miniskirts and bared midriffs.

ISRAEL

As a European-style society with a high standard of living, Israel is an easy place to travel with children. Apart from the unstable political situation, there are no real health hazards to speak of. The coastal resorts cater to families, with babysitting services and other child-friendly facilities widely available.

At the time of writing Israel is involved in civil unrest and parents should strongly consider the current situation when planning travel to Israel. Check Lonely Planet's Web site for up-to-date information and current travel warnings.

In conservative Orthodox Jewish areas or the Palestinian Territories, older girls should not expose legs and shoulders and breastfeeding should be done discreetly or in private.

information

Israel Loves Kids, Kids Love Israel: A Travel Guide for Families by Barbara Sofer gives some idea of what's on offer for children.

practicalities

Jerusalem is a difficult place to navigate with young children; in the Old City streets are narrow and crowded, while in the New City, roads are congested.

Disposable nappies and other baby supplies are easily available in supermarkets and pharmacies. Keep in mind that medical care in Israel is expensive and make sure you have adequate insurance before you travel. By law children under four must be restrained in a child seat, so car rental companies should supply them, but you should check first.

things to see & do

wild things The New Biblical Zoo in Jerusalem has a special children's zoo and creative play area. Older children might enjoy the Hai-Bar Arava Biblical Wildlife Reserve north of Eilat, where they can see biblical animals that have been re-introduced to the area. In Tel Aviv, the Ramat Gan Safari Park is another good place for children.

interesting & educational In Jerusalem, the Bloomfield Science Museum has hands-on exhibits. The Israel Museum has children's events, including singing and playing for pre-schoolers and cartoon screenings.

pure entertainment Attrakzia is a large water theme park on the shores of the Dead Sea with waterslides and splash pools to give the kids all the splashing fun they need in hot weather.

activities

To get the most out of a visit to Jerusalem, Kids' Jerusalem Adventures specialises in custom tours of the city for families with children. Kids of all ages will love having a mud bath and floating in the Dead Sea (just watch that the salty water doesn't get in their eyes). They'll also enjoy visiting the hill-top fortress of Masada. For littlies who don't want to climb the laborious Snake Path, the cable car is a fun alternative way to rise to new heights. There is another cable car ride to be had at the Monastery of the Temptation, near Jericho. Children will appreciate the breathtaking views of the surrounding area and the monastery's history: it's supposedly where the Devil tried to tempt Jesus during his 40-day fast.

parks & playgrounds

Liberty Bell Gardens in Jerusalem offers children green space to run as well as a puppet theatre in an old railway carriage.

books

Ann Levine's *Running on Eggs* is the story of an Israeli girl and a Palestinian girl, who reach across the hostility of their respective communities in friendship. Pack an illustrated retelling of classic Bible stories so you can explain the ancient sights.

cultural issues

It is important to clearly explain to your children the nature of the political situation in Israel so they can be sensitive to any local children they might meet or play with.

JORDAN

Jordanians love children and having them with you guarantees easy conversation with locals. There are few hazards to worry about, except the summer heat. Top-end and mid-range hotels usually let children under two stay for free and charge half for under-12s.

practicalities

Baby supplies – such as nappies, formula and food – are easily available in Amman but not in surrounding areas. Pharmacies in the capital are generally well stocked and medical facilities are good. Try to avoid the extreme heat of the summer months and make sure to bring high-SPF sunscreen with you, even in the cooler winter months. Traffic in Jordan is not as chaotic as in some surrounding countries and hiring a car can be a great way to explore.

things to see & do

There are good stables just outside Amman, although riding there is not cheap. Swimming can be done at any of the big hotels in Amman for a daily fee, and there are good beaches and snorkelling in Aqaba. Exploring the crusader castles at Karak, Shobak and Ajlun is an exciting activity for older kids. Camel riding is also popular and can be done in Wadi Rum. Most kids also enjoy floating in the waters of the Dead Sea.

LEBANON

Bringing the kids to Lebanon makes meeting people much easier because Lebanese people value children very highly. Finding space for children to run and play is perhaps the biggest challenge. Beirut has almost no parks and can be a difficult city to navigate with kids in tow, although there are a growing number of other child-friendly options. The other thing to keep in mind is that while most restaurants and resorts outside the capital are family-oriented, many of Beirut's hipper restaurants are not suitable for children. For babies and younger children, though baby food is freely available in most of the larger stores, as are disposable nappies.

information

At Home in Beirut, a practical English-language guide to living in Beirut, has some useful tips for keeping kids entertained, while listings in English of children's theatre and other activities can be found in the *Daily Star* newspaper or the *Guide*, a monthly magazine.

When you're born with a surname like Jordan, you wonder if there is a connection between the country Jordan, the River Jordan and you. According to my father, there is. Apparently, we're descended from a banner carrier in the Crusades who was knighted 'Jordan' after his return to France. Some 1000 years later, the Jordans set off to see the Holy Land again, but this time instead of liberating the Holy Land from the infidels, we went in peace to meet our Arab brothers.

jordan WITH the JORDANS

Kevin Jordan spent two weeks in Jordan with his wife, Myriam, and children, Kevin, six, and Daphne, 22 months.

We landed in Jordan and were convinced at the ferry port by a gentlemanly driver to go to a Bedouin camp on the coast of Aqaba. This camp ended up being a highlight for the kids as the Bedouin village was made out of palm tree trunks and blankets – with a few modern conveniences like showers, toilets and kitchen – and it was right on the beach, a much cooler choice than being in town. We ate Bedouin meals, sitting on the carpet-covered ground and jumped in the sea whenever we wanted to cool off. The snorkelling was great and the food superb. And we got to spend a lot of time getting to know the local people. The only drawback was we were a distance from town, meaning we always had to eat at the camp.

Snorkelling is a great way to teach kids to swim. I have been teaching my son to snorkel since he was three years old, because I knew some day we'd end up by a coral reef, and he'd miss a whole new world of discovery if he wasn't comfortable with a mask and snorkel on his face. We finally had our chance to take the plunge. The 18km coast of Jordan has some great snorkelling, and unlike much of the Red Sea, the sea life is all right at the shore. Though not quite as abundant in life as the Sinai coast on the other side of the Gulf of Aqaba, it's still a great place, especially to see coral heads, gars and lionfish.

If you take time to get to know the locals, they delight in showing you the treasures of their land, in more detail than a guidebook could ever hope to cover. Our host at the Bedouin camp was happy to take us out to a few of the secret snorkelling spots. He pointed out where a buoy marked a sunken ship, a short walk from his camp. His guidance added a great deal to our experience.

We felt absolutely safe in Jordan, which cannot be said for many of the places we have been in Europe and America. Everywhere we went, people wanted to help us and best of all to play with our kids. Kids don't need to speak the same language to communicate. They just want to play, and play is a universal language. We would be warmly invited to be part of a family group, to sing songs by the sea or to learn words in Arabic. One of my wife's most cherished moments came when she discovered while talking with a young woman that most Jordanians don't know how to swim. My wife, eager to repay her kindness, offered to teach her. The first attempts were hilarious, but after a short time, she was actually swimming. She was so thrilled, she gave lessons to her husband and kids.

Probably the greatest drawcard of the Middle East is Petra, the old Nabataean capital, made most famous by the closing scenes of the film *Indiana Jones and the Last Crusade*. The combination of Nabataean tombs, Roman ruins and breathtaking natural beauty makes Petra one of the world's greatest sights. The monastery is less famous than some other attractions, probably because to get there you have to climb for an hour in the sun, up a narrow path of more than 800 steps cut into a cliff. With young kids, this is formidable. Lucky for us, God invented donkeys. It's hard to imagine that a donkey can make its way up these treacherous paths, but they did. Petra is really the place for donkey, horse and camel rides. Distances are great, and the Bedouin children who lead rides are charming (once you've settled on a price). The young Bedouin girls would fight over who would get to take Daphne or Kevin on their donkey.

"If you take time to get to know the locals, they delight in showing you the treasures of their land, in more detail than a guidebook could ever hope to cover. Our host at the Bedouin camp was happy to take us out to a few of the secret snorkelling spots."

We went to Jordan in July and were concerned about the desert heat for the kids. But it was actually very manageable. The hottest area was the Jordan Valley and the Dead Sea. How hot was it? Our swimming masks melted and my sneakers shrunk, in the trunk (car boot). If you take a break between 1 pm and 3 pm – like lunch and a nap in the amphitheatre at Petra – you should be OK.

Overall, would we recommend Jordan? Yes, the Jordans loved Jordan.

practicalities

With a manageable climate and few health issues, Lebanon is an easy destination with children. Pharmacies are well stocked with nappies, formula and medicine. The one thing you might want to bring along is high-SPF sunscreen, which is very expensive. Another thing to keep in mind is that not all cars will have safety belts, so double check if you are renting a vehicle.

things to see & do

wild things Animal Encounter is a non-profit shelter for injured and orphaned wild animals and birds in Aley and is a great place for kids to learn about Lebanese fauna.

interesting & educational Lebanon has many ancient monuments, so there's no shortage of history on offer and ruins to explore. Planet Discovery is a children's science museum in downtown Beirut that centres on the theme of building and has a number of interactive exhibits. Outside Beirut, Jeitta Grotto – a surreal cavern that involves train and boat rides – is a good place to take children, as is the kitsch Castle Moussa in the Chouf Mountains.

pure entertainment A popular destination for Beirutis trying to amuse their kids are the seafront cafes in Ras Beirut. Raouda and the adjacent Macka Luna Park Funfair are both good choices. Too cool off too-hot kids, Splash Mountain, in Ain Saadeh, has waterslides and games.

activities

Skiing is growing in popularity in Lebanon. The Cedars and Laklouk resorts are known for being family-oriented, with good nursery slopes and kids' equipment on offer. For older children, trekking is a good pastime. Liban Trek, Lebanese Adventure and Greenline all organise weekend excursions, which are also popular with Lebanese families. La Reserve is a camp near the Afqa Grotto on Mt Lebanon that offers summer camps for kids aged between seven and 15.

parks & playgrounds

It can be tough finding room for kids to roam in Beirut. The public park at Saniyeh is cosy, but can become crowded on weekends. You can also try the grounds of the American University in Beirut, though they are very security-conscious.

festivals

Every July the Deir al-Qamar Estivales takes place in the Chouf Mountain village of Deir al-Qamar. The festival focuses on the family with a number of children's activities to entertain.

books

For younger children, *The Houses of Lebanon* by Nayla Audi is a pop-up book showing different styles of traditional Lebanese houses. *Sami and the Time of the Troubles* by Florence Parry Heide et al, is a sensitive look at a boy's experience during the civil war. Older readers should try *Once Upon a Time in Lebanon* by

Roseanne Khalof, a collection of three folktales. *Dances with Gods* looks at ancient myths, many of which date back to the time of the Phoenicians.

SYRIA

syria

Syrians, like their neighbours, love children and having them along with you will make it easy to meet people wherever you go. You will need to stick to mid-range and expensive hotels if you want decent bathroom facilities but they usually have discounts for children.

practicalities

Nappies, formula and other baby supplies are available in pharmacies and supermarkets in all major Syrian towns, although you may not find a large variety of brands on offer. Sticking to bottled water or UHT milk and avoiding unpeeled fruit or raw vegetables should keep diarrhoea at bay, but if kids do get ill, make sure you have rehydration salts on hand, which are usually readily available and cheap.

things to see & do

There are plenty of crusader castles to explore, but start with Krak des Chevaliers – an amazingly intact 800-year-old castle with 13 towers on its outside wall and a moat filled with stagnant water. With its commanding position on a rocky outcrop, it's perfect fantasy fodder for young knights and damsels. Just take care with some of the staircases and sheer drops. Camel treks and jeep safaris can also be done in the Syrian desert. For swimming, there's the Andalous – a private sports club in Ghoutah, on the Mezze road outside Damascus, and swimming here is much cheaper; there are a couple of tennis courts too. Away from the city, Lattakia and Tartus have a number of beach resorts that cater to families.

books

A Hand Full of Stars, by Rafik Schami, is an evocative novel for older children about a Damascus teenager, who expresses his frustration with the violence and corruption in Syrian society through his journal. Or check out Schami's latest book, *Damascus Nights*.

UAE

uae

As a conservative society with an emphasis on large families, the United Arab Emirates (UAE) is a good place to travel with children. Many mid-priced hotels have special large family rooms and family discounts are available on many activities. Fast-food restaurants abound and special children's menus exist in more upmarket restaurants. Best of all amusement parks and funfairs are in relative abundance. As with other Gulf countries, the UAE is conservative and breastfeeding should be avoided in public.

practicalities

Apart from the searing heat and sun in the summer months, there are few health issues to worry about and baby supplies are widely available. Baby-changing facilities are found in most toilets and there are nurseries or play areas in most shopping centres, although usually there are no attendants. Most amusement parks have grassy stretches for kids to run off extra energy.

things to see & do

wild things Dubai Zoo is set among lush gardens and houses many indigenous Arabian species, including the Arabian Wolf, which is no longer found in the wild.
interesting & educational Sharjah Science Museum and Planetarium is the only interactive museum in the UAE and is particularly aimed at children. The Sharjah Natural History Museum has a children's farm and desert park.
pure entertainment The Gulf has a surfeit of parks and playgrounds, so there is something to suit almost every age and taste. One of the best is Wild Wadi water park which claims to have some of the most exciting water rides in the world. Wonderland in Dubai has an amusement park with rides and video games. On Wednesdays the amusement park is reserved for women and children only. Dreamland Aquapark in Umm al-Qaiwaine is the largest water park in the Gulf and has a number of restaurants in addition to a go-kart track, video games and, of course, water rides.

activities

Dhow trips and desert camping safaris are good ways for children to experience something more than amusement parks and shopping malls. North Star Expeditions in Dubai specialises in educational and adventure trips for children around the UAE.

festivals

The Dubai Shopping Festival and Dubai Summer Surprises both offer special children's activities, although all take place in shopping centres and can have a commercial bent.

cultural issues

Nudity in young children is not appreciated, so make sure you bring bathing suits for even the youngest in the family. Older girls would also be advised to keep their miniskirts and midriff-baring halter tops for when they get back home.

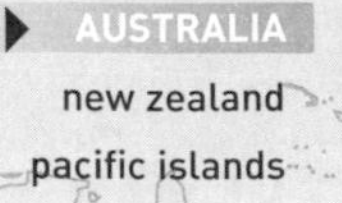

AUSTRALASIA

australasia

Children are generally well received and well catered for in Australia; relatively few places are reluctant to accept kids.

All cities and most major towns have centrally located public rooms where mothers (and sometimes fathers) can go to feed their baby or change its nappy – check with the local tourist office or city council for details. Disposable nappies are available just about everywhere and most department stores sell cloth nappies. In the Outback, disposable nappies are anything but disposable and are becoming a major item of pollution in the bush – carry used disposables away with you in a heavy-duty plastic bag on the roof rack (they won't smell much if rolled up tight).

In general, Australians have a relaxed attitude about breastfeeding in public, though there may be some who frown on it.

Most motels and the better-equipped caravan parks supply cots and baby's baths, and many have playgrounds and swimming pools – many motels also have in-house children's videos and child-minding services, as do top-end hotels. While a lot of cafes and restaurants don't exactly welcome small children with open arms, many have highchairs and kids' menus – or will happily provide small serves from the main menu.

In cars, you are obliged to use appropriate restraints for infants and young children. The larger car-rental companies will provide baby seats, but parents are expected to secure the seat in the car.

If you want to leave junior behind for a few hours, some of Australia's numerous licensed child-care agencies have places set aside for casual care. To find them, check in the *Yellow Pages* telephone directory or phone the local council for a list of local centres. Typically they look after children aged from one to five years during working hours; many do not accept very young infants. Licensed centres are subject to government regulation and usually have a high standard – to be on the safe side avoid unlicensed ones.

Child concessions often apply for such things as accommodation, tours, entry fees and transport. Discounts can be as high as 50% of the adult rate. However, the definition of child varies from under 12 to under 18. For accommodation, concessions generally apply to children under 12 sharing the same room as adults.

With the major airlines, infants travel free provided they don't occupy a seat. Child fares apply between the ages of three and 15 years old, but student and normal adult discount fares are usually more attractive. Bus companies have various discounting arrangements for children. Greyhound, for example, give a 20% discount to children aged between three and 14, as well as all students. Under-threes can travel free if they are nursed, or can have a seat for half the adult fare.

NEW SOUTH WALES

new south wales

sydney

information

Look for copies of *Sydney's Child*, a free monthly paper listing kids' activities – the Sydney Visitors Centre at the Rocks and the Powerhouse Museum are a couple of the many places that stock it.

practicalities

On public transport under-fours travel free. And as a bonus for big families – you only pay for your first child aged between four and 15, the rest travel free.

things to see & do

wild things The Sydney Aquarium in Darling Harbour is a beauty, older kids will enjoy walking through the transparent underwater tunnels. Taronga Park Zoo is home to more than 4000 animals and sometimes has night visits. At OceanWorld you can get (safely!) close to sharks and stingrays and see a seal show.

interesting & educational In Darling Harbour the Maritime Museum has a naval destroyer, a racing yacht and a refugee boat for kids to explore. Kids can have fun with the interactive displays at the Powerhouse Museum – check out the Australian rock music and space capsules displays.

pure entertainment In Darling Harbour, kids may want to visit Sega World, a virtual reality theme park with cool rides and cinema-style entertainment, and IMAX, reputed to be the world's largest movie screen. For those over 12, there's the Sydney Harbour Bridge Climb for the ultimate view of Sydney; safety regulations make this a no-go for younger kids.

activities

Harbour cruises and ferry rides are a great way to check out Sydney from the water, and kids will like seeing the city centre by monorail. Sydney's harbour beaches offer sheltered swimming spots, and for the more adventurous there are surfing lessons available at Bondi or sailing lessons on the Harbour.

parks & playgrounds

You can hire bikes, in-line skates or horses to explore Sydney's largest park, Centennial Park, and stop along the way to feed the ducks.

around new south wales

An hour from Sydney, kids will enjoy walks in the Blue Mountains or gliding along the Scenic Skyway 200m above the valley floor. Cave fans will like the nearby Jenolan limestone caves.

In Australia's capital, Canberra, the National Science & Technology Centre has 200 interactive displays – check out the lightning strikes and feel the earthquake tremor. Older kids will enjoy being shown around the Australian Institute of Sport by an elite Australian athlete and the chance to check out their own skills.

You can walk, bike or drive around the huge open-plain Western Plains Zoo in Dubbo, home to Bengal tigers and Asiatic lions. Further north, kids will enjoy a visit to the Koala Hospital at Port Macquarie and love the blowhole at Kiama which can spout up to 60m high. Older kids will like the underground mine tour at Broken Hill and checking out the School of the Air – the classroom for outback kids.

There's great national parks in NSW, the biggest is Kosciuszko National Park which has caves, lakes, forests and ski resorts. Ku-Ring-Gai Chase National Park offers walking trails, horse riding, Aboriginal rock engravings, beaches and a picnic area.

books

Two classics for younger children are Norman Lindsay's *The Magic Pudding* and May Gibbs' *Snugglepot & Cuddlepie*. Norman Lindsay's home, now open as a museum, is near Springwood in the Blue Mountains and there are displays relating to *The Magic Pudding*. Nutcote, May Gibbs' house in North Sydney, is also a museum.

NORTHERN TERRITORY

northern territory

darwin

things to see & do

Kids love hand-feeding the fish at Aquascene. At the Museum of the Northern Territory you can safely get a close-up look at a crocodile and the deadly box jellyfish. Checking out the gallows and cells at Fannie Bay Gaol Museum might appeal to the kids' gruesome side and they'll enjoy the Jumping Crocodile Cruises where the crocs leap clear out of the water for meat dangling on a hook. Just outside of the capital, the Darwin Crocodile Farm is home to about 8000 crocs and there are daily feeding sessions. The Territory Wildlife Park set in 1300 hectares of bushland is great for kids with its reptile house, walk-through aquarium, nocturnal house and nature trails to check out.

around northern territory

In Kakadu National Park, Aboriginal-guided East Alligator River trips keep kids interested with spotting crocs and checking out Aboriginal weapons. They'll like exploring the rocks and trails around Ubirr and Nourlangie, and will enjoy the spectacular rock art sites if they have a chance to read some Aboriginal children's stories beforehand (there's a good selection at the Bowali Visitor Centre).

Take the kids on a day trip to Manyallaluk, a former cattle station, to learn from local Aboriginal people about traditional bush tucker and medicine, spear throwing, and didgeridoo playing. At Tennant Creek, families can try whip cracking or boomerang throwing and wash down a witchetty grub with billy tea and damper on organised tours. In Alice Springs kids can take a camel ride at the Frontier Camel Farm and explore the Alice Springs Desert Park with its walk-through aviaries and brilliant nocturnal house (look out for the carnivorous ghost bats). Kids will enjoy scrambling around the rocks of Kata Tjuta (the Olgas).

QUEENSLAND

Queensland is one of Australia's top family holiday destinations and kids are well catered for. You don't have to look far for theme parks, wildlife sanctuaries, crocodile farms and safe swimming beaches. Queensland has a huge unspoilt wilderness in national parks which have lots of kid-friendly walking trails and swimming holes. Of course there's the Great Barrier Reef to explore via boat cruises, snorkelling or even diving for older kids. There's a proliferation of resorts in the Whitsunday Islands where children's activities are organised. Kids' clubs are offered on Daydream, Fraser Island, Hamilton, Brampton, South Molle, Club Crocodile Long Island and Hayman Island. Kingfisher Bay Resort has a junior eco-rangers program for six- to 14-year-olds. Mainland resorts offering kids' clubs include Laguna Quays Resort and Whitsunday Wanderers Resort.

brisbane

things to see & do

Kids will like playing around with the optical illusions and perception tunnel at the hands-on science museum, Sciencentre. In the South Bank Parklands are a cool swimming pool, IMAX theatre, lots of street performers and a wildlife sanctuary featuring hundreds of freely fluttering Australian butterflies, as well as a good collection of creepy-crawlies and native critters. Kids might like the collection of model ships and relics from old wrecks at the Queensland Maritime Museum. In Walk-About Creek in the huge Brisbane Forest Park kids can get up close to pythons, turtles, lizards and fish. They can cuddle koalas and picnic amongst tame kangaroos at the Lone Pine Koala Sanctuary. And dingoes and emus as well as exotic animals such as leopards and monkeys can be visited at the Alma Park Zoo.

around queensland

The Gold Coast has a huge variety of theme parks, most of them fairly expensive, though the ticket price usually covers all rides and shows so for a full day's entertainment they can be worthwhile and good fun. There's plenty to choose from including Sea World, Movie World, Dream World (actually 11 different theme areas) or the aquatic sports park, Wet 'n' Wild. When (if) the kids tire of theme parks, the Currumbin Sanctuary is probably the best wildlife sanctuary with a large bushland park with lots of Australian lorikeets and native animals.

At Underwater World in Maroochydore you can walk through a transparent tunnel and get up close to the fish. At the Big Pineapple close to Nambour (you can't miss the huge fibreglass pineapple) there's a train ride through a plantation and a themed boat ride. At the Ginger Factory at Yandina kids can learn about the processing of ginger, ride the Ginger Train and visit the native animals at Bunya Park Sanctuary.

At Airlie Beach and Hervey Bay you can watch crocodiles being fed or go on whale watching trips. Koorana Crocodile Farm, near Rockhampton, has hundreds of crocodiles. In Townsville, the Great Barrier Reef Wonderland has a living coral reef and you can check out the hundreds of fish, sharks, rays and other marine life which live in it (as close as you can get to snorkelling without getting wet).

In Cairns, kids can watch the sharks get fed at Undersea World. And for a re-enactment of a traditional corroboree, boomerang and spear throwing, and the telling of Dreamtime stories check out the Tjapukai Aboriginal Cultural Centre. Cairns has plenty of activities on offer including kayaking, canoeing, snorkelling, horse riding, and (if you can afford it) hot air ballooning.

SOUTH AUSTRALIA

information

The bimonthly publication, *Lollipop*, has information on what there is to see and do for kids in South Australia.

practicalities

It's a bonus for families that all South Australian restaurants and cafes are non-smoking and many pubs have restricted hours when smoking is allowed.

adelaide

things to see & do

Kids might like taking a boat trip to get to the Adelaide Zoo, home to 1500 native and exotic mammals, birds and reptiles, with its very own children's zoo. Who won't enjoy watching truffles being hand-dipped in chocolate on a tour of the Haigh's Chocolate Factory, and you can taste the goods. Adelaide has an indoor ice skating rink and ski slope where kids can ski, toboggan and snowboard. And for pure entertainment there's Magic Mountain in Glenelg, with a water slide, bumper boats and arcade games.

In the Adelaide Hills, kids can have their photo taken cuddling a koala at Cleland Conservation Park and see native wildlife, including endangered species, at Warrawong Sanctuary in Mylor. You can check out Victor Harbour on a Clydesdale-drawn carriage ride by day, watch the penguins come home from fishing at night and, if you're lucky, spot a southern right whale, sometime in between.

around south australia

In the beautiful wilderness of Kangaroo Island you can visit a sea lion colony, see pelicans being fed and watch sheep being milked (and then taste the delicious yogurt and cheeses).

In the Barossa Valley, the Whispering Wall at Lyndoch where conversations at one end can be heard clearly 150m away at the other end, is fun for kids. At Naracoorte, in the Wonambi Fossil Centre, kids will be intrigued by life-size reconstructions of some of the animals who lived there 200,000 years ago and enjoy the Bat Cave where you can see the bats in action on infrared TV cameras. The Eyre Peninsula is a popular summer holiday area with many good beaches, and sheltered bays (some scenes in *Jaws* were filmed here, but don't let that deter you).

Kids will enjoy exploring the rugged Flinders Ranges, where the national park has loads of kangaroos and birds. Further north, kids will be fascinated by the dug-out underground mines in Coober Pedy, Australia's opal capital.

TASMANIA

If your children enjoy national parks and beaches, they will have a wonderful time in Tasmania. The tourist office can provide you with information on walks ranging from less than two hours to a day.

hobart

things to see & do

Antarctic Adventure is a combination of theme park and science centre. Inside, you can take a simulated blizzard ride downhill at 120km/h, experience simulated freezing temperatures and view Antarctica's night sky in the planetarium. Another venue for families is Time Warp House which bills itself as Australia's first retro entertainment centre. Kids won't want to miss tours of the Cadbury Chocolate Factory. Littlies will like Alpenrail, a Swiss model village and railway with hands-on exhibits. To feed Tasmanian devils, wombats and koalas go to the Bonorong Park Wildlife Centre, Brighton.

around tasmania

At Hastings the underground cave tour followed by a dunk in the warm thermal pools is fun. On the east coast, at Freycinet National Park, there are evening tours to meet quolls, wallabies, wombats and Tasmanian devils.

In Launceston, kids will like the walk up Cataract Gorge or taking the long chairlift. Penny Royal World entertainment complex – with working 19th-century water mills and windmills, gunpowder mills and model boats – will appeal as well as the chance to take a ride on a barge, tram or paddle steamer. Around Launceston, kids will have fun finding their way out of the hedge maze at Westbury.

At Mole Creek, Marakoopa Cave features two underground streams and an incredible glow-worm display; there's also Trowunna Wildlife Park close by. Near Devonport there's the Don River Railway & Museum where you can take a vintage steam train ride along the banks of the river. In Burnie, the Pioneer Village Museum has an authentic blacksmith's shop, printer and boot shop.

VICTORIA

melbourne

information

Check out the Children's Activities section in the *EG* (Entertainment Guide), published in Friday's *Age* newspaper. *Melbourne Events* has a children's section in its free monthly magazine, available from tourist offices, and look out for *Melbourne's Child,* a free monthly paper listing all sorts of activities for children. Kids Tours specialises in full-day tours of sights in and around the city for kids or families.

practicalities

Large department stores and shopping centres usually have baby-changing facilities. Trains are easily accessible with a stroller, but the deep steps on Melbourne's trams make them a struggle. Board at the tram's front entrance and the driver, or a passenger, will usually help out. It's now illegal in Victoria for anyone to discriminate against women breastfeeding in public.

things to see & do

wild things One of the best in Australia, the Melbourne Zoo is a real treat for kids (and adults) – walk through the gorillas' rainforest and over the top of the lion enclosure. Healesville Wildlife Sanctuary is one of the best places around to get face-to-face with lots of Australian fauna.

interesting & educational Scienceworks museum in Spotswood has enough hands-on and interactive displays to keep the kids entertained for hours; the Polly Woodside Maritime Museum at Southbank has an old sailing ship to explore; and the Melbourne Aquarium opposite the Crown Entertainment Complex on the Yarra has the best of the ocean.

pure entertainment Melbourne has some good kids' entertainment including Luna Park with its famous big dipper and a stack of other amusement park attractions; the IMAX Theatre with its monster movie screen; and *Puffing Billy,* a vintage steam-train that puffs its way through the Dandenong Ranges.

Baby Harry was only six weeks old when we set off for the second stage of our journey, from Albany in Western Australia, up the west coast to Darwin. There were five of us now and suddenly a lot more gear to squeeze into our campervan and trailer; a portable carrycot (although mostly Harry slept between us), a lightweight pram, another car seat, nappies and clothes. After much discussion we included a fold-up rocker which turned out to be a real blessing because he loved it and would rock contentedly outside, surrounded by a mosquito net hung from the van's awning.

australia THROUGH the OUTBACK & BEYOND

Rosie Waitt and her husband, Tim, drove around Australia for 14 months with their children Nikita, 4, Freda, 2, and baby Harry.

It was great to be back in our van and experience once again the joy of leaving, and that wonderful but addictive feeling of freedom that comes with movement. Singing along to nursery rhyme tapes, we made our way slowly up the coast through Kalbarri and Carnarvon, towards the Pilbara region, where the normally harsh landscape was transformed by great swathes of wildflowers.

Once again we were surprised at how quickly Nikita and Freda adapted to life on the road. For them it was simple; everywhere was home. With few toys and rare access to television, they had become self-reliant and imaginative, learning to find fun and interest in everything around them. And now baby Harry was thriving too. Having spent most of my pregnancy on the road, the rhythm of the engine was like a lullaby for him so driving was easy. He was totally breastfed too, so we had no worries about sterilising bottles or plates.

But easy baby or not, with the new family dynamics it was difficult at first to rediscover the smooth pattern our previous journey had taken. The inevitably broken nights were taking their toll on Tim and me, and now there were three little voices demanding attention. Some days were so heavily punctuated with feed stops, burp stops and (with Freda just out of nappies) toilet stops, that it felt like we would never get anywhere.

Flies were a constant problem. Nikita would regularly become hysterical, start screaming and then swallow a few. We resorted to fly nets and found some relief. Inside the van we put a net over Harry's seat, but outside was a problem. As a deterrent I strung bright beads together into lots of strips and hung them from the top of his pram. Not only did they keep the flies away but the sound, the movement and the colours entranced him.

Then in the purpose-built mining town of Tom Price, we came under attack from giant kamikaze mosquitoes and tiny midges that flew right through the netting on our windows and stung us all over. It wasn't possible to use insecticides or burn coils because our eldest child had multiple allergies and was sensitive to chemicals. Tea tree antiseptic cream at least temporarily stopped the itching and ensured the bites didn't get infected. But our only defence against the bugs was to shut the windows and cover up. So we were all hot, stroppy and scratchy, and I was starting to wonder if it was all worth it.

Of course it was. My mood quickly passed as we drove into Karijini National Park and set up camp among the wildflowers and the extraordinarily fine red dust, that was like ochre and stained everything it came into contact with. Not surprisingly the children quickly discovered the amazing nature of the soil we were camped on. Just add water! Their clothes would never be the same again.

Coincidentally we arrived in Broome just in time for the annual Shinju Matsuri festival, or Festival of the Pearl; a celebration of ethnic diversity. We stayed for a week, watching national dances, fire eaters and jugglers and wandered around markets filled with local crafts and exotic foods. At the festival's spectacular final night concert, Nikita and Freda danced along to the music, were half-afraid of the Chinese Dragon, mesmerised by the thousands of candles held by spectators and asleep throughout the fireworks display. Harry slept through the lot.

"Flies were a constant problem. Nikita would regularly become hysterical, start screaming and then swallow a few."

Twenty kilometres outside of Broome, we heard Freda's little voice in the back, 'Doggy...I want my Doggy.' With sinking hearts we stopped and searched the car, to no avail. The worst had happened. We'd lost Doggy – Freda's special (once furry, now plucked), grubby friend that had accompanied her everywhere since the day she was born. Should we put it down to experience, to the inevitable process of growing up? No way. We were only too aware of the implications (tears, sleepless nights, a broken heart...broken hearts all round), as we drove back to Cable Beach, searched the caravan park and asked hopefully at the office, to no avail.

The air-con in our van was struggling and seated in the back, Freda and Harry weren't reaping its benefits. Both were developing prickly rash and getting pretty whingy. So we bought two small car fans which plugged into the cigarette lighter and rigged them above each child. This made a huge difference as we travelled deeper into the tropics, through the dramatic Kimberleys, to the Northern Territory, Katherine and finally Darwin.

Here we did a giant jumping crocodiles cruise, tentatively swam in icy cold, crocodile-free waterholes and visited the famous colourful Mindil Beach market. And when we went to the post office to collect our mail, there was Doggy, patiently waiting for Freda, with a pink ribbon tied around its neck. Freda has never really understood why Doggy got to fly to Darwin and we had to drive.

activities

You can splash around in hired row boats at Studley Park boathouse in Kew or cruise the paths in St Kilda on hire bikes. Melbourne's beaches are reasonably clean and fine for swimming, the most popular ones being St Kilda, Middle Park and Albert Park.

festivals

There's the 10-day Moomba festival carnival in Melbourne with fireworks and spectacular events on the water and Port Fairy Folk Festival, one of Australia's great music festivals and very family-friendly, both in early to mid-March.

around victoria

If you don't mind joining thousands of others, the kids will enjoy the penguin parade at Phillip Island. Kids can pan for gold in the mining township re-creation, Sovereign Hill, in Ballarat. Kids who've heard about the bushman and Australian icon Ned Kelly will enjoy a visit to Kellyland in Glenrowan.

Kids can get a real Australian experience with surfing lessons in Torquay. There's safe family beaches on the Mornington Peninsula and any of the state's public swimming pools are good value on a hot day – all reasonable sized towns have one.

If you want to take to the snow, skiing classes for kids aged three and over are available at Falls Creek, Mt Buller, Mt Hotham and Mt Buffalo.

WESTERN AUSTRALIA

perth

practicalities

In Perth, Little Hugger Hire rents all sorts of baby gear – car seats, cots, booster seats, prams and strollers – at reasonable rates. Many taxis have child seats, but it's wise to book ahead.

things to see & do

At the Perth Mint watch gold being poured and mint your own coins. The popular Perth Zoo has lots of Australian wildlife and a good nocturnal house. Kids will be kept amused for hours checking out more than 160 hands-on and large-scale exhibits at the Scitech Discovery Centre. You can walk through a tunnel at Underwater World and check out 2500 examples of marine life, including sharks and stingrays. There's the ubiquitous, and large, amusement park, Adventure World. And the Museum of Childhood might appeal with its interactive displays and collections of toys and games from bygone years.

around western australia

Not far from Perth, you can ride in a glass-bottomed boat to Rottnest Island and check out the local wildlife – quokkas. From Dwellingup take steam train trips through jarrah forests. You can wade with the dolphins at Bunbury in the south and Monkey Mia in the north. In Canarvon there are tours of banana plantations, finishing up with a chocolate-coated frozen banana; and kids can sit in on a lesson at the Canarvon School of the Air.

In the south, visit the stunning Leeuwin-Naturaliste caves – kids will like the fossilised jawbone of a giant wombat-like creature. Close by, are whale-watching tours. In the Outback, take a lift underground into a gold mine in Kalgoorlie or pan for gold. Up north in Broome, kids will like kicking back in the deck chairs at Sun Pictures, an open-air cinema with the latest releases. They'll also want to check out the 120-million-year-old dinosaur footprints at Gantheaume Point, just out of Broome.

New Zealand is an ideal country to travel with children. Health problems are not a major issue, getting around is easy and many attractions and activities cater for children.

Family passes are usually available at attractions, though all those theme attractions with hands-on activities and rides for the kids can be very expensive. Children's prices usually apply to children from four to 14 years of age. For children younger than four, admission is often free or only a token amount applies.

Families can get a four-bed share room to themselves in most backpacker accommodation. The YHA hostels are better set up for families and often have specific family rooms. Motels and particularly camping grounds are well set up for children and often have playgrounds and game rooms. Children cost extra, but the charge is usually half the adult rate and the real littlies may be free. Holiday homes and self-contained cottages are ideal for families. They are more spacious and often better value than tourist flats or motel units. The best way to find them is to inquire at information centres. Cots are often available but not necessarily modern, some readers have suggested taking your own.

Major car hire companies, at least, have car seats for children but they are not always high quality. Good cradle restraints for babies are hard to get – you're better off bringing your own. If you can get a good deal on a campervan, it can be an economical and enjoyable way of seeing the country.

You shouldn't have any problem breastfeeding in public in New Zealand. It isn't uncommon to see babies and toddlers of all ages being breastfed in public places such as cafes, restaurants, shops, parks, tourist facilities, and on public transport. Instances of breastfeeding mothers being asked to leave such places do happen, but very rarely and invariably make the news because it is so unusual! There are certainly those who don't approve of breastfeeding in public, but generally New Zealand society is supportive of the rights of mothers and babies.

auckland

information

A useful book to refer to is *Kids Go Auckland: A Fun Guide to Where to Go and What to Do* by Lynne Richardson, Nyla Breakspeare and Jennie Whyte. The visitor centre also has information on things to see and do with children.

practicalities

Supermarkets and pharmacies will have just about everything you may need. And strollers, backpacks and other equipment are all readily available in department stores.

things to see & do

wild things The primate and African animals' enclosures are particularly well done at the Auckland Zoo and you can feed the black swans at the Western Springs Lake (just outside the zoo). Kelly Tarlton's Antarctic Encounter & Underwater World may also appeal to older children with its simulated orca attack and moving footpath with fish swimming around you.

interesting & educational Kids can check out the dozens of sailing craft at the New Zealand National Maritime Museum or the Museum of Technology & Transport's infotainment science centre with lots of hands-on exhibits.

pure entertainment There is the new 3D-experience IMAX Theatre, at the Force Entertainment Centre and Rainbow's End theme park in south Auckland.

activities

Auckland offers umpteen opportunities for swimming and water sports. A good all-weather venue with lots of fun things to do is the Philips Aquatic Centre with its wave pool and slides. The Parnell Baths, only open during summer, has a small water slide and rafts in the shallow pool. The inner-harbour beaches are calm and safe; at low tide exploring the rock pools at places like St Heliers Bay can be quite absorbing. On the North Shore, beaches at Cheltenham and Takapuna are safe and popular.

Further out of the city centre there are working farms at Ambury, boat rides in historical vessels (at Kaipara Harbour, Waiuku) and horse rides along beaches.

parks & playgrounds

A good park near the city centre is the Auckland Domain – feed the ducks at the pond near the Wintergarden, or try flying a kite in the wide open spaces. Cornwall Park has a working farm as well as plenty of space in which to run around. Auckland's volcanic cones offer unlimited scope to burn off surplus energy; Mt Eden (a very steep crater) and North Head in Devonport, with its WWII tunnels and guns, are good spots. Kids 'n Action at Pakuranga is an indoor playground for younger children with plenty of challenges but still very safe.

around new zealand

New Zealand is a huge adventure playground in a beautiful setting – kids will love all the activities and there's plenty for thrill seekers. Activities range from tramping (bushwalking), cycling, horse riding, skiing and snowboarding to (for older kids) white-water rafting, kayaking, surfing, windsurfing, bungy jumping, canyoning, jetboating and zorbing (rolling down a hill strapped inside two spheres).

On the North Island, kids will like the gushing geysers and bubbling mud pools at Rotorua and checking out the Maori hangi (meals cooked in an earth oven) and the concerts with Maori dances (including a war dance), songs and hand games. The Waitomo Caves should impress kids with their magical underground limestone landscapes, complete with glow worms and rivers. In Wellington, kids will like taking the cable-car ride to the Botanic Gardens and the virtual bungy jump at Te Papa (Museum of New Zealand). And there's the chance to see kiwis at the Wellington Zoo.

On the South Island, kids will like checking out the amazing variety of wildlife in the Otago Peninsula – albatross, penguins, sea lions, seals and dolphins. At Kaikoura kids can swim with the dolphins or watch the whales backflip.

AUSTRALASIA

australasia

The climate, natural setting, aquatic games and lack of poisonous creatures make the Pacific a paradise for children. However, apart from major destinations such as Fiji, which is well set up for children, few travellers take their kids anywhere in the Pacific. In fact, some resorts and hotels ban small children for all or part of the year, so check when you make your booking. Ask about kids' discounts on everything from hotels to air fares.

Smaller towns and outer islands may have few resources. You will usually be able to buy disposable nappies, infant formula, long-life milk etc in the main town, but don't leave the capital without buying everything you need or checking the local situation at your destination.

Supervise your children when swimming or playing on beaches and make sure they understand not to touch fragile coral. Bring plenty of sunscreen and light clothes for sun protection. Make sure vaccinations are up to date and that your health and travel insurance also covers your child. It's important to keep small children well hydrated in a hot climate. Rehydration solution helps prevent dehydration and also masks unpleasant tastes in the water. If your child is sensitive to the local water, you can boil drinking water or buy bottled water. (See the Health chapter for further useful information.)

Children are highly valued in Pacific cultures. Locals will often be keen to talk to your kids, play with them and invite them to join activities or visit homes. However, local kids are expected to behave, so try to curb your child's crying and tantrums when visiting a village. Childcare is a shared responsibility in the Pacific and locals will sometimes correct your children for you if they misbehave!

FIJI

practicalities

Fiji is a major family destination and is very child-friendly. Some resorts cater specifically for children, with babysitting and child-minding services, cots and highchairs, organised activities and children's pools. Some of the family-friendly resorts also provide free accommodation and meals, and a supervised children's play area. However, many smaller exclusive resorts ban children or relegate them to a specific period during the year. Some resorts have lots of levels and sand paths, which make using prams and strollers difficult. Larger resorts that are well set up for kids include the top-end Shangri-La's Fijian Resort on Viti Levu and Jean-Michel Cousteau Fiji Islands Resort on Vanua Levu, or Plantation Island Resort in the Mamanucas for the budget-conscious.

Travelling around is fairly easy. Some car rental companies will provide baby seats. If you intend to take public transport, a backpack for carrying young children is a good idea. Long-life milk is readily available, as is bottled spring water and fruit juice. Nappies, formula and sterilising solution are available in pharmacies and supermarkets in the main cities and towns, but if you are travelling to remote areas or islands, take your own supplies.

things to see & do

Most of the islands offer great beaches and water activities. On Viti Levu there is the Coral Coast Scenic Railway which offers scenic rides along the coast on an old diesel sugar train; Kula Eco Park, a wildlife sanctuary and education centre for children which also has bushwalking paths through forests; and the Fijian Cultural Centre, where kids should enjoy the tour in an old-style canoe around the small islands which have an artificial traditional village.

activities

There are endless activities available which children can participate in, either provided at resorts or through private companies, including snorkelling, sea kayaking, horse riding, wind surfing and coral viewing.

cultural issues

Everyone will want to talk with your kids. Babies and toddlers are especially popular – they may tire of having their cheeks squeezed! Fijian men play a large role in caring for children, so don't be surprised if they pay a lot of attention to kids. Children are expected to be obedient, happy and spend lots of time playing outdoors. Backchat and showing off is seen as disruptive to the fabric of the community, so when visiting a village, try to curb any noisy behaviour.

MICRONESIA

Awash with children itself, Micronesia will welcome visiting children with warmth and curiosity. Micronesia is the area of the western and central Pacific basically starting in the Marshall Islands with Majuro Atoll and ending in the west with Guam, Yap and Palau. Guam has all of the brand name hotels plus a plethora of smaller hotels. Most have kids' rooms and day-care and babysitting services. In the less populated islands, most travellers find hotel staff willing to watch younger children and even infants. Many mid-range and upper-end hotels allow children to share the room at a reduced rate – often half-price for children under 12. Bring a baby carrier and also nappies if you need them as they can be expensive.

things to see & do

Micronesia has world-class snorkelling and diving and there's loads of places for kids to snorkel and swim. Kids will also get into beachcombing, kayaking and cultural events. On the most touristed islands, Guam and Saipan, there are water parks (at large hotels), horse riding and jet skiing on offer. On Guam, kids will also enjoy the fiestas – lively events brimming with local food and dances – and will like the dolphin watching tours.

On Kosrae, kids might like to explore the Lelu ruins, and on Pophnei there's lots of waterfalls, some with good swimming holes. On Yap, village tours offered by the hotels will give kids and adults a quick course in weaving coconut leaves or pandanus and kids will be fascinated by the traditional stone money. They'll enjoy traditional dancing on Kiribati, and on Rota the tropical zoo features coconut crabs, iguanas and fruit bats.

NEW CALEDONIA

practicalities

Many hotels offer discounted or even free accommodation for children. The top-end resort of Nouvata Parkroyal in Noumea lets young people under the age of 16 stay for free and at Le Méridien it's those under 12. Le Méridien also has a full day's program of kids' activities (ages five to 12), free for children of hotel guests.

things to see & do

There's no shortage of great beaches and snorkelling opportunities in New Caledonia and there's also kayaking and horse riding available.

In Noumea, the sculptured wooden totems, elaborate masks and spectacular weapons in the Musée Néo Calédonie will appeal to kids. The Noumea Aquarium is one of the most natural in the Pacific and has a good collection of rare and unusual species; kids will like seeing the sharks and sea snakes. Kids will enjoy chugging around town on the miniature train, *Petit Train*, and for littlies, there are several playgrounds dotted around Noumea. An assortment of children's rides – a toy train and merry-go-round – are usually set up at the southern end of Baie des Citrons. Pony rides can be taken from the Buffalo Ranch at Dumbéa and kids will enjoy a day's swimming and snorkelling or a trip in a glass-bottomed boat at Amédée Islet.

On Île des Pins, kids will enjoy taking a pirogue (traditional boat) trip and exploring some of the caves. On Grand Terre, they'll have fun checking out the great swimming holes at Chutes de la Madeleine and Wadiana Falls.

Pre-child we had travelled extensively throughout Fiji and written the Lonely Planet guide, so we had a good idea of what we were in for. A popular family destination, just a short flight from Australia and malaria free, it would be a relatively safe place for our first family trip overseas. For the guidebook update assignment we would visit about 30 of Fiji's 300 islands, ranging from tiny islets to the large mountainous islands of Viti Levu and Vanua Levu – an overly ambitious task according to many of our family and friends.

fiji ISLAND LIFE

Lonely Planet authors, Robyn Jones and Leonardo Pinheiro, spent three months travelling throughout Fiji when Alex was two.

We managed to pack lightly. We had no need for a port-a-cot, most hotels could provide one. Anyway, Alex thought he belonged in our bed, in keeping with the Fijian custom. We did take a large-wheeled stroller. It was useful for towns but absolutely hopeless on sandy paths and awkward for constant travel by small plane and boat. We ended up dumping it in hotel storage where it went mouldy in the humidity. So most of the time Alex rode on Leonardo's shoulders, with the exception of the villages where nothing should be carried on the shoulders out of respect for the chief.

Just getting around was fantastic entertainment for Alex – in fact for him Fiji was one big fun park. He loved the small inter-island planes and boats, and there began an obsessive fascination with propellers. Anyone with a two-year-old knows you have to constantly chase them to avoid disaster, especially as none of the resorts or hotels had pool fences. For all the small boat trips we took a child's life jacket. We hired cars and 4WDs (with a car seat) for getting around the larger islands, including the rough unsealed mountain roads. We only got bogged once and even that was fun for Alex. It was also great travelling around on the local open-air buses.

We had lots of 'homes', usually just for one night. Sometimes we wondered if moving so much would make Alex insecure, it was certainly different to the experience of our own childhoods. But as long as we were around he revelled in the changes. Alex also loved inspecting accommodation with us – bouncing on the beds, checking what sort of plugs were in the sink, turning on the taps, and switching on the ceiling fans.

Fiji has hundreds of safe, comfortable mid-range and upmarket resorts with kids' clubs and nannies – great for a short escape, but we were travelling for three months. While we avoided any boring, grimy, smelly dumps that perhaps we would have put up with in our pre-child life, we still managed to travel mostly at budget level. It was helpful if there was a fridge for the milk. Unexpectedly, the highlights of our trip were when we stayed in the budget resorts of the idyllic outer islands of the Yasawa and Kadavu Groups. The remote villages of the highlands of Viti Levu were also great. We stayed in rustic *bures* (traditional thatched houses) – a light or torch and a mosquito net were the only necessities.

While Alex was having a ball wherever we went, there were of course many times when we reminisced about the ease and relative freedom of the old days. Like snorkelling together rather than having to take turns watching Alex. He was the surprise result of our first research trip to Fiji. Eating at restaurants, once a pleasure, was often now a chore. With the exception of long-life milk, chips and bottled water Alex pretty much developed an aversion to food. And worse, he developed a spreading and persistent rash (nine doctors, nine different diagnoses). By day he would scratch his back like a horse on a fence. At night we were locked in small hotel rooms with at best interrupted sleep, at worst howling and vomiting. Although recently weaned, the breast became the only way to pacify him.

You meet lots of people when you travel as a family; somehow it breaks down the barriers and you must become more approachable. Fijians adore children of this age. Fijian men would carry him around and the ladies loved to squeeze his cheeks – usually more of an affectionate pinch. This would happen so many times a day that Alex began fleeing as any large colourful floral dress approached. Alex would impress people with his language skills: *Bula bula* (Hello); *Vinaka vakalevu* (Thank you very much); *Sega na lega* (No worries); *Moce* (Bye); *Sota tali* (See you later). When visiting remote villages he would be mobbed by other kids. Luckily his blonde head was easy to trace in a crowd of dark-haired local kids. At restaurants he would be whisked away to have his cheeks squeezed in the kitchen – bliss for us!

"You meet lots of people when you travel as a family; somehow it breaks down the barriers and you must become more approachable."

We made personalised storybooks with photos and a collage to help Alex relive his adventures. Two years have passed and he still has memories of the colourful fish through the glass-bottom boat, the hermit crabs on the beach, the kava ceremonies, swinging in hammocks, the fantastic singing, playing the huge wooden *lali* drums, the crew crying as he left the boat, the man scaling the coconut tree and tasting coconut water for the first time. How much remains as visual memories or how much has been reinforced by us recounting the stories and showing him the photos? It doesn't really matter.

COOK ISLANDS

practicalities

Children are loved in the Cook Islands and travelling with them presents no special problems. Some hotels allow children to stay free of charge, others have a reduced children's rate, and a few do not accept children at all. Nappies are expensive, so you might want to bring some of these along. There's a range of accommodation available on Rarotonga, from mid-range bungalows such as Lagoon Lodges, to reasonably priced rental houses, to large resorts such as Edgewater Resort, where accommodation for children under 12 is free, and there's a babysitting service.

things to see & do

Soft, sandy beaches on calm lagoons couldn't be safer for children to swim in and if they like snorkelling they'll be enthralled. There are plenty of other activities such as walking, cycling, horse riding and canoeing that children will like. Atiu, Mitiaro and Mangaia all have heaps of caves to explore, complete with stalactites and stalagmites. Kids will enjoy an 'island night' performance at one of the resorts, where local children sometimes perform in the dance troupes. Around Rarotonga, walks in the valley are suitable for children and there are tours on glass-bottomed boats and to see humpback whales. They'll like a visit to the Cook Islands Cultural Village to see traditional huts, demonstrations of music, dance and chants along with a traditional feast. And kids may acquire a taste for coconut water, Cook Island coconuts are particularly tasty.

SAMOA

Samoa doesn't have accommodation and specific activities geared for kids, but there are plenty of natural wonders to keep kids entertained.

practicalities

Children are highly valued in Samoa and childcare is seen as the responsibility of the extended family and community. Wherever you go, your children will be given lots of attention (not to mention plenty of sugary treats) and will be made to feel very much at home. Disposable nappies, formula and sterilising solution are available in Apia and Pago Pago. In the event of an emergency, you should be aware that medical facilities are limited in Samoa.

things to see & do

There are plenty of snorkelling, walking and swimming opportunities for kids in Samoa. On Savai'i kids will like seeing the enormous sea turtles at the Satoalepai Wetlands and one of the world's largest and most impressive blowholes at Taga.

On Upolu, kids will like the Fatumea Pool with its clean, clear springs and water-filled caves to explore; older kids will like the James Bond-type swim to the second cave pool. At Papasee'a Sliding Rock they'll also enjoy the 5m slide down a waterfall into a jungle pool (there are three smaller ones to chose from if that's too scary!) And they'll enjoy a *fiafia* night – a lavish presentation of Samoan dancing and singing staged at larger hotels.

TONGA

practicalities

Children are loved in Tonga. Nappies are expensive, so you might want to bring some along. Hotel policy varies with some places not allowing children, while others appeal to families with free accommodation for kids and babysitting. Check when you book.

things to see & do

Tonga offers plenty to keep children happy. Swimming, snorkelling, beach-combing, cycling or kayaking (for older children), short boat trips, visits to interesting places, cultural events are all possibilities.

Kids will love seeing the humpback whales in the Vava'u Group between July and November as Tonga is one of the best places in the world to see them. Experience traditional culture by joining a Tongan feast with traditional music and dance – they're especially good on Tongatapu and Vava'u.

On Tongatapu, the Tongan National Centre has a traditional lunch and fashion show of Tongan ceremonial dress, as well as displays and demonstrations. Anahulu Cave has a freshwater pool that is good for swimming. Kids will like a trip to the Mapu'a'a Vaca blowholes – a 5km stretch of blowholes with fountains of seawater up to 30m high.

VANUATU

practicalities

You need to be self-reliant in rural areas – village stores are most unlikely to sell such luxuries as formula and nappies. Ni-Vanuatu people love children, but they will correct them if they're misbehaving.

Several of the country's more upmarket hotels go out of their way to cater for families, particularly Le Lagon Parkroyal in Port Vila and the Bougainville Resort near Luganville. While guesthouses generally welcome kids they won't usually have special facilities for them. In villages you'll generally have no trouble finding a babysitter.

things to see & do

Kids will enjoy swimming with the local marine mammal, the dugong (and will also like the fact it's called 'the sea cow'), at Lamen Bay, Epi. And they'll love the 'fireworks' display of lava at night from the active Yasur Volcano, Tanna – if it's particularly active avoid getting up close, as people have been killed by flying lava. On Tanna there are short guided walks to traditional villages and a bat cave.

Vanuatu has hundreds of safe swimming beaches but you'll need to check that you book accommodation near safe ones, sharks and currents can be a problem. In Port Vila there's horse riding and the chance to go on a glass-bottomed boat tour as well as night coral touring. The Melanesian feast nights in villages near Vila are a good opportunity to sample traditional cooking and watch traditional dancing – the feast night at Ekasup is particularly good. Mele-Maat Cascades near Port Vila is a good place to swim and explore. And kids might enjoy a trip to see Feles Cave and hear the story about the Polynesian chief who died there.

TRAVEL GAMES

Most of these games use few props so they're very mobile and require little preparation. This is not a definitive list and we left off classics like I-Spy; Rock-Paper-Scissors, Charades and Simon Says in favour of games that will give you ideas for more games. Think of these games as suggestions and change the rules to suit your family.

anywhere

The best games rely on imagination – a fantastically portable commodity found in most kids

copycat One player pulls a face or makes a movement (like a robot, a monkey or a ballerina, for example) and the next player must copy it. Play around by giving kids roles they're not used to and working in characters you've met on your travels. More advanced games can use noises.

two truths and one lie Each player takes it in turns to make three statements, two of which are true and one of which is a lie. The other players try to guess which statement is a lie, holding up one, two or three fingers to indicate the lie.

You can keep a score over a couple of rounds or let whoever guessed correctly take the next turn as liar.

clapping categories Clapping hands, snapping fingers or slapping thighs, create a rhythm that all the players can keep up (younger players will be better at easier rhythms, such as simple 1-2-3-4 clapping). Now introduce a simple category (such as vegetables, colours or films): each player takes it in turns to say something in the category at a point in the rhythm (try clap-clap-clap-'apple' for starters). Harder than it sounds and it gets harder.

I went to the shop and I bought... Each player chooses something they bought at the shop with the next player having to recite everything the previous players bought at the shop as well as adding something to the list. When a player forgets something they are out of the game and the remaining players battle it out. Longer things might be easier to remember, but try throwing in left field things like 'a stinky, hairy, man-eating piano' or 'a nice new suit and tie for my pet chimp, Gilbert'.

word association Not just for psychiatrists, this is a quick game to play anywhere with two players. Say a word and the other player responds with the first word that comes into their head. Keep it quick to keep it fun.

same name One player chooses the full name of a famous person, the next player has to think of a famous person whose name begins with the first letter of the last person's name. For example Player 1 might say Winston Churchill and the next player would have to follow with someone whose first name begins with C, say Charlie Brown, and so on.

rhyme time Think of a word (children's names can keep it interesting) and go around the group finding words that rhyme with it. Younger players might need hints. The player who thinks of the most rhymes gets to choose the word next round.

talk to the animal One player chooses an animal character to be for the round and the other players ask it questions until they guess what kind of an animal it is. First to correctly guess the animal gets to be the next animal. Throw in family pets, animals you've seen along the way and mythical monsters to keep it tricky.

odds and evens A quick easy game for two players. One player chooses to play odds and the other plays evens. Both players shoot by saying '1-2-3-shoot' and sticking out a chosen number of fingers. Add up both hands to see if the total is odd or even with whoever guessed correctly winning that round. It's such a simple game that it can be played with local children in playgrounds throughout the world.

cars

Games that take attention outside the car often prevent car sickness as well as making the trip go faster. Games with activity can stop kids from squirming in the backseat and mean you can drive further without grumpy kids. At night, substitute talking games or use night landmarks like neon signs or tail lights for spotting games.

singing in echoes This is a noisy one, so avoid it if you feel a headache coming on or if you've still got a long journey ahead. Take it in turns to make up a line of a song (nonsense words work best) with the rest of the family repeating it as a chorus. Another player sings the previous line and adds one on. Keep adding until your memories fail.

passing cars A nice easy creative game. Get the kids to make up stories about the people in other cars that pass you based on the quick look they get as they pass. Ask questions to get them thinking – What are their names? Where are they going? Is one of them a superhero travelling in disguise?

buzz words Gets kids concentrating on the radio and keeping quiet. Choose a word (start with easy ones like 'song', 'listening' or 'news') and listen out for it on the radio in songs or DJ's announcements. Shout out 'Buzz' when the word comes up. Readers can look out for buzz words on road signs and advertising.

licence plate games Make a phrase out of the letters in a licence plate with the first one to make sense winning. Have kids spot their initials in passing plates (first to get all their initials wins). Choose a word and spell it out using license plate letters (use familiar things like pets or school friends to ground kids in unfamiliar territory). Use the numbers in licence plates to play car twenty-one – get the kids to add up all the numbers on a number plate in passing cars. GMZ 421, for example, would add up to 7, while 969 would break the bank with 24. Players can ask for another card (the first number of the next passing car), but if they go over 21 they break the bank. Take it in turns with the closest to 21 (but still under) winning. Or for an easier game, see how many different countries or states you can collect on licence plates.

planes, trains or buses

Getting from A to B doesn't have to be a journey to boredom for kids. The added pressure of other passengers might restrict the kinds of games you can play, but many of the games from the Cars section can be adapted for other types of journeys.

geography games Expand your kids' geographical knowledge by taking turns to name a capital city and its country. If this is too easy, try thinking up one for each letter of the alphabet.

would you? Read up about the country you're visiting and prepare some questions for your kids that will challenge their cultural ideas. Try concepts like 'In Sri Lanka they wash elephants in a river after a long day's work. Would you?' or 'In Chile they eat *chupe de cóngrio* (or conger eel soup). Would you?' This a fantastic way to introduce your kids to different customs, languages and foods

before arriving in a country to reduce culture shock. Use a Lonely Planet guidebook to find out more about a country.
maps Get kids to trace out your journey on world, country or local maps. Some tourist information centres offer free maps, which can be coloured in or cut up.

waiting

Kids don't believe everything comes to those who wait. Longer games come in handy in restaurants, queues and at public transport lines, because they distract kids from the time it's taking for something to happen.
storylines A good game for the whole family that is limited only by imagination. Start a story with a sentence ('Once upon a time...' might be a good place to start) with the next family member adding the next sentence. Add one that doesn't make sense or finish your sentence with a cliffhanger to keep it interesting.
alphabet games Alphabet games can run for hours if need be, so they're perfect for undetermined waits. Name a category, then run through the alphabet naming something from each category. Animals (eg 'aardvark', 'bumble bee', 'cat') are easy, but harder topics can be famous people or song titles. Double points for double letters, like bumble bee. In other alphabet games you can choose a category and all the players have to name something beginning with that letter before moving on to the next letter (eg 'apple', 'asparagus', 'artichoke'). For older kids make up a structure, like 'My name is blank from blank where they make the best blank' filling in each of the blanks with a name, a location and an object starting with each letter of the alphabet.
guessing games Guessing games can be good for shorter waits, as kids can get frustrated or bored. Most guessing games are based on simple yes or no questions, using general questions ('Is it alive?') to narrow it down to specific guesses ('Is it a rabbit?'). In Guess the Food, one player will nominate a describing word ('crunchy', 'sweet' or 'red') with other players asking questions to guess the food. Use other categories like animals or famous people. You can prepare some cards with categories or names on them. Locate the games in your travels by using famous people or animals from the country you're visiting to keep kids excited about life on the road.

quiet places

Sometimes you might just want your little treasures to keep quiet. Quiet games can teach children that loud behaviour is not always okay, as well as buy a few moments of peace in a hectic day.
guess the letter Another one for readers. Draw a letter on the palm of another

player with their eyes closed. Try whole words if guessing a letter is too easy.
whispers Pass a whispered message from one player to the next saying the message only once. As players pass it on from one to the next the message will become garbled. In a reasonably sized group (usually more than five) the message should end up as nonsense when the last player says it out loud to the group.

outdoors

Exploring the great outdoors is easy (kids love to run and frolic after long journeys). Using simple games can help them to appreciate their surroundings even more or calm them down after too much running around.
touchy feely tree Walk a blindfolded player to a tree and let them explore it using only touch for a few minutes. Then spin them around and lead them away from their tree. Removing the blindfold, ask the player to find their tree.
statues A good game to relax with. Move around until the caller says 'freeze', then stay still the longest to win. Another version involves players sneaking up behind the caller to steal a token. (A rock or anything that's handy will do fine.) Rather than call freeze, the caller turns and sees who is still moving. Anybody caught moving gets sent back to the start.
clouds What do the clouds look like? Can you find a cloud that looks like: a person, your car, your pets, your breakfast?

museums or galleries

Although many museums are becoming more interactive there are still many old-fashioned museums that will have a 'look, don't touch' feel that frustrates kids. With a bit of preparation, these games can get children to appreciate looking in a museum as much as you will.
did you see? A game that might involve a bit of preparation. Make a list of things to see in a gallery or museum by asking the kids what they think they'll see or prepare a list beforehand based on a guidebook. Kids can check off their list with a prize or treat for the most complete list. Remember to have a range of items that are both common (so kids achieve something easily) and rare (to challenge them). You can debrief and talk about items on the list. More complex versions of the game might involve getting more than one of each item (eg, seven paintings with a blonde man in them).
how many? Guess how many of an object you'll see on your visit and get the littlies to count them up as they go. Good objects include sculptures, gold frames or security guards.

what was it? A simple game that will get kids looking at exhibits or paintings. Give the kids a minute or two to look at an exhibit, then ask 'What was it?', 'Who used it?', 'When did they use it?'; or if it's a portrait ask, 'Who was it?', 'What did they do?' Ask any other questions to stimulate the imagination. Be prepared to answer some tricky questions yourself.

walking

Kids need to focus on something other than how far they're walking, so it's a good idea to have a few games you can play to take their mind off things. These games also highlight differences between their own culture and the culture being visited.
what you saw When passing through scenery ask kids to look around for a minute, then have them close their eyes and tell you what they remember. An observational game that will have kids appreciating their surroundings.
counting games These are easy games to make up in a hurry. Select a frequently occurring local feature – say windmills in Holland or bikes in China – and two players can count all of these features on one side. First to 100 wins. To keep the game interesting you can count down from 100. Count several things with various points for each sighting and the game can be about addition. If you're near a roadway counting arrows on signs is always a good one.
stepping out A quick game, but a good distracter. See who can take the biggest steps, the smallest steps, the silliest steps, the straightest step, a sideways step or the most backward steps (without running into anything).

WEB SITES

planning

www.lonelyplanet.com Lonely Planet's Web site has a popular Kids to Go section on the Thorn Tree and destination profiles to supply up-to-the-second information on countries.

www.travelwithchildren.com This site covers a variety of issues from planning to destinations and travel games. It also has a wealth of links to other helpful sites on the Web.

family.go.com/ This site covers a whole range of general issues relating to families, including travelling with children. It has some interesting articles on issues such as travelling with babies or teens and holiday ideas as well as flight offers.

www.travelwithyourkids.com/ Lots of articles and tips as well as good links to other sites with a focus on international travel. Includes sections on moving abroad and a few of the more popular destinations.

www.travelguides.com This US-oriented site has holiday ideas, tips and deals for families. Some sensible advice on first aid, food and general safety.

www.worldhop.com Devoted to one family's travels through 18 countries on their year off around the world. It's full of photos, journal entries and humour. Includes links to similarly inspiring sites.

www.familiesontheroad.com This site covers issues facing families doing RV (recreational vehicle) trips with their children. It looks at issues such as what kind of vehicle and what to do about schooling. It includes a practical forum/chat section.

www.travel-news.org This online generalist travel agency has information on good-value family package holidays departing from the UK.

www.thefamilytravelfiles.com Complete with its own vacation finder and regular e-zine this site is crammed with information and stories.

www.gobabies.com/ An enthusiastic online magazine that focuses on infants with articles and advertisements for baby-related products.

www.familytravelforum.com A useful site which covers everything from travel news to pediatric health issues. Family travel deals are listed and there's an on-site forum to pitch your questions to like-minded parents.

www.familytraveltimes.com A subscription-based bimonthly online magazine on family travelling that goes beyond the easy alternatives and encourages adventure.

places to stay

www.childfriendly.co.uk A great UK site listing hotels that cater especially for kids.

www.holiday-rentals.co.uk This Web site advertises more than 3500 vacation properties worldwide with details and photos. Most of the properties are upmarket and in great locations.

www.goldray.com/hospitality/index.htm The Hospitality Exchange is a worldwide directory listing travellers prepared to offer one or two nights' accommodation in their home to travellers. Members can stay with other members and then host travelling members themselves.

www.intervac.com This Home Exchange organisation has thousands of houses available for long- or short-term stay, though many of them are in Europe. It provides details of their properties, including photos and has a search engine to plan destinations around.

on the road

www.cyberschool.k12.or.us/ This American-based set of courses is a good example of a cyberschool, offering a variety of subjects for young adults, including mathematics, literature and biology. Fees are paid online and courses are carefully designed to supplement of American high school subjects.

www.choiceineducation.co.uk A simple UK site that makes for a good place to start if you're thinking of educating your kids outside the typical school system.

distancelearn.about.com/education/distancelearn/ A great source of information on all kinds of home schooling which provides links to all stages of education.

members.aol.com/parklinks/links.htm If you're thinking of taking the kids to an amusement park then this is the site for you, especially if you are travelling to the USA. There are even links to prominent manufacturers if you want to own your own rides, as well as ride safety instructions for the more cautious.

www.cbsg.org/ For your own little wild things check out this site that has a worldwide zoo listing and some great images to whet their appetites.

www.kidsdomain.com/ A great source for younger kids' games online, some educational and some just good clean fun. Snakes and ladders to games that emphasise nutrition are all included.

www.tpwd.state.tx.us/adv/kidspage/kidsout.htm A page of good advice for parents taking their kids into the great outdoors with tips on safety, expectations and exploring.

www.gorp.com/gorp/eclectic/family.htm An offshoot of the popular outdoors site, this page covers family travel issues such as camping from your car and videotaping the trip.

www.diabetesmonitor.com This site has articles on travelling with diabetes and good links to other relevant sites.

www.holidaycare.org.uk A UK charity which provides information on travelling with a disability including details of accessible hotels and attractions in 40 countries as well as information packs on topics such as equipment hire companies in various destinations.

www.makoa.org/travel.htm A good special needs resource page with loads of links to other sites including American-based camps and travel companions. Also has country specific information about accessibility.

www.tmvc.com.au/info10.html All the info you need on healthy travel including vaccinations and articles by doctors about possible risks.

www.who.int/ith/english/country.htm The official World Health Organization guide by country of the current health risks.

healthlink.mcw.edu/travel-medicine/ Based on articles supplied by doctors, this is a good general health site which includes some information on travelling while pregnant and with children.

www.lalecheleague.com The official site of La Leche League International, this site has everything you need to know about breastfeeding, including information on travelling and weaning.

INDEX